Danes on D-Day

Danish soldiers, sailors and airmen in the invasion of Normandy 1944

Jakob Tøtrup Kjærsgaard

Helion & Company

Helion & Company Limited
Unit 8 Amherst Business Centre
Budbrooke Road
Warwick
CV34 5WE
England
Tel. 01926 499619
Email: info@helion.co.uk
Website: www.helion.co.uk
X (formerly Twitter): @Helionbooks
Facebook: @HelionBooks
Visit our blog at helionbooks.wordpress.com

Published by Helion & Company 2025
This book has been made possible by the generous donation of Boghandlers Clausens Fond, Bjørnows Fond and Frihedskampens Veteraners Mindefond.
Designed and typeset by Mach 3 Solutions (www.mach3solutions.co.uk)
Cover designed by Paul Hewitt, Battlefield Design (www.battlefield-design.co.uk)

Originally published in Danish with the title *Den Røde Brænding: Danske beretninger fra D-dag og invasionen i Normandiet 1944* (Aarhus: Turbine Forlag, 2019).

ISBN 978-1-804518-78-6

British Library Cataloguing-in-Publication Data.
A catalogue record for this book is available from the British Library.

For details of other military history titles published by Helion & Company Limited, contact the above address, or visit our website: http://www.helion.co.uk

We always welcome receiving book proposals from prospective authors.

To Vester: ***Sic Parvis Magna***

Contents

Preface

The history of World War II and the invasion of Normandy in 1944 are still fascinating and relevant topics that continue to capture our interest and curiosity. As more and more literature is published on the subject, history is also viewed with new eyes and new angles of history come into focus. History is alive, history is constantly evolving and new material is emerging from literature, archives and private individuals at home and abroad. In relation to the Danish efforts during the Normandy invasion, these new sources in context with existing materials and research are precisely the background for this book.

The Normandy invasion was codenamed Operation Overlord. An operation that became one of the most decisive battles of the entire Second World War. The invasion was launched in Normandy on 6 June 1944 under the military term D-Day, and the scale of it was huge! The outcome of Operation Overlord was thus decisive for the outcome of the Second World War. The Danish interest in the Battle of Normandy has not diminished since 2014, the 70th anniversary of the Normandy invasion. This was the first time that Denmark was represented as a contributing nation to the Allied countries during Operation Overlord. The Dannebrog flew side by side with the other Allies' flags, and that this was possible was due in no small part to the efforts of the more than 800 Danish sailors during the invasion. The recognition has sparked public debate about Denmark's role in the Second World War, but has also generated even more interest in the Danish efforts during the Normandy invasion. Regardless of Denmark's status after the 70th anniversary of D-Day, the story of the Danish invasion participants deserves to be told. They made an invaluable contribution to Denmark, to the Allies and to the free world.

The purpose of this book is to give the reader a clear and richly illustrated picture of the Danish efforts before, during and after D-Day, 6 June 1944. In order to tell the story of this fateful day, it is also necessary to tell the story of both the prelude and the aftermath of the invasion. The book is first and foremost an account of people, Danes and some descendants of Danish emigrants, who fought for the Allies before, during and after the Normandy invasion. Much of the source material is based on the perspective of the sailors, but much of it also deals with the Danish pilots, paratroopers and infantrymen at the front lines, on the invasion beaches and in the later offensive of the operation. The book tells of many of the Danes who were an active part of the Allied effort in Normandy – but the book also uses and brings to the public previously unpublished Danish accounts. In addition, there are accounts from both Danes and their descendants that have still not been truly researched and publicised.

The Danish flavour is thus a crucial concept in the book, as the stories show that even if you had recently become a citizen of another allied country for various reasons, that special Danishness was still part of your identity.

The book focuses on the gripping first-hand accounts and lets the characters tell the story from their personal perspective. It considers the accounts in relation to the period from the occupation of Denmark in April 1940 to the invasion of D-Day, 6 June 1944, as well as the subsequent period of Operation Overlord – arguably one of the most important of the twentieth century. Finally, the post-war period will be covered briefly to illustrate the impact of having been part of the war and what it was like to return to Denmark. For many after more than 5 years of fighting in the Second World War.

From working on this book, I would like to thank the many people who have helped me. First and foremost, I would like to thank the book's sponsors who have made this project possible: Boghandlers Clausens Fond and Bjørnows Fond. I would also like to thank the staff at the Coastal Museum, and not least Henrik Gjøde Nielsen for keeping the project on track and for the important personal support he has provided. I would like to thank Turbine, Ulrik Skafte and Ole Steen Hansen for a good and inspiring collaboration. I would also like to give a big thanks to Helion for the opportunity and a special thank you to Duncan Rogers and Stephen Ede-Borrett. Finally, I would like to thank Jakob Sørensen for his solid professional sparring.

I would like to extend a huge thank you to all those who have contributed to the content of the book in terms of general help, passing on information and collecting the amazing stories that are included in the book: Simon Bang, Ian Gardner, Anette Eggert Frydenberg and Cicerone, Ebbe Kyrø and Nexus Kommunikation, Morten Bach, Donald Galbraith, Karl Ravn, Mikkel Plannthin, Claus Arboe-Rasmussen, Henning Brinckmann Kristensen, Jakob Andersen, Jørgen Flintholm, Frederikshavn City Archives, Skagen Archives, Aalborg City Archives, Bornholm Island Archives, Hadsten Local Archives, Kim Ørsted Iversen at Vesthimmerlands Museum, Nordby Sognearkiv, Frihedsmuseet and Henrik Lundbak, M/S Museet for Søfart and archivist Henriette Gavnholdt, Chrestina Dahl at Vendsyssel Historiske Museum, Jens Andersen at Museumscenter Hanstholm, Wendy Hanson Hudson at DANE – Danish Archive North-East, Timothy Jensen at Danish-American Archive and Library, Faye Kjearsgaard at Danish Canadian Museum, Vivian Rogers-Price at National Museum of The Mighty Eighth Air Force, Janet M. Larocco at the 91st Bomb Group Memorial Association, Megan Harris (Veterans History Project), Linda Steffensen at The Danish Pioneer Newspaper, and Tova Brandt at the Museum of Danish America.

And not least, a big thank you to the families and relatives of the sailors and Normandy veterans: Finn Wiesneck, Aksel Bødker Knudsen, Kis Bødker, Lis Nielsen, Jørgen Aarlo Jensen, Søren Egebak, Ole Moustgaard, Ann Nørregaard, Anne Paludan, Jason Gibbs, Mary Christensen, Mary Jo Nørgaard, Carl Steffensen, Charlotte Updike, Krish Harsh and Torben Vildner Pedersen and his family.

A huge thank you to my former colleagues at the Musée du Débarquement Utah Beach in Normandy: Séverine Letourneur Diaz, Ed Diaz, Marie Hoguet, Benoît Noel, Charles De Vallavieille, Henri Milet, Veronique Baugin, Clare Uden Comrie, Rodolphe Passera, Marion Coquoin and Bertrand Ledan.

Special thanks also go to Bill Galbraith, Jack Port, Erik Kragelund, Jørgen Linnet and Evald Brinck, who all experienced World War II in Allied service. They are the real reason and inspiration that these stories should continue to be told.

Finally, the biggest thanks to my family for their tireless and indispensable support.

It has been a great privilege to be able to work on a subject that I am very passionate about. I am especially grateful for the opportunity to tell the story of the Danish efforts during the Normandy invasion and to place these unique stories in the context of the history of the Second World War, thus helping to preserve them for posterity.

Introduction

'*Navigare necesse est, vivere non est necesse.*' (It is necessary to sail, but not to live.)[1] As the Roman commander Pompey allegedly proclaimed regarding the vital transport of grain ships to Rome. These words can be put into perspective with the role of Danish sailors in transporting supplies for the Allies during the Second World War. Vital supplies that were crucial to focal points and front lines around the world. A task they took on based on their conviction that they could make a difference for the Allies, despite already knowing that the outcome for the individual sailor could be fatal. The Danish merchant seamen in the national and international merchant fleet were the first Danes to become an active part of the Second World War. Throughout the war, these sailors were prominent representatives of fighting Denmark and thus contributed to opening the eyes of the free world to Denmark's sympathy for the Allied struggle. The war meant that all Danish ships' crews were now separated and scattered around the world's oceans. The warships sailed individually or as combined crews, but they had no real overall leadership.

The sailors had only guidelines from the shipping companies, words of encouragement and guidance from the Danish champions of the free world, such as Captain Røder and John Christmas Møller, as well as the sailors' own fighting spirit to combat the superpower.[2]

Even before Denmark's occupation, the Danish merchant fleet and Danish fishermen were already severely tested and suffered heavy losses, despite Denmark not yet even being part of the war. In the period before Denmark was occupied on 9 April 1940, 387 Danish sailors and 36 Danish fishermen had died as a result of torpedoing or the explosions of mines. They were aboard the 35 Danish ships and 11 fishing cutters that had been sunk. In addition, more than 200 other Danish sailors on other countries' ships had also died as a result of acts of war.[3] These tragic fates attracted national attention, and Danish Prime Minister Thorvald Stauning even included the seamen in his New Year's speech on 1 January 1940: 'On this New Year's Day, let us gather in thanks and in a promise that the deeds of the seamen will

1 Christian Tortzen, *Søfolk og Skibe 1939–1945, bind 1* (Copenhagen: Lindhardt & Ringhof, 1981), p.224.

2 Christian Tortzen, *Søfolk og Skibe 1939–1945, bind 1* (Copenhagen: Lindhardt & Ringhof, 1981), pp.395–541.

3 The late Erik Kragelund, chairman of the Danish War Sailors' Association, worked on the statistics for the last 25 years of his life before his death in 2016. After reviewing these statistics with the author and Erik Kragelund before his death, it must be concluded that these statistics are as up-to-date and complete as is currently possible. The wartime sailor statistics have generally been inaccurate for many years, but these are now the closest thing to complete.

not be forgotten!'[4] A speech that resonated throughout the Danish merchant fleet and gave the sailors a belief that despite the otherwise uncertain fate of the Danish merchant fleet, it would probably receive support from the Danish Government.

Stauning's promise in his speech would prove to be remembered among war sailors to this day.

However, the sailors were far from the only ones who chose to take up the fight in Allied service against the occupying forces. Several chose to join the Allied air force, and others chose to sacrifice their citizenship to join and fight alongside the forces of the Allied countries.

It is estimated that in 1940 there were 138,174 Danish-born Americans living in the USA.[5] Many of those who volunteered for service had in common that they wanted to make a difference and refused to witness an occupied Denmark and a Europe on its knees.

Hundreds of sailors, Danes in Allied service and other Danes who had now emigrated and become citizens of Allied countries would meet their fate during one of the largest landing operations in living memory – the invasion of Normandy in June 1944. This book conveys a sample of their efforts before, during and after the decisive invasion of Normandy.

4 Christian Tortzen, *Kampen på Havet* (Copenhagen: Information, 2011), p.56.

5 Torben Grøngaard Jeppsen, *Danske i USA 1850–2000: En demografisk, social og kultur- geografisk undersøgelse af de danske immigranter og deres efterkommere* ((Odense: Museum Odense, 2005), pp.324–331.

Part 1

9 April 1940 – Denmark is occupied

Early in the morning of 9 April 1940, countless German planes flew over Denmark. The planes had a very specific task: to drop leaflets with the headline *Oprop*, which made it clear to the Danes that war had come to their homeland. Denmark was swiftly occupied by Germany. The majority of the Danish population was still asleep when the German occupation took place, and apparently only a few had fully woken up before the fighting to stop the Germans crossing of the Danish-German border was actually already over. Danish Prime Minister Stauning and the other ministers in the Danish Parliament chose to surrender to the Germans early in the morning of 9 April for fear of a bombardment of Copenhagen and the rest of Denmark. Despite the shock of the German occupation of the country, daily life continued shortly afterwards for the Danish population. Public transport worked, people went to work and the government was still intact.[1]

9 April and the War Sailors
'Early this morning the damned Germans attacked Denmark'

The situation for war sailors was at the same time very similar and very different when the news of Denmark's occupation came on 9 April. Their fates depended largely on the waters they were in and the harbour they were near. What many of the wartime sailors had in common, however, was that in the days around 9 April 1940, none of them had any real overview of the situation and what the occupation would mean for them. The ship owners had different statements about how the captains on board the ships in the foreign fleet should relate to the occupation. The majority of the shipping companies gave orders to sail to the nearest Allied harbour and to enter Allied service. Ship councils were held on many ships, and on almost all Danish ships it was decided to sail to Allied ports. On a few Danish ships, the crew had to mutiny to force the ship's captain and officers to sail to an English harbour, because they would rather follow the shipping company's orders from Copenhagen to go to a neutral or German-controlled port. Other Danish ships were seized by the British Navy and impounded for use in the British merchant fleet. The war sailors experienced 9 April very differently, and a majority of the school ship students shared the

1 Christian Tortzen, *Kampen på Havet* (Copenhagen: Information, 2011), pp.57–67.

same fate when *Skoleskibet Danmark* was in the USA at the time of the occupation. The school ship had been on a circumnavigation of the globe, including a visit to the USA, where the crew participated in the World's Fair in New York. The return trip to Denmark was scheduled for 10 April 1940. On 8 April, the Danish school ship students were invited to a ball at the American-German Association in Jacksonville when, as Erik Egebak recalls, the news of Denmark's occupation was announced:

> At one point we got the impression that the captain had been called to the phone and an important message had been received, but we were not aware what that message was. The party continued, but later there were rumours that the captain had been informed about the German occupation of Denmark on 9 April (8 April in Jacksonville). But we continued our party so as not to spoil the good mood and then boarded our ship just before midnight. As soon as we got on board, we were all called together and our captain informed us of the message he had received and that Denmark was now occupied by the Germans.[2]

Jørgen Linnet, who attended the ballet in Jacksonville with Erik Egebak, also remembers how the students received the fateful news of the Danish occupation:

> We were in Jacksonville on 9 April and we were called on deck where the captain explained the situation. He did not know what the outlook was and what was going to happen next. We did not know very much at all. But we were now stranded in Jacksonville. It was quite unexpected for us. The occupation was quite unexpected for us, as we did not expect it to happen. There was no prelude to anything, and we were supposed to sail home to Denmark shortly afterwards. But that was brought to an abrupt end.[3]

Good advice was expensive as the Danish school ship students were now cut off from their homeland like the other Danish sailors in the Danish foreign trade fleet. The renowned Captain Røder gave a speech on 12 April over the BBC, in which he asked the free Danish sailors to make an effort to liberate their country by sailing their ships to Allied ports and join the fight against the aggressor.[4] Captain Røder's speech and the fact that the young sailors' homeland was now occupied stirred the emotions, as Erik Egebak recalls:

> The only thing on the minds of the Danish students on the ship was to go to England and take part in the war. We tried to convince our captain that we should disembark and go out and take part in the war. Officially, he couldn't go in favour of that idea, because he had been entrusted with looking after us, but he fully understood our decision. In any case, it was not long before we were allowed to disembark. This

2 Quote from Cicerone ApS and Nexus Communication's interview with Erik Egebak and archive material in connection with the production of the documentary 'The War Sailors'.

3 Interview with Jørgen Linnet, February 2016.

4 Christian Tortzen, *Kampen på Havet* (Copenhagen: Information, 2011), p.64.

> happened in small groups, which then mustered out on ships on the east coast of the USA.[5]

At the end of 1939, Niels Wiesneck received a call at home in Copenhagen. It was from the shipping company Østasiatisk Kompagni / East Asiatic Company, who asked Wiesneck if he would like to be hired on one of the ships sailing on the west coast of America. He accepted and signed on the ship, which sailed across the Atlantic. World War II had broken out at the same time, when Germany invaded Poland on 1 September 1939. The outbreak of war put things into perspective and Wiesneck began to consider his situation:

> We had already painted the Dannebrog flag on the side of the ship *Jutlanta* so that any belligerent nations would not start torpedoing us. When we sailed home with the EAC ship, we could see the large troop transports that also sailed past us. The question for me was whether I should run away in such a war situation. I talked to a good friend and my parents, and we agreed that I should continue employment at EAC.[6]

The former *Skoleskibet Danmark* trainee Wiesneck had already gained plenty of experience of life as a sailor after his discharge as a school ship trainee when he joined the Danish Navy on 1 January. On 9 April 1940 he was on board the EAC ship M/S *Europa*. The occupation of Denmark came unexpectedly for him, as it did for the other Danish sailors:

> We sailed to New York, where we unloaded and sailed back to Denmark. On the way across the Atlantic we met a large Dutch passenger ship that put up a lot of signalling flags to tell us something. He couldn't use the radio because he was afraid that the submarines would pick up the signal. The signal flags told us that Denmark had been occupied and that we should turn round, as the Dutchman thought there were submarines further out waiting for us.

Wiesneck kept a diary throughout the war and often vividly described the experiences he was part of. On Tuesday 9 April 1940, he wrote in his diary:

> This was a sad day. Early this morning the damned Germans have attacked Denmark… But by all that is good and bright we shall regain our country and all that has been given to us.[7]

Niels Wiesneck's ship was taken into Canadian custody and handed over to the Canadian government for direct military service. This meant that they would now sail in military service in convoys to England.

---

5 Quote from Cicerone ApS and Nexus Communication's interview with Erik Egebak and archive material in connection with the production of the documentary 'The War Sailors'.

6 The quotes come from Kystmuseet Bangsbo Arkiv's material about Niels Wiesneck, in which a taped interview is available.

7 Excerpts from Niels Wiesneck's unpublished diary, courtesy of Finn Wiesneck.

Of course, the crew discussed the prospects of being an active part of the war, but there was little they could do about the situation. A few travelled home to Denmark, but others, including Wiesneck, touchingly agreed that they should stay on board.

Henrik Bødker Knudsen from Frederikshavn was on board M/S *Uranienborg* as an ordinary seaman when news of the German occupation of Denmark arrived on 9 April. After their ship had left the Panama Canal and entered the southern seas, Bødker Knudsen had not given the war a second thought. On board *Uranienborg*, opinions on the war were divided, but most did not expect it to affect them. In any case, many of the sailors on board did not think the war would last until they got home. Some even believed that the equipment and tanks they had observed while at sea were just cardboard cut-outs – mere scenery in a grand theatre of war. But when 9 April came, reality also reached *Uranienborg*, as Bødker Knudsen recalls:

> On 9 April 1940, heading for the Red Sea, we received a message over the ship's radio that Denmark had been occupied by Germany and that we had to go to a Danish or a neutral port as soon as possible.[8]

For the rest of the day, the debate and discussions were very loud at *Uranienborg*. How should we relate to Denmark's occupation? Some of the older sailors had wives and children back home in Denmark, which created major dilemmas for them, as everyone knew that the war would now have consequences for the sailors. However, Bødker Knudsen had no trouble at all deciding how to relate to the Danish occupation:

> I immediately made it clear to the others that if there was a choice, I would sign up for British service. I thought that I best fitted into the pattern of life that the English had.

Holger Christen Jensen from Hou, north of the entrance to the Limfjord, was on board Det Forenede Dampskibs-Selskabs export boat S/S *Diana* on 8 April 1940. A few months earlier, he had been home with his wife after a long trip at sea. The war was smouldering, and Jensen's wife noticed this too, as several Danish ships had been torpedoed during the same period that Holger had been away shortly before:

> I came home and rang the doorbell, as my wife and I had agreed, to let her know that it was me she was opening the door to. But instead of happily welcoming me as she usually did, she snuggled up to me and said with emotion: 'You are not going to sea any more.' Of course, I spoke well to her, because I had to go to sea, and a few days later I had to go again.[9]

On the same day, Holger Jensen said goodbye to his wife at the quay at Christiansgade in Copenhagen, where the S/S *Diana* was to sail from. Little did either of them realise that it

8 The quotes are from Henrik Bødker Knudsen, *Krigssejler* (Copenhagen: Frihedsmuseets Venners Forlag, 1992).

9 The following quotes are from Jørgen Aarlo Jensen's documents regarding his father Holger Jensen.

would be five years before they would see each other again. On 8 April 1940, *Diana* was due to sail from Denmark with 500 tons of coffee, but, as was the case with many other Danish ships, *Diana* was also seized by the British authorities on 9 April for Allied war service. The news of the occupation of Denmark came as a shock to Holger Jensen and the rest of the crew on board S/S *Diana*:

> In the morning, an English Army officer and a couple of privates arrived. The officer boarded the ship – the two enlisted men remained at the gangway. The officer said that the Germans had occupied Denmark and from now on the ship would be considered enemy territory by the British. It is not easy to explain what you feel at a time like that. It was hard for us.

Evald Brinck was just 17 years old and on board M/S *Boringia* near Marseille when Denmark was occupied. The French authorities seized the ship two days later and interned the entire crew. The first weeks after 9 April were spent in internment for the crew before they were ordered to sail under the French flag to Port Said, after which the ship was seized by the British and came under British custody in Singapore in June 1940. It was a tough day for the Danish crew when they were informed of the events of 9 April:

> I remember that there was a tense atmosphere throughout the ship when I turned in at 6 o'clock in the morning on 9 April.
>
> The telegraph operator had intercepted a message that German troops had invaded Denmark both by sea and across the land border. We on *Boringia* felt that we had been lured into the lion's mouth at night, because we later learnt that the major Danish shipping companies had tried to warn their ships over Lyngby radio on 8 April – well aware of the Germans' intentions – but the shipping companies had been refused permission, presumably on orders from the Danish Government. This was the direct cause of us being locked up, and as a 17-year-old, I would have been happy to do without it.[10]

Brinck later wanted to become a soldier in the British service and in 1942 was declared fit to join The Buffs (Royal East Kent Regiment), which was known to be a Danish regiment. After six months in the regiment, Brinck moved on to Glasgow, where he joined the armed crew of the ship *Highland Princess*, which was fitted with depth charges, guns and a rocket battery. Brinck then moved to various other ships, and he took part in the invasion of Sicily on 10 July 1943. Brinck was later ordered to embark on an Empire boat to take part in D-Day on 6 June 1944, and subsequently made 25 convoy trips during the Normandy invasion.

The occupation of Denmark on 9 April affected not only Danish citizens and sailors, but also Danes who had emigrated to other countries and were now living there. One of them was John Andreasen from Bornholm. He had emigrated to Canada to work as a farmer and settled in South Saskatchewan, where he ran a small ranch of 2,000 acres of grass. There

10 Evald Brinck, ... *de vil aldrig blive husket – beretning om danske søfolk 1940 – 1945* (Tåsinge: Evald Springeren Brinck, 2007), p.10.

was no compulsory military service in Canada, and there was talk among John Andreasen and his friends about signing up for service after Canada declared war on Germany on 10 September 1939.[11] When the news of Denmark's occupation reached Canada, there was no longer any doubt in John Andreasen's mind whether he should volunteer for the army:

> Everything went smoothly until the spring of 1940, when Germany occupied Denmark, and being from Bornholm, I got a little excited; the first few days after the occupation I hardly left the radio, and then I agreed with myself that I would volunteer for the Canadian Army.[12]

John Andreasen was 31 years old when he joined the Canadian Army. He had been living in Canada for 13 years and despite still not being a Canadian citizen, he managed to join the army. After four months of basic training, he was shipped out of Halifax to train as an anti-aircraft gunner in an artillery regiment that would later take part in the Normandy invasion in 1944. His strong feelings towards old Denmark were unmistakable when the ship *Empress of Japan* sailed from Halifax with around 2,000 soldiers on board:

> We were all standing on the decks looking inland as we sailed out of the harbour, and many of us thought, 'Will we see Canada again? I didn't think about Canada as much as many of the others, because the further I got from Canada, the closer I got to Denmark.[13]

German-Friendly or Allies?
'He was knocked out like a Dane'

The situation for the Danish merchant fleet and Danish sailors, however, was completely different to the Danes, who saw the German soldiers marching into Danish cities. When Germany occupied Denmark, a barrage of mines and submarine nets was laid in the North Sea along the west coast of Jutland and further up through the Skagerrak to Norway. Due to the blockade, the Danish merchant fleet was divided into two, and these were labelled the home and away fleet. Within the German blockade, there were around 7,000 Danish sailors.

Outside the blockade, there were 245 Danish ships and around 6,300 Danish sailors. These made up two-thirds of the Danish merchant fleet's ships and seamen.[14]

In addition to the fact that the approximately 6,300 Danish sailors in the Danish Merchant Navy faced a fateful choice regarding their future in Allied service, their role as an active player in the war was also hotly debated among the countries that were officially considered allies. The Danish sailors found themselves in a difficult political situation, since Denmark

11 David J. Bercuson, *Our Finest Hour: Canada fights the Second World War* (London: Harper Collins, 2015), p.8.
12 John Andreasen, unpublished war diary, p.1.
13 John Andreasen, unpublished war diary, p.5.
14 Erik Kragelund, *Overlord – Den Danske Deltagelse i Invasionen i Normandiet i 1944* (Copenhagen: Radius, 2013), pp.2–4.

as a nation had chosen not to take up the fight against the Germans, as the Norwegians had done, and the Danish Government had chosen to cooperate with the German occupying forces to avoid further conflict with them. This perspective was viewed very negatively by the Allied countries, and as the sailors were the only ones outside of Denmark who were directly involved in Allied service at this time, there were many conflicts and a lot of mistrust shown towards them. The Danes in particular had to listen to a lot from their Norwegian colleagues who, unlike the Danes, had defied the Germans and refused to cooperate. Furthermore, the Norwegian royal family and government had managed to flee to England and establish a government in exile.[15] The British Merchant Navy subsequently issued instructions for the recovery of Danish ships to be used in Allied war service. The Danish ships were technically labelled as hostile, but due to the shortage of both ships and British sailors, the Danish sailors in the British Merchant Navy were still allowed to man the Danish ships themselves.

Jørgen Linnet noticed the mistrust first-hand when he was on board the ship *Nordvest* in 1941:

> One day the Coast Guard came alongside the *Nordvest*, went on board and took all the men ashore except the skipper and the first mate. We then boarded this Coast Guard boat, where we were sailed up to Seattle and put in immigration detention there. This was because they had discovered that the German ships that were laid up in America had been sabotaged so that they could not be used by the Allies, and they were afraid that the Danes were not loyal to the Allies either. So they went through the Danish ships but discovered that they were in perfect order.[16]

Niels Wiesneck also noticed the growing distrust of Danish sailors. In 1942, Wiesneck's ship was loaded with war material and the destination was Liverpool. After unloading, the crew spent a couple of weeks in the city and then the ship set course for Canada. Wiesneck had long wanted to study to become a first mate, and he intended to realise this dream in Canada. This would prove to be extremely problematic, as he recalls:

> It turned out to be completely impossible as we were considered best friends with the Nazis. Then I tried to get down to my uncle in Chicago. But immigration wouldn't allow me to go down there with a Danish reputation. We had enough trouble with the Canadian authorities, but it was really bad in America. I then tried to get into the Norwegian Air Force, which was set up in Canada. The Norwegians didn't think much of us Danes either; several of us were spat on because we gave up so easily when Denmark was occupied. They did not like us, and that was one of the reasons why I did not join the Norwegian Air Force.[17]

---

15 Christian Tortzen, Christian, *Søfolk og Skibe 1939–1945, bind 1* (Copenhagen: Lindhardt & Ringhof, 1981), pp.395–436.

16 Interview with Jørgen Linnet in February 2016.

17 The quotes come from Kystmuseet Bangsbo Arkiv's material about Niels Wiesneck, on which a taped interview is available.

However, other Danish sailors managed to become part of the Norwegian Air Force, which was known in Canada as Little Norway. One of these was Kjeld Rønhof, who also experienced the growing distrust of the Danes when he volunteered for service with a captain at the recruiting office in Toronto: 'I am surprised, I would not have thought that about someone from such a docile people as the Danes,' the captain said boldly.[18] Elsewhere, boxing commentators also often used the phrase: 'He was knocked out like a Dane.'[19]

There was no mistaking the trust in the Danes who tried to enter Allied service. Despite the reluctance and mistrust, the sailors and other Danes in Allied service continued to assist the Allies.

Some Danish sailors, such as Kjeld Rønhof, chose to take a different path when Denmark was occupied. He was born on 12 May 1920 in Bromme, was educated at Sorø Academy and was then hired on board an EAC ship with the intention of becoming a first mate. When Denmark was occupied on 9 April 1940, he was on board the M/S *Kina II* on its way to the USA. He was subsequently admitted to the Norwegian Flying School in Toronto. Two years later, he received his pilot wings and was transferred to England to complete his training.

> I always had a dream of becoming a pilot. I tried to join the air force at the Norwegian Embassy in Washington, and then I was told to join up in Toronto. We then started flight school, where I skipped the recruitment period. I was part of the first joint flight team in the Norwegian Air Force (FTL1). It was a flight team that had a very sad fate, as only three of them survived the war.[20]

Rønhof flew his first solo flight in a Spitfire in May 1942. He would later take part in the Dieppe raid in 1942, Normandy in 1944, and he experienced being hit near Rotterdam in late 1944. He flew his last mission on 3 May 1945, where he took part in the bombing of German ships in Danish waters.

The Fall of France and the Evacuations During Operations Dynamo and Ariel 'You could see it was impossible to save all those people'

Just like Denmark, other European countries also came under German occupation in April and May 1940. The Netherlands, Belgium and France surrendered relatively quickly. The Netherlands surrendered after five days of fighting, while Queen Wilhelmina and the rest of the government fled into exile in England. Similarly, the Belgian Government arrived in England on 28 May, with the exception of King Leopold, who chose to stay in his homeland to sign the surrender papers to the Germans. Neither country wanted any form of cooperation with the German occupying forces and instead created governments in exile based in England. Similarly, the Norwegian Government had chosen to establish a government in exile in England, all in stark contrast to the Danish Government's policy of cooperation with the Germans.

18 Kjeld Rønhof, *Vi fløj for Friheden* (Copenhagen: Four Stripes,1991), p.20.
19 Kjeld Rønhof, *Vi fløj for Friheden* (Copenhagen: Four Stripes,1991), p.21.
20 Kjeld Rønhof, *Vi fløj for Friheden* (Copenhagen: Four Stripes,1991), pp.5–7.

The aggressive and rapid advance of the Germans in Europe meant that Hitler's troops had already reached the Channel coast by 21 May 1940. As a result, the Allied front line was cut in half and the Allied forces were split in two. Thus around 215,000 British, French and Belgian soldiers of the British Expeditionary Force and French and Belgian Armies were cut off and pushed further and further north-west until they reached the coast at Dunkirk in France. This put maximum pressure for their quick and efficient evacuation. A lightning operation codenamed Operation Dynamo was carried out between 26 May and 4 June. The operation was highly successful and managed to evacuate not only all British troops and equipment, but also 123,000 Belgian and French soldiers.[21]

All available vessels were used for the evacuation at Dunkirk – from large ships to smaller cutters, from military vessels to private civilian boats. Several Danish ships were involved in the evacuation, including *Marie Toft*, *Edvard Nissen* and S/S *Holland*, which were all sunk at Dunkirk harbour.[22] The Danish ship S/S *Dagmar* was also involved, as it was in England when word came that the massive evacuation mission at Dunkirk was imminent.[23] *Dagmar* was enlisted to transport the beleaguered soldiers back across the Channel to England. The Danish sailor J. P. Sørensen was on board *Dagmar* and clearly remembers the large-scale evacuation:

> We were told to sail over to Dunkirk, and we were given nets mounted down the side of the ship and various provisions and blankets on board. The whole Channel was full of boats, small yachts, anything that could sail, ventured across. At Dunkirk we saw lots of soldiers heading out into the water. We got several of them on board with us and they were taken back to England. It was a terrible experience because you could see it was all helpless – you could see it was impossible to save all those people. They came wading into the water with their rifles over their heads and kept holding this gun over their heads – until the white foam came out of their mouths. They kept holding the rifle over their heads like it was a life raft for them.[24]

Shortly after the Dunkirk evacuation became a reality, Churchill gathered all MPs in the House of Commons to announce the success of the evacuation. Churchill spoke passionately about the need to stand together during this period and ended his speech by saying:

> We will go on to the bitter end. We will fight in France, we will fight on the seas and oceans, we will fight with increasing faith in ourselves and increasing strength in the air. We will defend our island, whatever the cost. We will fight on the beaches, we will fight on the landing places, we will fight in the fields and in the streets, we will fight in the mountains. We will never surrender![25]

21 Hugh Sebag-Montefiore, *Dunkirk*: Fight to the Last Man (London: Viking, 2006), pp.497–507.

22 H. C. Røder, *De Sejlede Bare* (Copenhagen: Høst & Søn,1974), pp.137–142.

23 Christian Tortzen, *Søfolk og Skibe 1939–1945, bind 2* (Copenhagen: Lindhardt & Ringhof, 1982), p.372.

24 Interview with J. P. Sørensen: Interviewer: Ulrik Brandt. Photo: Ebbe Kyrø – Nexus Kommunikation A/S. Recorded at Bombebøssen in Christianshavn on 9 August 2005.

25 Winston S. Churchill, *Erindringer om Den Anden Verdenskrig, Bind 1, 1939–1942* (Copenhagen: Rosenkilde, 2010), pp.310–311.

However, Churchill probably never imagined that it would be another four years before the British would set foot on French soil again on a more permanent basis.

Between 15 and 25 June 1940, another large-scale withdrawal codenamed Operation Ariel was carried out. The mission was another large-scale evacuation to rescue approximately 190,000 Allied soldiers located at Cherbourg and Brest. Several Danish ships participated in Operation Ariel.[26] All Danish ships escaped unharmed from this evacuation, but the experiences were not to be forgotten, as Captain Hartmann on board *Lifland* recounts:

> On the last trip, we sailed right behind a large liner that had several thousand people on board. It was hit by a direct hit and sank in an instant. We sailed past the sinking wreck at a distance of five feet, and it was terrible to see the many terrified people lying in the water screaming for help. However, we could not stop and save them.[27]

The evacuation during Operation Dynamo at Dunkirk as well as the evacuations during Operation Ariel at Cherbourg and Brest, despite the loss of life and material, were an overall success. The success of the evacuations was of utmost importance to Britain, not only because of the blow of losing its most important ally, France, but also because a large part of the British Expeditionary Force was still intact with the hope of returning to France to fight another time.

Paris was taken by the Germans and on 14 June 1940, an armistice was agreed between France and Germany following a request made by French Prime Minister Marshal Henri Pétain shortly beforehand; it came into effect on 25 June. The armistice effectively divided France into two parts. An occupied part, ruled from Paris, and an unoccupied part, where Pétain would act as political leader, based in the city of Vichy. As part of the armistice agreement, the Vichy regime retained control of the French colonies, which meant that part of the French navy was released to control the French colonial empire. This meant that the rest of the French navy would be demobilised and under German and Italian administration. The armistice also meant that the French merchant fleet had to cease all activity and recall all ships or sail to the nearest neutral harbour. This message was almost identical to the Danish Ministry of Trade's announcement to Danish merchant ships on 10 April 1940. The fall and collapse of France had consequences for hundreds of Danish seamen and 25 Danish ships that subsequently came under the French flag. These were effectively forced to sail for the Vichy regime.[28]

The Danish ship *Cyril* was boarded by French marines, which caused a lot of unrest among the crew, as telegraphist Hans Mathiasen recalls: 'We are interned. Now we are really a part of this mess ... What would they do to us who have promised to work for the Allies?'[29] However, a few ships managed to escape the Vichy regime's control, including *Cyril* with Hans Mathiasen on board. He later participated in the Normandy invasion in 1944 aboard the Danish-manned ship *Empire Beatrice*.

26 Christian Tortzen, *Søfolk og Skibe 1939–1945, bind 2* (Copenhagen: Lindhardt & Ringhof, 1982), p.372.

27 Report by Captain Hartmann, reproduced in Christian Tortzen, *Søfolk og Skibe 1939–1945, bind 1* (Copenhagen: Lindhardt & Ringhof, 1981), p.374.

28 Anders Bjørn Hansen, *Breve fra Anders* (Copenhagen: Gyldendal, 2012), pp.129–130.

29 Quoted in Christian Tortzen, *Søfolk og Skibe 1939–1945, bind 2* (Copenhagen: Lindhardt & Ringhof, 1982), pp.388–389.

After Britain's evacuations from France, it was clear that the country's continued warfare depended on keeping merchant ships under British control. At all costs, the French, as well as other merchant ships in Europe, had to be kept from falling into German hands. The British subsequently launched several actions to gain control of the Vichy-controlled ships. In July 1940, the French fleet was docked in Algeria, where a British ultimatum to hand over the fleet to Britain took place. The British demand was rejected, resulting in a resolute British attack on the fleet, resulting in the deaths of 1,300 French marines and two British soldiers. The action caused a stir, especially in the US, and showed that Britain was still fighting. Several similar British actions were subsequently carried out, including at Dakar in French West Africa, but without the same success that was achieved at Algeria. On 15 July 1940, a formal decision was made by the British to round up all merchant ships under the French flag and transfer them to the British merchant fleet. The utilisation of the merchant ships for further warfare was of paramount importance to the Allies. Five French-flagged Danish ships that were in British-controlled harbours at the time of France's surrender came under British administration and subsequently sailed under the flag of the British Merchant Navy – the flag is commonly known as 'The Red Duster'.[30]

The Second Front

Britain's focus on the importance of the merchant navy to the wider war effort and the success of evacuations during Operation Dynamo and Ariel meant that the UK now had its full focus on defending the homeland against the *Luftwaffe*, which repeatedly attacked the country to achieve air supremacy with the ultimate goal of conquering Britain as planned in Operation *Seelöwe.* The battle for air supremacy over Britain raged throughout 1940 and 1941, but Hitler's appointed leader of the *Luftwaffe*, Hermann Göring, realised that the battle could not be won. As a result, Hitler chose instead to focus on attacking the Soviet Union in the east, and Operation Barbarossa was launched on 22 June 1941. This created breathing space for the British, who were able to offer the Soviet Union arms aid. However, Stalin did not need much of these additional supplies, but instead demanded that a new front be opened in Western Europe to take the pressure off the Russians. The British promised to intensify their efforts, and this took the form of a landing in Africa, codenamed Operation Torch, in November 1942.

However, the opening of the second front in Western Europe still had a long way to go, and not until the US entered the war after Pearl Harbor was attacked by Japan on 7 December 1941 did the prospect of a potential opening of the second front become more likely. Hitler declared war on the US four days after Japan's attack on Pearl Harbor, and American war production kicked into high gear. The Soviet Union and Great Britain now had access to the vast resources of the US to defend themselves against Germany. However, the prospect of opening another front had to wait, as US war production had to be on a better war footing than it had been when Pearl Harbor was bombed. The opportunities became a lot greater when the Russians stopped the German offensive in the east and the

30 Anders Bjørn Hansen, *Breve fra Anders* (Copenhagen: Gyldendal, 2012), p.132.

British pushed the German troops back in North Africa. This left the Western Allies free to focus on opening a front in Western Europe or attacking in the Mediterranean.

Despite disagreements among the Allied countries, the focus on attacking the Mediterranean was established. The British had strong interests here, but the Americans favoured a focus on opening the Western Front in Northern France and hitting Hitler in the heart, which could potentially shorten the war. The US feared that if the Soviet Union collapsed, the Germans would be able to use soldiers and equipment from there to defend the Western Front. This would greatly decrease the chances of a successful Allied entry into Western Europe. Due to the strategic disagreements, a large-scale landing in 1942 was therefore ruled out. This was also largely due to an attempted and ill-fated raid at Dieppe in 1942, which proved fatal for those involved.[31]

The Raid at Dieppe
'...the last I saw of him was that he was diving rather abruptly over Dieppe with smoke pouring out of the aircraft.'

By 1942, it was obvious to the Western Allies that a landing was necessary to open up the front in Western Europe, but at this point there was no experience of a land invasion on the scale they imagined would be necessary to gain a foothold. Therefore, it became necessary to conduct various smaller raids to test how the attack strategies would work in practice. The first Allied raid took place at St Nazaire in April 1942 and aimed to sabotage the port's harbour. This was done by running the American destroyer *Campbeltown* directly aground at the mouth of the harbour, after which the crew on board had to flee the scene. The ship was loaded with three tons of explosives, which were then detonated by a timer, but the charge did not go off. The operation was an immediate failure, but the day after the raid, the Germans wanted to investigate the strange ship that had run aground and detonated the explosives. As a consequence of the raid, the harbour's functionality was severely reduced for the rest of the war.

However, the largest and most disastrous raid, codenamed Operation Jubilee, took place on 19 August 1942 at Dieppe, located on the Channel coast between Le Havre and Calais. Dieppe was clearly intended by the Allied planners to be attacked because the harbour town was a stationary target with a significant defence by German troops. In other words, similar to the fortifications you would expect to attack during an invasion. The overall goal was to attack the harbour at Dieppe directly, but with support for the attack from both sides of the harbour. This was based on the theory that the success of a major invasion depended on the capture of a harbour to keep the supply lines going. The 2nd Canadian Division was selected to make the assault, with soldiers from the Canadian Essex Scottish Regiment strongly represented. In addition, various commando units were deployed to attack artillery batteries aimed at shelling the beaches during a landing. Furthermore, attempts would be made to land tanks directly from the sea so that the infantry had additional support when they landed.

31 Christian Tortzen, *Søfolk og Skibe 1939–1945, bind 2* (Copenhagen: Lindhardt & Ringhof, 1982), pp.355–375.

The commandos quickly and effectively defeated the German artillery positions – except east of the town, but the infantry and tanks attacking the beach area were just as quickly and effectively stopped by the German defences. Several of the Canadian troops from the Royal Regiment of Canada managed to fight their way to the sea wall east of Dieppe and got through the German defences, but the majority were held on the beach by the massive German defences. Shortly thereafter, the second wave of Canadian soldiers attacked, and soon afterwards the third wave. None of the attacking waves managed to advance from the beach, and three hours after the first wave, the attack was stopped by the German defences. The result was disastrous: 554 Canadian soldiers attacked this sector, of which 227 were killed. The western assault at Dieppe was more effective, but still left 200 dead and wounded. The Churchill tanks that were landed on the beaches also failed to defeat the German defences and as a result, all the tanks were left behind at Dieppe.[32]

The attack at Dieppe was supported by various forms of air support, including from the Royal Air Force, where Danish pilots Kaj Birksted (331 Squadron) and Kjeld Rønhof (332 Squadron) participated in the attack in Spitfires. Flight Commander of Blue Section, 331 Squadron, Kaj Birksted, wrote in his after action report on the Battle of Dieppe:

> I was patrolling with Blue Section over Dieppe at 6,000 feet when a general fight took place between Red and Blue Sections and approx. 20 enemy aircraft. I attacked an FW [Focke-Wulf] 190 diving towards Red Section, started the attack at about 70-degree angle, 250 yards range. Right behind him and at somewhat longer range I followed him and gave him a 4 second burst until the aircraft went down vertically, out of control, just NE of Dieppe. Blue 3 and 4 cancelled their attack. (½ shot down, shared with Sergeant Fearnley). When I had climbed to 5,000 feet again, I saw an FW 190 attacking Red 4 at very close range, dived to attack this aircraft and warned Red 4 over the radio. I fired the rest of the ammunition at this 190 from various angles and 200–300 yards away, the last I saw of him was that he was diving rather abruptly over Dieppe with smoke pouring out of the aircraft. I lost sight of him; as I pulled my aircraft out of the dive, I lost consciousness and levelled off 50 feet above the sea. (1 shot down). Blue 1 and 2 then returned to base."[33]

Birksted regained consciousness shortly afterwards and regained control of the aircraft.

Kjeld Rønhof clearly remembers the raid at Dieppe:

> The army came ashore in the wrong place and came under fire, so they never actually got over the wall (tank barrage) at the beach. In another place, however, they got further inland. There was an airfield we had agreed to use over there and the Canadian Army took it. We did what we could up in the air and I think we actually won the battle up there that day, and that's a claim I still stand by. When I came over the second time that day, there was no more opposition. No aeroplanes at all.[34]

32 Will Fowler, *The Commandos of Dieppe: Rehearsal for D-Day* (London: Collins, 2002), pp.20–70.

33 Reproduced in Susanne Zima Feierskov, *Med vinger og våben* (Copenhagen: Gyldendal, 2011), pp.124–125.

34 Interview with Kjeld Rønhof in the DR programme 'D-Dag Den Længste Dag', rebroadcast June 2004.

Kaj Birksted and Kjeld Rønhof flew three and two sorties respectively during the raid at Dieppe. The raid was costly for the Royal Air Force, as 100 aircraft were lost during the raid. RAF reports stated that 43 German bombers and 49 fighters were shot down – in addition to 10 potentially shot down bombers and 29 fighters, 56 bombers and 84 fighters were damaged. The reports were greatly exaggerated, just as the German reports stated that the Luftwaffe had only lost 23 fighters and 25 bombers during the attack at Dieppe. The correct figure is probably somewhere in between.[35]

When the order to withdraw came at 9 a.m., just three hours after the attack had begun at 6 a.m., as many people as possible were evacuated. However, the commanders realised that not everyone could be brought off, resulting in 3,164 enlisted men and 215 officers being left behind, around 2,000 of these were taken prisoner.[36]

The attack at Dieppe was a costly exercise for the Allies, but also an instructive one. Hitler's theory that the success of an Allied landing would depend on the Allies' ability to capture harbours to keep the supply chain going would prove crucial to the Allied invasion of Normandy two years later in 1944. The heavy loss of life and material in the attack on Dieppe caused Allied commanders to completely abandon plans for a direct attack on the harbours in a potential invasion. However, the Germans still clearly believed that by maintaining a well-established defence of the various ports, an Allied invasion would be stalled. One of the most heavily fortified harbour areas was to be in the Pas-de-Calais region, as it was the shortest distance from England to France, so there was a 'natural' assumption by the Germans that a potential Allied invasion would take place here. The definitive result of Hitler's assumption to resist an Allied invasion by focusing on the defence of ports would come in June 1944.[37]

Fortress Europe *The Atlantic Wall*

According to German propaganda, by 1944 the entire west coast of Europe had been transformed into a completely impenetrable fortress. Thousands of bunkers, guns and mines along the west coast made up Hitler's *Festung Europa*. This huge Atlantic rampart, manned by the finest soldiers of the German Reich, could repel any invasion. However, the reality was quite different, as the elite soldiers were only a minority of the units that actually manned the Atlantic Wall at the Normandy section.

Construction of the Atlantic Wall did not begin until March 1942, when Hitler began to fear an invasion along the west coast of Europe due to the war's progress. As the Allies had already attempted several smaller raids, such as at Dieppe, Hitler was forced to focus on a more concrete construction of the seaward defence. The Atlantic Wall project became a reality, and the project would be extremely large scale, as the fortifications and bunkers

---

35 Svein Heglund's estimate in Susanne Zima Feierskov, *Med vinger og våben* (Copenhagen: Gyldendal, 2011), p.132.

36 David J. Bercuson, *Our Finest Hour: Canada fights the Second World War* (London: Harper Collins, 2015), pp.85–107.

37 Stuart C. Robertson & Dale Booth, *Following in the Footsteps of Heroes: D-Day June 6th 1944*, (Devizes: Sabrestorm, 2014), p.22.

would stretch all the way from the North Cape in Norway in the north to the Franco-Spanish border in the south. Hitler clearly believed that the key to resisting an Allied invasion would depend on the ability to defend harbours that would be vital to keeping the Allied line of supply in place. However, by the end of 1943, the construction of the Atlantic Wall was not satisfactory to Hitler, so he sent Field Marshal Rommel to inspect the fortifications, which he found to be seriously deficient. Subsequently, in February 1944, Rommel assumed full authority over the continued construction of the Atlantic Wall. At this time, Normandy was primarily protected at the harbours, Cherbourg, Le Havre, Pas-de-Calais and other smaller areas in Normandy. This made it Rommel's primary task to raise the standard of defence of the structures, which not only had a significant effect on the Atlantic Wall in Normandy, but also on the rest of the Western European coastline. Rommel made countless inspections across Europe to assess the state of the defences, and in most places he demanded significant improvements in order that the structure could withstand an Allied invasion from the sea.

Rommel ordered the gaps between the Atlantic ports filled with thousands of bunkers, guns, mines, beach defences and barbed wire for the Allies to get through in an attempted invasion.[38]

Rommel had a doctrine that, in the event of an invasion, the Allies should be stopped at the beaches and then thrown back into the sea. Therefore, *Wiederstandsnests* (resistance nests) were established as part of the Atlantic Wall. These were tactically placed positions that could lay down crossfire on top of each other to protect the beach sectors and the approaches from the beaches. Each line of resistance was protected by a belt of obstacles to ensure maximum protection, whether it was high or low tide. Up to 50,000 obstacles and mines were placed on the beaches of Normandy.

In addition, more than 100,000 anti-personnel and anti-tank mines were placed directly behind the Normandy coastline.[39] Establishing coastal defences was a demanding and slow process, and despite Rommel's intense efforts to complete it as quickly as possible, there were still gaps in the defences along the Normandy coast. Rommel made a final inspection and delivered his report to Hitler on 30 May 1944. Unaware that the Allied invasion was imminent, Rommel noted in his report to Hitler that 82 percent of the fortifications in Normandy were incomplete. He made this assessment after a thorough inspection of the sector that would later become known as Omaha, where only 44 percent of the 167 emplaced weapons, including guns, mortars and machine gun emplacements, were covered in concrete – the majority of the guns were still in open and unprotected positions. In contrast, the fortifications at Pas-de-Calais, the shortest road between England and France, were 68 percent complete.[40]

In the unlikely event that the Allies managed to break through the Atlantic defences, Hitler wanted the attackers to come face to face with the Third Reich's very best armoured divisions. The idea was to maintain mobility during an invasion so that the armoured divisions could quickly and efficiently carry out a counter-attack, regardless of where along the coast the attack took place. According to Hitler, the advantages of a possible German

38 Stuart C. Robertson & Dale Booth, *Following in the Footsteps of Heroes: D-Day June 6th 1944*, (Devizes: Sabrestorm, 2014), pp.21–28.

39 Steven Zaloga, *D-Day Fortifications in Normandy* (Oxford: Osprey, 2005), Fortress series, p.16.

40 Steven Zaloga, *D-Day Fortifications in Normandy* (Oxford: Osprey, 2005), Fortress series, p.13.

counter-attack were also due to the fact that the Allies would not have the opportunity to land as many tanks at the start of a given invasion, and thus the chances of throwing the Allies back into the sea quickly were significantly increased.[41]

For the Allies, who were watching from afar the growing threat that the building of the Atlantic Wall posed to the success of a future invasion, this meant that they had to focus intensely on how to penetrate Hitler's *Festung Europa*.

Danes Regain Respect
'... we had to fight for it, if there was to be a change'

Ever since Denmark had been occupied on 9 April 1940 and the Danish Government had chosen to cooperate with the German occupying forces, the Danes who chose to enter Allied service, and especially the sailors, had worked under difficult conditions. Respect for the Danish sailors was nonexistent to say the least, as the Danish Government's policy of cooperation had a negative impact on the lives of the sailors on board the ships. Danish sailors had to listen to a lot from their foreign colleagues on board the ships, especially the Norwegians. Niels Wiesneck, who started out as a sailor and later joined the Canadian Army, was very aware of the sacrifices it took to restore trust in the Danish people:

> We could see that there was a war going on and it was crazy to get involved, but on the other hand, we HAD to get involved. It was our duty somewhere. Otherwise there would be no end to it. We didn't know how long Denmark would be occupied, and it was us Danes that had to fight for a change in Canada's attitude if there was to be a change. In the end, I joined the Canadian Army, and despite my very poor English in the beginning, I settled in very quickly and was accepted. I was very happy about that, as up until then we had been called all sorts of things such as foreigners and Nazi sympathisers.[42]

However, Danish sailors and other Danes in Allied service gained a form of recognition and respect again in connection with various events in Denmark during 1943. On Christmas Day, 1943, Danish ships in the British Merchant Navy were once again allowed to sail with the Dannebrog flying over their ships. Before this, they were forced to fly the flag of the British Merchant Navy, The Red Duster. This was not only because the Danish sailors had worked tirelessly for the Allied supply effort from the occupation of Denmark in 1940 to the end of 1943, but also because this effort was now more visible to their colleagues and, in the case of the sailors, to the higher authorities in the international merchant navy.

29 August 1943 was also a turning point for the Danish people, as a real showdown with the German occupying forces took place in Denmark; the reasons for this showdown were due to important events at home and abroad. The difficult battles on the Eastern

41 Jakob Sørensen, *D-Dag – Operation Overlord 6. Juni 1944* (Copenhagen: People's Press, 2014), pp.20–21.

42 The following quotes come from Kystmuseet Bangsbo Arkiv's material about Niels Wiesneck, where a taped interview is available.

and Mediterranean fronts, where Hitler's troops suffered more and more defeats, would have a massive impact on the Danish people's relationship with the German occupying power. When Hitler's Italian ally, Mussolini, was deposed on 24 July 1943 as a direct consequence of the strong Allied advance in Italy, this greatly affected the mood of the Danish people. In Denmark, there was a feeling that the war would soon be over, and this created a strong reluctance to cooperate with the German occupying forces. The resistance movement's sabotage activities, primarily against railways, were greatly increased, which led to several curfews from the Germans. The increased bans led to large protests from the Danish people, which they showed by stopping work, going on strike and creating actual street riots against the German soldiers. As a result of the violent rebellion, the Danish Government was pressurised by the German occupying forces to calm the population. However, Hitler was not satisfied with how the riots were handled and ordered the Reich Plenipotentiary in Denmark, Werner Best, to call for a state of emergency. The Danish Government was to issue a ban on gathering in groups, a ban on strikes and a curfew after dark. The most prominent demand was a faster trial and the introduction of the death penalty for sabotage against the German Wehrmacht's assets in Denmark.

The parties in the Danish unity government rejected the German demands, which meant that the Danish Government was now deposed and its functioning ceased. Instead, the Germans launched Operation Safari, which meant martial law – the Danish defence was disarmed on the morning of 29 August 1943. The operation resulted in 23 Danish and 5 German soldiers being killed. All Danish war material was taken by the Germans and all Danish officers were interned. In addition, 90 communists were arrested by the Germans and taken to German camps, and 250 prominent Danes, such as politicians, writers, scientists, et cetera were interned in the Horserød camp. At the same time, the Germans attempted to take over the Danish fleet at Holmen in Copenhagen. Four Danish ships and nine cutters managed to escape to Sweden, the crews aboard 32 vessels managed to sink their ships, but the majority of the Danish ships fell into German hands. The events in Denmark were seen as a serious offence against the German occupying power, which meant that Denmark now had to be controlled under much stricter conditions, as was also the case in Norway. The German martial law ended six weeks later, but the Danish Government still refrained from returning and resuming work.[43]

The significant events in Denmark in the last half of 1943 were of great importance to Danish warships in Allied service. As a result of the Danish people's rebellion against the German occupation, Danish ships in British service were allowed, from 25 December 1943, to sail with the Dannebrog hoisted again – but still subject to British regulations. The symbolic significance of being able to represent Denmark again after having witnessed the government's collaboration with the German occupying forces was of great importance to the Danish sailors. At the start of the Danish occupation in 1940, the Danish sailors had been declared 'friendly enemies' by the Danish Government. The same support the sailors had given to the Allied merchant fleet had now directly contributed to Denmark regaining some respect from the British perspective.[44] British Foreign Secretary Anthony Eden paid

43 Claus Bundgård Christensen, Joachim Lund, Niels Wium Olsesen, Jakob Sørensen, *Danmark besat – krig og hverdag 1940–1945* (Copenhagen: Gyldendals, 2005), pp.412–433.

44 Anders Bjørn Hansen, *Breve fra Anders* (Copenhagen: Gyldendal, 2012), pp.245–251.

tribute to the Danish efforts after the events of August 1943 in a speech at the Anglo Danish Society in January 1944:

> You are front-line fighters in the ranks of the united nations. Like the Danish ships in our service, you help to hoist the Dannebrog by the work of your hands side by side with the Allied Flags. It has been the efforts of the Allied war and trade flags that have made victory possible. And Danish ships and Danish sailors have bravely taken part in this great eruption of power.[45]

The symbolic recognition of the Danish sailors' efforts in the first three years of the war was generally a welcome thank you, as the Danish sailors, like their foreign colleagues in the Allied merchant fleet, had done the same work and, significantly, had been exposed to the same dangers as them. The incessant threat of torpedoing and mine explosions to the cargo ships was a constant threat to the sailors, and even when they were in what was presumably a safe harbour, the danger was ever-present, as Danish sailor Viggo Hans Nielsen found out when he was on board the *Ville D'Amiens*:

> We were moored at Liverpool when the sirens suddenly sounded. We hadn't been told anything about these bombings, but suddenly the sirens sounded... And then all of a sudden it started to roar and thunder around us. I shouted to my mate: "We have to lie down in the gutter, there's nothing else to do." The bombs were dropping close by.[46]

During the war, the Germans developed the infamous V weapons, which were used for terrorist bombing of London in particular. Nielsen experienced this first-hand, even though he was in what he described as relatively safe areas:

> During the war, we also became familiar with the V-1s. We called them 'doodle-bugs'. At one point we were down near Southampton when one of these V-1s came whizzing over our heads with a Spitfire right behind it. We also had another time when we were at Dagenham and we were at the racecourse and one of the V-1s flew over us and suddenly we could hear the engine stop and we all dropped down, but thank God it kind of skidded instead of crashing straight into us, so it got out and went straight into the Thames. We were lucky...

Viggo Hans Nielsen would later experience even more of the reality of war aboard *Thyra III*, which took part in the Normandy invasion.

---

45 Repoduced in Anders Bjørn Hansen, *Breve fra Anders* (Copenhagen: Gyldendal, 2012), p.251 from Radioreferat den 13. January 1944 (London radio's Danish broadcasts). The Danish National Archives, Ministry of Foreign Affairs H 84–346 (1909–45), j. No. 84.X.6 Principielle Akter om Behandling af Danske Skibe og Ladninger (indenfor de Allieredes Magtområde).

46 This and the following quotes are from an interview with Viggo Hans Nielsen conducted by Kjeld Sasbye on 16 February 1984.

It was not only the Danish sailors abroad who felt the impact of the major events in Denmark in August 1943. The previous national shame was now being reversed for Danes in Allied service, and they could afford to be proud of their resistance to the German occupation, as Kjeld Rønhof of the Royal Air Force recalls:

> There was finally good news from Denmark. Our countrymen had finally had enough. The navy had sunk its vessels in Copenhagen harbour. The army had been disbanded. Many of the officers had gone underground and the Germans were hunting them everywhere. The King was now considered a prisoner in his own Kingdom. Even though things would now be tough for Denmark, they had shown themselves to be men and taken a stand against the tyrant. That same day, I painted a Danish flag on my Spitfire to show that I was proud of my countrymen.[47]

The regained respect for the Danes after the events of 1943 would not only be of great importance for the Danes who later participated in the Normandy invasion in 1944 and especially for the sailors who had to sail with the Dannebrog hoisted, but the events of 1943 would also be of great importance for Denmark's post-war legacy.

47 Kjeld Rønhof, *Vi fløj for Friheden* (Copenhagen: Four Stripes,1991), p.72.

German bombers over Copenhagen on 9 April 1940. On the street are air-dropped leaflets, 'OPROP'. The Palads Cinema is in the background. (Freedom Museum)

The good-natured laxative
LIXEN
ELIXIR Bottles 1/2 & 2/-
LOZENGES Tins 8½d, 1/2

CLOSING PRICES — EVENING STANDARD April 9, 1940 — FINAL NIGHT EXTRA

Evening Standard

Amusements 12
Radio 14

BLACK-OUT 8.15 pm, 5.48 am
MOON
Rose 7.4 am ; Sets 9.38 pm

Ingersoll
THE WATCH FOR THE
AIR FORCE
INGERSOLL POCKET & WRIST WATCHES
Sold by Ingersoll Dealers Everywhere

No. 36,066 — LONDON, TUESDAY, APRIL 9, 1940 — ONE PENNY

NORWAY AND DENMARK INVADED: THE ALLIES WILL GIVE FULL AID

Nazi Battle-Cruiser Reported Sunk

"BRITISH FORCE ON WAY," SAYS NEW YORK

IT WAS REPORTED IN STOCKHOLM TO-NIGHT THAT NORWEGIAN COASTAL BATTERIES SANK A GERMAN BATTLE CRUISER, BELIEVED TO BE THE GNEISENAU, IN OSLO FIORD, SAYS BRITISH UNITED PRESS.

THE British and French Governments are to extend full aid to Norway, following the invasion of Norway

"PROPHECY FULFILLED" —PREMIER

Nazi 'Mining' Excuse Is Exploded

MR. CHAMBERLAIN told the House of Commons this

The occupation of Denmark and Norway made headlines around the world, as seen here in the *Evening Standard*. (*Evening Standard*)

Above: Erik Egebak (Historisk Arkiv Vendsyssel)
Right: Jørgen Linnet who was onboard the training ship *Denmark*. He would later participate in the invasion of Normandy in 1944.. (*Evening Standard*)

Niels Wiesneck in Canadian uniform. (Finn Wiesneck)

Henrik Bødker Knudsen. (Aksel Bødker Knudsen)

Holger Jensen in 1938. (Jørgen Aarlo Jensen)

One of the many drawings in Wiesneck's diary. Here of an unnamed harbour from the period around the occupation of Denmark. (Finn Wiesneck)

Danske Skibe skal søge til neutrale Havne

København. Torsdag.

Handelsministeriet meddeler Onsdag:

Danske Skibe opfordres til at søge ind til neutrale Havne. Skibe i Middelhavet skal saavidt muligt søge til italienske eller spanske Havne.

From the Danish side, the order was: 'Search for a neutral European harbour. Preferably Italian or Spanish'. Danish captains realised that it was most likely the Germans who were behind this order. (Nordby Parish Archives)

Evald Brinck in British uniform. (Evald Brinck)

Kjeld Rønhof. (Freedom Museum)

John Andreasen in Canadian uniform. (FamilieJournalen / Karl Ravn)

Danish propaganda poster used in England. (M/S Museet for Søfart)

British soldiers wade into the sea to board a destroyer during the evacuation at Dunkirk. (Imperial War Museum)

British troops under attack by German fighter planes on the beach at Dunkirk, 20 June 1940. Not all troops managed to return to England during evacuation of 26 May to 4 June; up to 100,000 British soldiers found themselves south of the River Somme after Operation Dynamo officially ended. (Imperial War Museum)

Captured British and French soldiers who did not make it to the evacuation ships. (Freedom Museum)

J.P. Sørensen in 2005. Sørensen was involved in evacuating British troops at Dunkirk as well as the invasion of Normandy in 1944. (Ebbe Kyrø)

S/S *Dagmar* of Esbjerg participated in the evacuation at Dunkirk in 1940. The ship was sunk in the English Channel on 9 June 1941 by an air raid. (M/S Maritime Museum)

Dieppe 1942 then. (Library and Archives Canada)

Dieppe 1942 now. (Private collection)

THE GLOBE AND MAIL, TORONTO, WEDNESDAY, SEPTEMBER 16, 1942

2,547 Canadians Listed Missing After Dieppe Assault

Defense Department Issues Official List

(Continued from previous page)

Missing

Ontario Officers Missing

Newspaper headline in the Canadian newspaper, *The Globe and Mail* after the disastrous raid at Dieppe. (National Archives of Canada)

Kaj Birksted (first row, second from right) and other pilots from the Norwegian 331 Squadron, November 1942. (Tvedte)

A German officer inspects a Thompson sub machine gun abandoned by the Canadian forces at Dieppe. Many vehicles, weapons and equipment were subsequently taken over and used by the Germans. (Freedom Museum)

Above and right: Hans Erik Jepsen was reported missing in Canadian service on 19 August 1942 during the disastrous Dieppe raid. It was subsequently assumed that he perished in the bloody attack. Jepsen was born in Odense on 10 August 1920. He wanted to become a sailor, after which he became student No.84 aboard the training ship *Denmark*'s voyage to America in 1940. When Denmark was occupied by Germany, he found himself in Jacksonville among many other young school ship students, and like many of his peers, had a burning desire to fight the Germans and sign up for Allied service. He subsequently enlisted in the Canadian Army and The Essex Scottish Regiment on 25 June 1940 in Windsor, Ontario. Jepsen's name is on the plaque at Brookwood Memorial in Surrey, England. (Photo left: Hadsten Local Archives – Photo on the right: Canadian Virtual Memorial) (Photo left: Hadsten Local Archives)

Henning Rudolph Calberg was also part of Canadian Essex Scottish Regiment that attacked Dieppe. He died during the attack on 19 August 1942, aged 20. Calberg was born in Copenhagen and enlisted for Canadian service when the war broke out. He is buried in the British cemetery near Dieppe. (Photo: K. Falconer & J. Stephens)

German soldiers quench their thirst after the successful defence of Dieppe. (Freedom Museum)

Rommel's first stop on the inspection tour of the Atlantic Wall was Denmark. In this photo he is making an inspection on 8 December 1943 at 'Pikkerbakken', part of the Atlantic Wall near Frederikshavn. (Kystmuseet Bangsbo. Lokalhistoriske Arkiv)

During the inspection of the Atlantic Wall, Rommel ordered a sketch of what the ideal coastal defence should look like. Rommel's 'asparagus' with mines on top of wooden piles, Belgian gates, 'Spanish horsemen' and miles of barbed wire were some of the elements Rommel demanded be introduced. (US National Archives)

Cannon bunker located on 'Pikkerbakken' near Frederikshavn. (Kystmuseet Bangsbo Fort – Photo: F. G. Tillisch)

Part of the Atlantic rampart at Longues-sur-Mer in Normandy where one of the original guns still exists today. The battery was in action on D-Day, 6 June 1944, when it fired 170 shells. (Private collection)

V-1 bomb on its way to its launch pad. (Bundesarchiv)

Left: One of the most significant symbols for Danish sailors in the Allied Merchant Navy – the Merchant Navy emblem. This was a visible proof for the Danish sailors that they were officially part of the Allied cause. This emblem belonged to the Bent Ørberg. (Private collection)
Right: Danish sailor on board *Avance* in Normandy. (M/S The Maritime Museum)

Viggo Hans Nielsen, 1943. (Lis Nielsen)

The Dannebrog hoisted over the aft anti-aircraft gun on board *Avance* during the invasion of Normandy in 1944. (M/S Museet for Søfart)

Danish warships after the navy's sinking at Holmen in Copenhagen in connection with the state of emergency on 29 August 1943. From the right are the artillery ship *Peder Skram*, heating boat *Vb. 2* and the motor torpedo boat *Hvalrossen* (of which only the masts are visible). In the background is the frigate *Fyn*. (National Museum of Denmark)

Part 2

The Grand Plan – Operation Overlord

In the period from 9 April 1940 to early 1944, the sailors had already experienced the horrors of war. They were scattered far and wide during those years, from the Pacific to the Atlantic. Torpedoing, mine explosions and the constant danger of German E-Boats were an ever-present threat to them. Their fates were also very different, which ultimately determined their role in the Normandy invasion. One of the factors that became crucial to the success of a major invasion was the vital need for transport ships – thousands of ships that could transport troops, equipment, vehicles, weapons, ammunition and other essential supplies. Many Danish ships in the Danish Merchant Navy were used for this purpose. In early 1944, the war was turning in the Allies' favour, but an invasion was necessary for them to penetrate and gain a firm foothold in Western Europe. There was a need to open the second front, which could push Hitler's troops back into Europe and all the way to Berlin.

The Allied commanders had not yet launched a large-scale invasion of Western Europe, largely because the Battle of the Atlantic had to be won first. This only happened finally in May 1943, after the German E-Boat fleet had been diminished. The Battle of the Atlantic involved the E-Boats and armed merchant ships of the German Navy against the Allied convoys. Despite the German Navy's defeat in the Battle of the Atlantic, there was still a constant threat of attack from German E-Boats in the North Atlantic, although these were nowhere near as intensive nor as dangerous due to the increased anti-submarine weaponry and tactics of the Allied navies. Additionally, the Russian army had crushed the German offensive at Kursk in early July 1943, and Stalin now called for firm invasion plans from his allies into Western Europe.

After a meeting between Stalin, Roosevelt and Churchill in Tehran at the end of November 1943, it was finally decided to focus on opening the second front. After careful consideration, they decided that the invasion would take place in Normandy in May 1944. The operation was codenamed Operation Overlord and General Eisenhower was chosen as the Supreme Commander of the Allied Forces.[1] The decision to open the second front with an invasion had a major impact for the transport ships that would carry supplies to Normandy.

The overall plans for the upcoming operation would be drawn up by a select group of men under the Chief of Staff to the Supreme Allied Commander (COSSAC). In March 1943,

1 Christian Tortzen, *Kampen på Havet* (Copenhagen: Information, 2011), pp.176–206.

British General Frederick Morgan was appointed commander of this group of planners. The group's work was crucial to the outcome of the largest landings in history.

The first drafts of the plans were delivered to Generals Eisenhower and Montgomery in the autumn of 1943, and it was finally decided in January 1944 that the operation in this form should be expanded to five landing sectors if Normandy, as a landing site, was to be used as a base for the final objective of the war, Germany. In February 1943, General Eisenhower initially proposed to set the date as 31 May 1944. For the operation to take place on this date it would still be dependent on several factors, such as optimal weather, as an operation of this magnitude ideally depended on as much daylight as possible, making the time of year relatively ideal. In addition, low tide would also be desirable, as the mines and underwater obstacles of the Atlantic Wall would then be visible to the attacking Allied forces. Additionally, paratroopers could rely on a full moon to orientate themselves in the darkness before the infantry troops attacked the landing sectors on D-Day itself. As time progressed and the date of D-Day drew nearer, these factors became decisive in setting a new date for the operation. The choice was now 5 June. The invasion planners in charge would meet daily during this period, and they soon realised that the weather would have a huge impact on the invasion date. On 2 June, a weather report was delivered to General Eisenhower and the forecast for 5 June was not promising. A storm was coming and it could be disastrous, especially for the airborne troops. The launch of Operation Overlord was therefore postponed.[2]

By this time, thousands of Allied ships had already been launched to transport the invasion troops to the Normandy coast. They had to drop anchor and wait for better weather. The Allied troops aboard the ships were not used to the rough seas and they suffered greatly – the seasickness weakened them for the coming invasion. The storm gradually subsided and Operation Overlord was officially launched on 6 June, which became D-Day. (This designation is not specifically a definition for the Normandy invasion, as is perhaps widely believed, but the D-Day designation is a general military term for the start day of any major military operations. Furthermore, the exact launch time of the operation was labelled H-hour.)

The many Allied troops that were part of Operation Overlord were distributed to attack five beach sectors. These were codenamed, from west to east: Utah, Omaha, Gold, Juno and Sword. The American forces were given responsibility for Utah and Omaha. The British were responsible for taking Gold and Sword, while the Canadians were responsible for Juno. All five beach sectors were supplemented by troops, airmen and sailors from many other countries: Norway, The Netherlands, France, Australia, New Zealand, Czechoslovakia, Greece, Belgium, Poland and Denmark, despite the latter not actually being an Allied country.

Five divisions were to attack the Normandy coastal area over a stretch of more than 100 kilometres. Another four divisions were to act as reserves.[3]

---

2 Stuart C. Robertson & Dale Booth, *Following in the Footsteps of Heroes: D-Day June 6th 1944*, (Devizes: Sabrestorm, 2014), pp.14–16.

3 Antony Beevor, *D-Dag: Kampen om Normandiet* (Copenhagen: Lindhardt & Ringhof, 2009), pp.19–51.

Preparations for Invasion
'There was no hiding the fact that the invasion and the second front had moved pretty close'

In preparation for the impending invasion the majority of the transport ships had to be upgraded to handle the invasion supplies. Despite this, the ordinary Danish sailors were not told what was happening, as the invasion plans were still top secret. Erik Egebak clearly remembers how he began to realise something was up when he was on board the American Liberty ship *Joseph Pulitzer* in April 1944:

> Speculation was already rife at the time, because for a very long time the Russians had been telling all the Allied forces that the second front was about to be opened. It was on everyone's lips.
>
> So it may well be that we were already thinking at that time that this has something to do with some kind of landing... Things started happening in Liverpool. We were probably around April by then. Preparations were already very far advanced. So we were sent to the shipyard in Liverpool to have some radical changes made to the ship. We were adapted to sail with a certain number of troops. One of the holds was converted into accommodation for soldiers. Our crew went on some courses in advanced firefighting and protection against gas attacks.[4]

In May 1944, Henrik Bødker Knudsen from Frederikshavn boarded the Danish ship M/S *Gudrun Mærsk* as third mate. The ship was well suited for an invasion as it was very manoeuvrable and could carry significant amounts of supplies. *Gudrun Mærsk* was converted for use in the invasion so that it could transport 3,500 tons of petrol in metal cans, the so-called 'jerrycans'. In addition, the middle deck was also converted to carry troops to the landing areas. In early June 1944, *Gudrun Maersk* lay in the Bristol Channel and was loaded with the many tons of petrol cans to be transported. All smoking was forbidden and working with tools had to be done with extreme caution as the slightest spark could ignite the vapours from the petrol cans. This was a constant stress factor at first, but quickly became part of the routine, as Henrik Bødker Knudsen recalls:

> At first we walked like we were walking on a bomb, but it quickly became a daily routine and we got used to travelling with the risk of explosion and eventually didn't give it a second thought.[5]

Once the pilot had disembarked from a transport ship and that ship had left the harbour, a boat would dock alongside and an officer from the Admiralty would board the ship and deliver a sealed envelope with strict instructions not to open the envelope until the ship had sailed. This letter contained the final orders for the invasion, it indicated the ship's place

4 Quote from Cicerone ApS and Nexus Communication's interview with Erik Egebak and archive material in connection with the production of the documentary 'The War Sailors'.

5 Henrik Bødker Knudsen, *Krigssejler* (Copenhagen: Frihedsmuseets Venners Forlag, 1992), p.97.

in the convoys and the specific destination on the invasion coast.[6] On a sunny summer morning, Knudsen and the rest of the crew aboard *Gudrun Maersk* were told to weigh anchor and place the ship in a fixed position off the Bristol coast. The captain had previously received a sealed letter that was not to be opened under any circumstances until the ship was in a holding position off the British coast. He opened the sealed letter shortly afterwards, and the suspicions of the sailors on board *Gudrun Maersk* were now realised. In the letter was a specific and clearly described order that they were to sail to Normandy and specifically unload at the Omaha Beach sector. The letter also included a map and a detailed description of the invasion area, with specific buoys and routes marked so that the route to 'Omaha' was unmistakable.[7]

Viggo Hans Nielsen was on board *Thyra III*, and as early as the end of May 1944, the crew had strong suspicions that something big was afoot when the ship was ordered into harbour. Here, the bow was reinforced, the propeller was replaced and an extra engine pump was fitted for firefighting. The booms were reinforced and the ship was equipped with three anti-aircraft guns. After a while, Nielsen realised what was in store:

> We had guns on board, but there weren't enough men, so I went to gunnery school to learn how to operate the guns. We learnt how to clean it all, take it apart and put it back together again, and of course how to shoot at the target. We wondered what all that was for, but one day shortly afterwards we were suddenly told that we were not allowed to contact other ships. Shortly afterwards, we painted a number on the ship and sailed down to Portsmouth, where we were loaded with soldiers and vehicles. There were lots of ships, so we knew something was going on, but we didn't know what exactly. On 5 June 1944, we were told to leave without knowing exactly where to. At night we could hear one wave of aeroplanes after another flying over our heads, and we could hear bombing from Pomerania to over there.[8]

Further east, off the coast of London, Jørgen Linnet was on board *Alan A. Dale*. The ship was originally called *Nordvest*, but when war broke out, it was taken into the American merchant fleet and renamed. In the period leading up to the Normandy invasion, the ship lay off London for a few days while the captain awaited orders on what to do. *Alan A. Dale* was ordered to sail down the Dover Strait with dozens of other ships. During the journey down the strait, Jørgen Linnet saw how the Germans sent the dreaded V weapons towards London. *Alan A. Dale* was ordered to wait at the Dover Cliffs, and here the crew could just lie there and witness the countless guns placed on top of the Dover Cliffs trying to shoot down the V-1s. Confusion reigned as several of the transport ships anchored at Dover suddenly began sailing eastwards towards Normandy. At this point, *Alan A. Dale* had not yet received orders. After a few anxious days, during which several V-1s detonated around Dover Cliffs and scattered metal shrapnel across the ship's deck, Jørgen Linnet and the rest of the crew were finally ordered to sail for Omaha on 10 June 1944:

6 Erik Kragelund, *Overlord – Den Danske Deltagelse i Invasionen i Normandiet i 1944* (Copenhagen: Radius, 2013), p.10.
7 Henrik Bødker Knudsen, *Krigssejler* (Copenhagen: Frihedsmuseets Venners Forlag, 1992), pp.96–101.
8 From an interview with Viggo Hans Nielsen conducted by Kjeld Sasbye on 16 February 1984.

> At that time, the invasion was already underway, but we were never really informed that the invasion was actually underway. In general, there wasn't really any information for the enlisted crew. There was no radio or anything to let them know about it. Everything was very secret, and you weren't allowed to say anything on the air. Therefore, we were always unaware of what was going on.[9]

The development of the war from 9 April 1940 to the beginning of 1944 also meant that it was often a coincidence which ships the sailors were hired onto during this period. Coincidences that even led several young sailors to join other Allied services. Niels Wiesneck had served on board several ships in the Allied international merchant fleet when he ended up in Canada in 1942. At this point, he could not find employment on a ship, so he made the decision to enlist in the Canadian Army. He joined the Essex Scottish Regiment, which was generally a colourful bunch of French, Germans, English, Irish and a few Indians. What Niels Wiesneck and the rest of the regiment did not realise at the time was that the Essex Scottish Regiment would serve as a replacement regiment during the Normandy invasion in July 1944 – about a month after D-Day. 22,000 Canadian soldiers, including Niels Wiesneck, were shipped out of Halifax in early June 1944 on the huge troopship *Queen Elizabeth I*. None of the soldiers knew their destination, but as they approached Scotland, they were all unloaded onto cattle trains and shipped south at night. Wiesneck now knew that something big was happening:

> Suddenly we were ordered to move further down the coast at Eastbourne. That's where we saw the Germans come roaring in to bomb London. We were then sent out into the Channel to do exercises with small landing craft, so we could sense that something big was coming. We were then moved all the way down to the coast by the beach in some large forests. Here, all communication with the outside world was completely shut down. No letters came in or out, and we had previously been warned that we should write a letter home, because it would be a long time before we could send new ones. As we waited and were trapped down by this forest, we realised more and more that we might have to cross to the other side of the Channel. We were given 24-hour rations and extra bandages and water boots.[10]

Elsewhere in England, Holger Jensen was travelling south on a train. At the time, he had no idea where exactly he was going, but he knew that something big was happening. He had spent several years as a sailor, including, in 1942, being torpedoed by a German submarine in the North Atlantic aboard the M/S *Diana* and spending 91 hours in the icy sea clinging to a piece of driftwood, and after which he was treated in a hospital in Reykjavik.

He was then assigned to the US Army Maritime Transport. Subsequently, he was transferred to England as a naval inspector, which would give him a pivotal role during the Normandy invasion. Jensen knew nothing of this when he arrived in an unnamed wooded area in England:

9 Interview with Jørgen Linnet, February 2016.

10 From Kystmuseet Bangsbo Arkiv's material about Niels Wiesneck, where a taped interview is available.

> There were sentries walking so close to each other behind 4 or 5 rows of barbed wire that they could touch each other with their rifle barrels. We lived in tents in there in straw and lived well the days we were there, and as some put it: "It's the fattening up before we're slaughtered." One morning we got ready and then we had to go. There was a terrible racket in the air with airmen, and we got to Southampton. We got on a ship there in the late afternoon. It must have been the 6 of June.[11]

Shortly thereafter, Jensen was ordered aboard a ship with the other marine inspectors and placed in the front convoy ship with the role of convoy commander. He was informed that the destination was 'Omaha' and that there had been brutal and heavy fighting on this particular beach sector during the day.

The Danish pilots in the Royal Air Force also noticed the increasing activity and sensed that something big was happening. Kjeld Rønhof was told that the fighter pilots' Spitfires should be fitted with 250kg bombs so that the fighters could also function as fighter-bombers. By the end of April, Danish pilots in the Norwegian Air Force began carrying out small-scale bombing raids in France, including against the German V-1 bomb sites at Calais. Rønhof then participated in bombing raids at Reims, Rouen and Paris. On 10 May, Rønhof's squadron was ordered to carry out a bombing raid on the railway at Valenciennes as part of the strategy of destroying the German supply lines for the upcoming Normandy invasion:

> There were a lot of trains gathered at the station, and our bombs hit the middle of the railway yard. There must have been an ammunition train in the centre of it all, because the explosion that followed was tremendous. We saw locomotives and railway wagons flying through the air, and it all developed into a gigantic ball of fire. The process of softening up France continued. Day after day we bombed railway stations, cut railway lines.[12]

Lieutenant Colonel in the Norwegian Air Force, Kaj Birksted, on the other hand, was in no doubt about the prospects of the coming invasion when he was given responsibility for planning all daytime fighter operations of the Norwegian squadrons. Birksted had already received the British DSO in 1943, and as Operations Officer, he was now responsible for fighter operations for the upcoming invasion. Birksted's planning for these operations included the initial attacks on airfields, radar stations and railway stations in the weeks leading up to D-Day, 6 June. In addition, the Norwegian squadrons were tasked with supporting the heavy and medium bombers during bombing raids on bridges, bunkers, gun positions and other tactical targets. The heavy bombers were Lancasters, and the medium bombers were Bostons, Marauders and Mitchells, usually flying in formations of 36, 72, 144 or in special cases up to 200 aircraft at a time with fighter cover.[13]

---

11 Quoted from Holger Jensen's account from the DR radio programme 'Den Store Landgang' by Poul S. Poulsen, 6 June 1969.

12 Kjeld Rønhof, *Vi fløj for Friheden* (Copenhagen: Four Stripes,1991), p.98.

13 Susanne Zima Feierskov, *Med vinger og våben* (Copenhagen: Gyldendal, 2011), p.212.

Andreas Moldt was on board the training ship *Danmark* when the news of Denmark's occupation came on 9 April 1940. He subsequently served on various Scandinavian ships in convoy service, but returned to the training ship as an assistant instructor after it was taken over by the US Coast Guard in 1941. In 1943, Moldt enlisted in the Canadian Air Force and was transferred to England the same year for final training in the Royal Air Force's Bomber Command, where he was promoted pilot officer in 1944 and then worked for a short time as an instructor in Canada in air traffic and gunnery. Moldt's skills served him well when he was later transferred to England and subsequently took part in the invasion of Normandy, where he acted as a rear gunner in a Lancaster bomber and took part in 30 sorties over occupied Europe. After the 30 sorties, the *ITEM* Lancaster was handed over to a new crew (*ITEM* was the name that the crew had given their aircraft), who were shot down shortly afterwards over the French-Belgian border. During the same period that Moldt flew in 166 Squadron, the squadron lost 45 aircraft and 22 crew members. On 27 May 1944, Moldt and the crew aboard *ITEM* received word that it was 'ops on' and that they were going on another bombing mission. They had previously participated in bombing raids over France, but this time the target was a freight railway station near Achen. For Moldt, this meant that the Lancaster had to be prepared as quickly as possible – the engines had to be cleaned and the machine guns adjusted. By the end of May, however, there was no doubt that an invasion was coming, as Moldt recalls:

> There was no hiding the fact that the invasion and the second front had moved pretty close. Every night, other groups took care of targets related to coastal defences and the transport routes to the western part of France. But exactly where on the coast the invasion was to take place, we could not draw any conclusions.[14]

The bombing raid at Achen was a foretaste of what awaited *ITEM* and the other Lancasters during the Normandy invasion. *ITEM* and the other bombers came under heavy fire from German anti-aircraft guns, but *ITEM* escaped unharmed. The *ITEM's* load consisted of 13 x 500kg bombs, all of which hit railway wagons and destroyed important German supply routes. Three of the other Lancasters that *ITEM* flew with did not make it home, and all crew members were killed. After the bombing raid, the *ITEM* crew were given a few days of leave, which proved to be much-needed, as in June 1944 they flew 15 bombing raids, or every other day, as Moldt recalls:

> The month of May ended with a short trip across the North Sea, where we had to fire all the machine guns and correct any faults. I was certainly glad of that, as I was going to need them to work very soon.[15]

John Andreasen had become a hardened anti-aircraft artilleryman in the Canadian Army in the run-up to the Normandy invasion. In May, Andreasen's regiment was positioned

14 Andreas P. Moldt, *Natbomber: Slaget om Europa som en Dansker Oplevede det i Invasionssommeren 1944* (Copenhagen: Gyldendal, 1985), p.55.

15 Andreas P. Moldt, *Natbomber: Slaget om Europa som en Dansker Oplevede det i Invasionssommeren 1944* (Copenhagen: Gyldendal, 1985), p.56.

on the south coast of England. Attacks from German fighter planes and the infamous V weapons continued. As a result, there was a constant need to defend the airspace against the enemy, a defence that the Canadian artillerymen also took part in. At the end of May, John Andreasen's regiment was relieved by a British anti-aircraft battery, and this was the last time Andreasen was involved in the defence of the British coast. When the regiment returned to their camp, known simply as 'The Bog', they were told that a major new operation was underway and each man was issued a new Lee Enfield rifle direct from the factory. In addition, each man was given a lifejacket, which fuelled rumours that the invasion was imminent. As Andreasen recalls:

> One day we were called in to see the commander, and we were told that our division would be part of the first day of the invasion of 'Hitler's Fortress'. Now we had to train in earnest, mostly command and landing exercises, but mostly how to kill our enemies. Rumours were rife again, but this time it was to be very secret. We were ordered to get everything ready to leave the next day morning, never to return to The Bog again, so that night most of us went down to the pubs, we wanted to have a last glass of beer with our English friends in town.[16]

Evald Brinck had joined the British Navy after war broke out in 1939. In March 1944, he received orders to report to a naval station in Scotland, where he was trained to operate Bofors machine guns, which were typically installed on board British ships.

He was then sent to Sunderland, where he and the rest of the crew had to prepare a British Empire boat. They were told that the ship had to be able to handle tons of supplies and soldiers. It was here that Brinck realised that something big was about to happen:

> Everyone suspected that something was going on. It was common knowledge. When we sailed into Sunderland, we could see that the transport ships were fully crewed. You don't have that much crew on board for fun. At the end of May, we loaded the ship with soldiers and tanks. I don't think we were officially aware that we were going to Normandy in the days leading up to the invasion. It was only early in the morning via the radio that we were told it was Normandy.[17]

The success of the upcoming invasion depended on several things, including conducting small raids on the Normandy coast to find out what types of defence installations the Germans had. This involved taking German soldiers prisoner to get information. This intelligence could be crucial to the success of the Allied attacks on the coast. A Dane, using the invented name of 'Jens Jensen', took part in these raids in the dead of night:[18]

16 John Andreasen, unpublished war diary, p.25.

17 Evald Brinck, ... *de vil aldrig blive husket – beretning om danske søfolk 1940 – 1945* (Tåsinge: Evald Springeren Brinck, 2007), p.21.

18 Jensen's account is based on an interview by Poul S. Poulsen in the DR radio programme 'Den Store Landgang', first broadcast on 6 June 1969. The following quotes are taken from the programme. Jens Jensen is a fictitious name in connection with the interview.

> We were called in and given a fixed task. The task usually consisted of getting two or three men, either enlisted men or officers. We usually sailed across the Channel on a dark night. We hit a point on the coast that was predetermined and that we knew from aerial photographs or other information was a good spot. Then we captured – to put it bluntly – with the devil's violence and power, three or four men, maybe five, maybe not more, because we didn't have room for that. And if we got more, God have mercy and comfort the poor souls. We indeed had cases where the Germans rightly said that we had left them in handcuffs, but it wasn't too bad and we managed to avoid any reprimands. But with handcuffs and tied up, and with three bullets in the chest, it was not a pretty sight for the Germans to find the next morning on the beach. Although this only occurred if we captured too many to take back.

These specially trained groups also aimed to gather important information about the Normandy coastline. These raids tested the soldiers' discipline, as the slightest misstep could put the Germans on their trail, so the men were trained to kill first and find information later – but live prisoners were of course an advantage. As you would expect, these raids were by no means without danger, even for your own men, as Jens Jensen recalls:

> We had a Polish guy with us and there's nothing to say about it, he couldn't resist the temptation. He shouted: "Kill them, kill them", and we had been ordered to do it all quietly, and we had every chance to surprise a patrol and just take the three or four men we needed and leave as it should have been done. But then comes the discipline, then comes the sadness and the brutality. The raw. The Pole couldn't control his mentality, or to put it another way, his hatred was so great that he couldn't shut his mouth, keep silence and obey the order – because the order was 'silence'. Our officer grabbed the only means available, a knife. One blow and there was silence. We were one man down. That raid could have gone off without casualties. But we had one man missing – by our own hand.

Jens Jensen actively participated in several raids on the Normandy coast as part of the important gathering of information for the upcoming invasion. In 1945, he was sent to Burma, where he fought against the Japanese forces. When he returned to Denmark in 1946, he held the rank of captain. He lived isolated on a farm for the rest of his life, far away from the horrors of war.

The V Articles

The efforts of warships in the upcoming invasion would be crucial to keeping supply lines moving. The potential dangers of participating in an operation of this magnitude could undoubtedly cause cold feet for the sailors in the various Allied merchant fleets. Participating in the Normandy invasion was voluntary for the British Merchant Navy, thus, the Merchant Navy authorities feared that some sailors would back down at the prospect of a potentially hazardous invasion. For this reason, a maritime contract, known simply as the V Articles, was drawn up for Danish sailors to sign – it came with a hefty bonus for signing it. This was enough for the majority of the Danish sailors whose ships were selected to participate in the invasion to sign. But their signature on the maritime contract and the many benefits that came with it also had a downside. The V Articles dictated, among other things, that the Danish sailors had to sail supplies to any area designated by the British merchant fleet. This meant they had to sail supplies for the duration of the invasion, and there was no such thing as overtime. It also meant that the warships were closer to the dangers of the Allied offensive than had previously been the case.[19] Henrik Bødker Knudsen from Frederikshavn also remembers that the V Articles had to be signed if he wanted to participate in the invasion on board *Gudrun Maersk*:

> Only when you signed a document called 'LIBERATION OF EUROPE' were you subject to the discretion of the British Ministry of War Transport. The conditions were a little better than those we had when we sailed otherwise. I received the hefty sum of 1 pound, 1 shilling and 10 pence a day, all inclusive. In addition to the wages, we were given a weekly ration consisting of a bottle of whisky, 200 cigarettes and four bars of chocolate, so we were never short of something to smoke, but we never drank on board when sailing, so there was plenty of that too.[20]

J. P. Sørensen was also on board the Danish ship *Gudrun Mærsk* shortly before the Normandy invasion. He clearly remembers the importance of the V Articles:

> I was at the muster office, and a man came and asked me: Would you sign the V Articles? I thought, V Articles, V for Victory, of course I would. I didn't really know what I was signing, but it turned out that I was signing something that said I was bound to all forms of military service – which I realised later![21]

The provisions of the V Articles quickly made it clear to the Danish sailors considering signing the contract that the tasks associated with the coming invasion would by no means be harmless, as Captain Strøh on board the Danish ship *Avance* described it:

> We were 7 captains at a conference in Swansea before sailing; after it had been impressed upon us that we had duties and rights like everyone else belonging to the Royal Navy, we had to realise that we could not all expect to come back again, it was a bit hard to swallow...[22]

19 Christian Tortzen, *Søfolk og Skibe 1939–1945, bind 4* (Copenhagen: Lindhardt & Ringhof, 1985), pp.396–399.

20 Henrik Bødker Knudsen, *Krigssejler* (Copenhagen: Frihedsmuseets Venners Forlag, 1992), p.96.

21 J. P. Sørensen interview: Interviewer: Ulrik Brandt. Recorded at Bombebøssen in Christianshavn on 9 August 2005.

22 Christian Tortzen, *Søfolk og Skibe 1939–1945, bind 4* (Copenhagen: Lindhardt & Ringhof, 1985), p.396.

The Big Exercise – Exercise Tiger 'We trained and trained endlessly'

Before the final plans for the invasion were finalised, the Allies had already conducted a realistic exercise to prepare for the coming invasion. At the end of April 1944, the Allied forces completed Exercise Tiger, which was intended to be a dress rehearsal and as realistic as possible for the Normandy invasion. The exercise took place at Slapton Sands in England, which is geographically similar to the Normandy invasion areas.

The beaches consisted of gravel and were located in a bay, there were also high cliffs similar to the Pointe du Hoc area in Normandy. Slapton Sands thus provided the most realistic training terrain for the real invasion areas to come. Niels Wiesneck was a private in the Canadian Essex Scottish Regiment at the time and clearly remembers the exhausting exercise leading up to D-Day:

> Later on, we were sent down to the coast to practice with the landing craft. We were then sailed out a few miles and sent back to see what it was like to run out onto the beach. Then we were put in charge of storming the hills and practising taking enemy positions. We trained and trained endlessly.... And we were getting really tired of just waiting.[23]

Artillery and air support were part of the exercise, and the smaller landing craft that Wiesneck was aboard were also covered by minesweepers and various warships. Realism was paramount to give the Allies the best possible preparation for the day of the real battle. The rural areas of Slapton Sands were also evacuated, not only to make the exercise as secret as possible, but also to allow the Allies to simulate the capture of cities during the invasion. Exercise Tiger began, as it would in real life during Operation Overlord, by dropping paratroopers from the 82nd and 101st Airborne Divisions over the coast at Slapton Sands. The fleet approached the coastal area on the morning of 27 April, after which the infantry was ordered into landing craft to attack the beach area. Kjeld Rønhof in his Spitfire was to take part in Exercise Tiger as part of the fighter escort of the bombers and recalls the major exercise and its importance:

> The manoeuvre lasted a whole week in cooperation with the army and navy. Who knows, one of these days we might fly out on an exercise like that and then suddenly turn round and go straight for the French coast!
>
> The Germans were of course on their toes everywhere, but they had no chance of getting anywhere near the training area. Europe, indeed the whole world, was holding its breath waiting for us. But to avoid disaster, we had to train and train and train. We had to make sure it was possible to get ashore and then stay there.[24]

23 Interview with Niels Wiesneck in the DR programme 'D-Dag Den Længste Dag', rebroadcast June 2004.

24 Kjeld Rønhof, *Vi fløj for Friheden* (Copenhagen: Four Stripes,1991), p.96.

However, the exercise was not the decisive dress rehearsal that the Allied commanders had hoped for – quite the opposite. There were long delays for some units, and others began attacks on the beach without air support. The engineer troops that arrived on the beach took a very long time to clear obstacles, which led to the tanks idling on the beach for an extended period. It was not until five hours after the attack that the first tank managed to leave the beach. Several soldiers seemed disengaged and strolled across the beach instead of storming it. The purpose of Exercise Tiger was also to create a functional beachhead with troops to defend the area.

There were eight troop ships full of soldiers on their way to participate in the exercise; it was the soldiers' first ever exercise. The eight troop ships were supposed to be escorted by a destroyer, but the destroyer had been superficially damaged by a mine, prompting the captain to order the ship back to harbour. The eight troop carriers were now unprotected and a disaster happened: nine German E-boats had entered English waters to attack Allied merchant ships, but the German E-Boats instead found the eight troop ships and promptly fired their torpedoes at them. Two ships were hit and caught fire. The E-Boats attacked two more ships, which also caught fire. After some time, reinforcements arrived and drove off the German E-Boats, but the damage was already done. There were close to 1,000 soldiers on board the ships, of which almost 750 died during the attack. Despite the great disaster and the loss of 750 men, the main concern of the Allied commanders was whether the Germans had intercepted the Allies' plans for an upcoming landing.[25]

The Great Deception – Operation Bodyguard

The Chinese warlord Sun Tzu proclaimed around 500 BC that 'All warfare depends on deception.'[26] Tzu's statement would prove to still be true in one of the greatest invasions in history almost 2,500 years later. The Allies knew that securing a solid beachhead after the Normandy landings was almost impossible unless they could divert the German armoured divisions from where the invasion would actually take place. Without a diversion, the German armoured divisions would quickly, and probably effectively, carry out a counter-attack where the Allied landings took place, pushing the Allies back into the sea. This is why perhaps the biggest bluff in history was launched with Operation Bodyguard.

Bodyguard was to function as an overarching operation with several subordinate operations, all aimed at confusing the German defenders in the run-up to the launch of the invasion in June. There were two very specific purposes of Bodyguard: one was to give Hitler the impression that the Allies were going to attack certain areas along the west coast of France. The Allies hoped that Hitler would keep his troops in places that were only sporadically attacked as a diversion. The second aim was to keep the German defenders of the Atlantic Wall believing for as long as possible that the Normandy landings were really just a diversionary action and not the actual invasion. Operation Bodyguard contained six main points, including 36 sub-points, all of which were designed to mislead Hitler's troops. For

25 Edwin P. Hoyt, *The Invasion Before Normandy* (London: Robert Hale, 1987), pp.92–100.
26 Sun Tzu, *Kunsten at Føre Krig* (Copenhagen: Gyldendal Business, 2015), p.67.

example, point 3 was directly related to Denmark, as rumours were to be spread that the Allies were planning an attack on Norway with the support of Russian troops, either to force Sweden over to the Allied side, or to capture the Norwegian air bases and harbour facilities, or to begin an Allied invasion of Denmark during the summer of 1944.[27]

The challenge of Operation Bodyguard was to create total confusion and misdirection on many fronts, but the big question was whether the information the Germans intercepted was credible enough for them to actually believe it. If it was not, it could cause the entire Operation Bodyguard to fail. However, the plan appeared to succeed; for example, out of the 300 divisions Hitler had at his disposal in early 1944, 16 were held in Norway and Denmark, so the Germans had certainly not written off Scandinavia as a potential landing destination for an Allied invasion.[28]

The Inflatable Army – Operation Fortitude

Operation Fortitude was one of the largest and most complex hoaxes under Operation Bodyguard. As with Bodyguard, the aim of Fortitude was to confuse the Germans and disperse the German defences as much as possible before the Normandy invasion began.

Operation Fortitude was divided into two different operations, one of which, Fortitude North, was very much linked to Denmark. The aim was to keep the German divisions in Finland, Norway and Denmark by setting up a major diversionary manoeuvre that would make the Germans believe that an invasion in these areas was a real possibility. To create this illusion, a fictitious British 4th Army was set up in Scotland, which on paper comprised 350,000 soldiers who, along with the American 15th Corps (which was a real corps) would invade the north-west coast of Scandinavia during the early summer of 1944. The Allies had no intention of invading Norway or Denmark, but by setting up the fake force in Scotland, they kept the Germans' idea of a possible landing in the north alive. The deception succeeded. All of the German divisions on Norwegian soil were retained in Norway and even expanded. In the spring of 1944, there were 13 infantry divisions, 60,000 Luftwaffe troops, 6,000 SS troops, 90,000 marines and 12,000 other German military personnel with various tasks. The large force was even largely retained in Norway until the surrender in 1945 because of the continuing suspicion of an invasion in Scandinavia.

Fortitude South involved another fictional army – the First US Army Group with, on paper, a huge force of 50 divisions and a million men, which, according to the false intelligence, was to be concentrated in the south and south-west of England. The real invasion army was also in this part of England in the run-up to D-Day, but the false intelligence associated with Fortitude South was designed to convince Hitler that this huge fake army remained after the real invasion had begun. This was to make the Germans believe that once the serious landings had begun, it was really just a diversionary invasion, a diversionary manoeuvre. The intention was for the Germans to wait for the 'real invasion' by this huge fake army, which would attack at the shortest distance from England to Normandy, the

27 Anthony Cave Brown *Bodyguard of Lies: The Extraordinary True Story Behind D-Day* (New York: The Lyons Press, 2007), pp.432–435.

28 Jakob Sørensen, *D-Dag – Operation Overlord 6. Juni 1944* (Copenhagen: People's Press, 2014), p.78.

Pas-de-Calais. General Patton, much to his own annoyance, was put in charge of the tasks associated with Fortitude South. Despite preferring to be on the front lines, he became a very important part of the misdirection of the German defence. Part of Fortitude South consisted of setting up a huge amount of fake military equipment, including inflatable tanks, ships, vehicles and dummy aircraft. False radio traffic was also an important part of the hoax, which caused German reconnaissance planes to fly over the area to take photos of the fake army. Patton's role was to visit both the troops and the areas where the fake military vehicles were set up to make the illusion more believable.[29]

The most important thing was to keep the Germans believing that the fake army was the real invasion force, and it all rested on keeping the Germans supplied with false information. This was done with the help of various spies, one of whom was the Dane Hans Hansen.

Hansen had initially been a spy for the Germans, but after the British intelligence service got hold of him, he had been turned. In this way, he acted as a double agent during Operation Bodyguard and Fortitude. Hansen played two key roles in particular. In January 1944, he was able to tell German intelligence that Eisenhower was coming to England, confirming the Germans' suspicions that an invasion was imminent. Hansen's intelligence was correct and Eisenhower arrived in England on 16 January. The Germans' faith in Hansen was paramount. The intelligence he passed on in connection with Operation Fortitude's deployment of the fake army at Dover was to convince the Germans of the build-up of this huge army at precisely specified cities and locations in England. The Germans had no doubt that there was now a massive force in England and that the most obvious target for the coming invasion was Calais. Fortitude South, like Fortitude North, can be considered a success because the German troops at Calais were held there even when the real landing in Normandy was well underway.[30]

The Invasion Begins – Operation Neptune
'What a sight, ships were everywhere and more were arriving all the time'

Before launching Operation Overlord, it was crucial to prepare. These preparations were aptly named Operation Neptune, after the Roman God of the sea, and included the huge armada of ships and the gigantic logistical puzzle that had to be solved to transport 132,715 soldiers and tons of supplies to the Normandy beaches. In addition, 23,000 paratroopers aboard nearly 1,000 transport aircraft were flown over on the night of 5/6 June. The navy's role in Operation Neptune was thus of the utmost importance, as the troops on board the transport ships had to be protected during the journey from England to Normandy. Among other things, the Channel had to be cleared of mines so that the flat-bottomed landing craft could sail directly onto the beach. In the year leading up to the Normandy invasion, there was a strong focus on having the British shipyards upgrade and arm Allied transport ships, including Danish ones, so that they could carry troops, vehicles and other war material. The

---

29 Joshua Levine, *Operation Fortitude: The Greatest Hoax of The Second World War* (London: Collins, 2011), pp.65–85.

30 Jakob Sørensen, *D-Dag – Operation Overlord 6. Juni 1944* (Copenhagen: People's Press, 2014), pp.83–84.

most important change in the conversion was that they had to be able to unload their cargo directly onto amphibious vehicles and barges at the coastal area. This required both new unloading booms on the ships and the ability to lock the barges to the sides of the ships so that the cargo could be unloaded quickly under fire.

The order to launch Operation Neptune after the stormy June weather and subsequently enter the Operation Overlord phase came on 4/5 June, when meteorologists reported that the weather was clearing on 6 June. This was the starting point for the huge armada of ships to begin sailing towards Normandy in the early morning hours of 5 June.[31] Nerves were on edge for everyone – there was no doubt about how much was at stake in the invasion. The Danish sailor, Bostrup, on board *Fanø* recalls:

> It was a dark night, but the weather was good. All lights and lanterns were switched off, a sharp lookout was kept on the bridge, bow and stern, everyone listened and watched, because it was important for each ship to keep its place in the line and be exactly where it was supposed to be, and where the other ships expected it to be – still in the right place at the right time! In between this mighty fleet, speedboats and message ships raced back and forth, but everything went as it should…[32]

Although the extremely dangerous Operation Overlord had not yet begun, there were still constant dangers associated with transport during Operation Neptune. Erik Egebak was on board the American Liberty ship, *Joseph Pulitzer*, when the ship suddenly hit a mine:

> As we entered the English Channel, something very unexpected happened when there was a sudden explosion close to us, with the result that the stern of the ship was lifted out of the water and all the troops we had on board in the stern were knocked out of their bunks.[33]

Joseph Pulitzer had hit an acoustic mine, but the ship was still intact and able to continue sailing. A diving survey was conducted to determine if there was any damage to the propeller shaft or rudder, but everything was intact. The ship docked at Southampton, where several American troops boarded, and then headed to Normandy to take part in Operation Overlord. The losses associated with Neptune were primarily due to the bad weather, with less ships sunk due to enemy action. The biggest loss associated with Neptune was the American minesweeper USS *Osprey*, which struck a mine and caught fire on the afternoon of 5 June. Six men died and the ship sank a few hours later.[34]

In Neptune, the navy's 1,213 different warships played a particularly important role in D-Day. A total of 6,939 ships and boats of all sizes were involved in the operation, and it was

31 Kenneth Edwards: *Operation Neptune: The Normandy Landings, 1944* (Stroud: Fonthill Media, 2013), pp.48–58.

32 Sven Arvid Birkeland, *Sænket af tyskerne – Danske krigssejlere i 2. Verdenskrig* (Copenhagen: Gyldendal, 2012), pp.360–361.

33 Quoted from Cicerone ApS and Nexus Communication's interview with Erik Egebak and archive material in connection with the production of the documentary 'The War Sailors'.

34 Jakob Sørensen, *D-Dag – Operation Overlord 6. Juni 1944* (Copenhagen: People's Press, 2014), p.138.

the task of the warships to pave the way for the troops to land.[35] The warships were to assist and provide fire support before the actual landing began, and then act as support during the infantry assault to establish the beachhead. The bitter lessons learnt from the Dieppe raid in 1942 were in the minds of Allied naval commanders, as a failed bombardment from the warships could have catastrophic consequences for the landing troops. However, the Allies' greatest fear was that the Germans would discover the huge armada that was crossing the Channel.

The element of surprise was of the utmost importance to the invasion force, as just one German reconnaissance aircraft's information could determine the outcome of the initial attacks on the German batteries. However, there was no word of the invasion from either German aircraft or ships. The stormy weather meant that the Germans did not expect the Allies to begin a landing, so the German airmen remained on the ground. Danish sailor Georg Unger was aboard the replacement ship *Fort St Croix*, which was part of the huge invasion fleet that would dock at the Canadian sector, 'Juno', on D-Day. In his diary, Unger described the uncertain and nervous atmosphere leading up to the launch of Operation Neptune:

> We are a crew of 40 men, mostly Danes who have volunteered for the invasion; also 24 English soldiers who belong to the ship. We are in Scotland waiting for orders to leave. We are all impatient to get going. We have been waiting for the invasion for two years now, and we want to put an end to it so we can get home. We are ready with 24 hours' notice. One day it will be reduced to half an hour. It won't be long now. We all go and lurk. We don't like to be among the first...[36]

Unger also realised the seriousness of the coming invasion when the ship sailed south to Dover to be part of the upcoming Operation Neptune:

> Off Dover, a couple of violent explosions tell us that it is serious. It's the Germans' long-range guns sending us a greeting. We get two shots to starboard and three to port, but they don't hit us. I throw myself on the deck with the soldiers as shrapnel and water rain down on the ship. When we've been lying down for a while, I lift my head to see if there's more to come, but I get a thump on the head from the soldier behind me. He swears at him, I have to stay down.[37]

J. P. Sørensen was on board the Danish ship *Gudrun Mærsk*, which had Omaha as its destination when the huge squadron of ships arrived in Normandy on D-Day. *Gudrun Mærsk* carried both fuel and soldiers, and one of Sørensen's clearest recollections of the trip from England to Normandy was a conversation with an American soldier:

35 Kenneth Edwards: *Operation Neptune: The Normandy Landings, 1944* (Stroud: Fonthill Media, 2013), pp.36–48.

36 Christian Tortzen, *Søfolk og Skibe 1939–1945, bind 4* (Copenhagen: Lindhardt & Ringhof, 1985), p.390.

37 Morsø Folkeblad, 6 June 1994.

> I distinctly remember an American soldier I stood with at the stern on the trip over to Normandy, who said something to me I'll never forget: "Do you think I'll ever see America again?" I said, "Yes of course you will. You've come this far, so you'll probably come all the way home again." I still hope he made it back to America.[38]

Rear gunner Andreas Moldt and the rest of the crew aboard the Lancaster bomber *ITEM* took part in a bombing raid targeting a heavy battery in the south-west corner of Normandy – a battery at Crisbecq, which could almost reach Le Havre. Frequent bombing raids were not unusual during this period, but when the crew was strictly instructed not to deviate from the course, it caused some debate among the *ITEM*'s crew. Deviations from the course were normally accepted. The reasoning behind the order was that there would be a lot of traffic in the air that night. *ITEM*'s navigator, Jack, reported an unusual number of spots on the radar – hundreds of bright dots over the Channel, and he decided that something was probably wrong with the radar. When the Lancaster had bombed its target at Crisbecq, the coast was illuminated by other bombing raids from other bombers. Moldt later estimated that close to 1,100 aircraft were deployed against 11 targets, all bombing their targets simultaneously. The crew discussed whether this could be the start of the real invasion. The answer came on the return flight from the bombing raid, as Moldt recalls:

> We talked again about all the radar targets on the screen, and I sat in my cupola at the stern looking down towards the lake. It was a clear night and I could only see the dark water, but halfway across I saw long white stripes. My experience at sea told me that these were not wave crests and I told the others what I thought they were. Jack moved down the nose of the machine again. From his position he could see a bit behind and agreed with me. He said there were hundreds of ships, and as we approached the English coast, I could see more and more. Then there was another shout from Jack: "Aircraft with navigation lights on!" They came in small groups of three or four below us at different altitudes. We realised then that this must be the invasion.[39]

Canadian Army anti-aircraft gunner John Andreasen was on board an LST (Landing Ship Tank) which, instead of transporting tanks and heavy vehicles to Normandy, was loaded with 30 anti-aircraft guns and Canadian soldiers to land at 'Juno'.

In addition, there were tons of ammunition on board, which caused a great deal of fear among the soldiers, as rumours of underwater attacks were a constant topic of conversation on board the ships. At 4 a.m. on the morning of 5 June, the LST sailed from the south coast of England. The invasion was a reality and the image of the invasion fleet made an indelible impression on Andreasen:

---

38 Interview with J. P. Sørensen by Ulrik Brandt. Recorded at Bombebøssen in Christianshavn on 9 August 2005.

39 Andreas P. Moldt, *Natbomber: Slaget om Europa som en Dansker Oplevede det i Invasionssommeren 1944* (Copenhagen: Gyldendal, 1985), pp.60–61.

> What a sight, ships were everywhere and more were arriving all the time, large and small, warships, aircraft carriers, Liberty ships and all sizes of landing craft, I am sure there were thousands of ships, yes, the world's greatest armada on the world's greatest crusade, it was a beautiful sight for poor eyes. Above us in the air, fighter planes circled continuously... Every man was handed a letter from General Dwight D. Eisenhower with the following content about the great crusade we were about to begin. The eyes of the world were on us and there would be no retreat, only victory, and that the Germans were the best trained soldiers, but that we had the best equipment and air supremacy. The Germans of 1940 were not Germans of 1944, and that he expected a total victory for us.[40]

During the trip to Normandy, Andreasen and the rest of the regiment were told that half of the anti-aircraft guns were to keep an eye out for enemy fighters, and the other half were to watch out for German E-Boats.

While Operation Neptune was underway and the 6,939 ships and boats were heading towards Normandy, the 23,000 Allied paratroopers were preparing to board nearly 1,000 transport aircraft to be dropped over Normandy in the dead of night.

Behind German Lines: The Danish Paratroopers
'We ask only this, that if die we must, that we die as men would die...'

One of the defining elements of Operation Neptune was to drop more than 25,000 paratroopers. 13,000 of these were from the US 82nd and 101st Airborne Divisions, which were to be dropped behind Utah. In addition, 12,200 paratroopers from the British 6th Airborne Division and the 1st Canadian Parachute Battalion were dropped in the area of Sword. The primary objective of the paratroopers was to capture access roads and bridges to the beaches and destroy German guns. The purpose of destroying the German guns located behind the coastal areas was to provide more security for the infantry who landed on the beaches on D-Day itself. Pathfinders were dropped before the rest of the paratroopers to mark the landing zones. The largest force of paratroopers would then be dropped into Normandy about an hour and a half after the pathfinders. The British 6th Airborne Division's main task was to take the towns of Ranville and Bénouville, as important bridges for the Allied advance were located near the Orne River, the Caen Canal and the Dives River. There was also a highly effective German battery at Merville, which was crucial to defeat as the guns here could reach all the way to the landing beach at Sword. The two important objectives of the British and Canadian troops were both achieved on D-Day, as was the capture of the Merville Battery despite heavy fighting in the area. The capture of the bridges over the Orne River and the Caen Canal meant that the British were subsequently able to attack Caen from two sides.[41]

---

40 John Andreasen, unpublished war diary, p.33.

41 Jakob Sørensen, *D-Dag – Operation Overlord 6. Juni 1944* (Copenhagen: People's Press, 2014), pp.94–110.

Otto Hjalmar Antoft helped transport the paratroopers across the Channel on D-Day. He had initially participated in an earlier mission where the crew was to drop supplies to the Special Operations Executive on 6/7 May 1944 near the Pyrenees in France. He emigrated to Canada with his family in 1930 at the age of 11 and enlisted in the Canadian Air Force on 5 March 1942. On 22 June 1943, he was transferred to service in England. At the beginning of 1944, he was a Flying Officer with 190 Squadron, which was trained to transport troops for the coming invasion. On 5 June 1944, Antoft and the rest of the crew that he was a part of were briefed for their D-Day mission. They would be part of phase 2 of Operation Tonga, which was to transport paratroopers to the invasion coast. Phase 1 of the operation involved gliders carrying British soldiers from the Oxfordshire and Buckinghamshire Light Infantry to attack the bridges over the Caen Canal and the Orne River east of Bénouville.

Then phase 2 of the operation would begin, with 23 Stirlings dropping 887 paratroopers from the 7th Parachute Battalion near Ranville. Antoft's aircraft took off at 23:25, heading towards the drop zone. As they approached the French coast, the Stirlings were met by German anti-aircraft fire and some of the aircraft were forced to change course to avoid being hit. This meant that some of the troops were scattered when they finally landed on the ground, but many of them still managed to find the bridges and capture them. Antoft returned to base unharmed at 2.35 a.m. on 6 June. From 14 June to 11 September 1944, he took part in 14 missions involving troop and supply drops and then four missions during Operation Market Garden in The Netherlands in September 1944. On the fourth mission, on 21 September 1944, Antoft's aircraft was heading towards Oosterbeek, but due to the critical situation for the hard-pressed British troops at Arnhem, Antoft's crew was not ordered to any specific drop point. The aircraft came under heavy German anti-aircraft fire and Antoft's aircraft was hit and caught fire. The crew tried to extinguish the fire, but without success. Two crew members parachuted out, but Antoft and the rest of the crew did not make it out of the aircraft before it crashed north of Zetten and died in the crash. He is today laid to rest at the Airborne Cemetery in Oosterbeek. Antoft was posthumously awarded several Canadian medals and a Danish medal for his actions during the war.[42]

The tasks for the American paratroopers of the 82nd and 101st Airborne Divisions at Utah would not be without problems. Their goal was like that of their British counterparts in capturing several exit routes and bridges and destroying German gun positions inland. The drop zones were centred behind the Utah Beach itself, and securing the roads away from the beaches was essential for the 4th Infantry Division's advance on D-Day. However, this proved to be a major problem for the paratroopers as the Germans had flooded several large areas along the Merderet River, with fatal consequences. Several of those who landed directly in the flooded areas drowned. Securing the town of Sainte-Mére-Église was of great importance on D-Day because the main road from Cherbourg to Bayeux passed through it. Whoever controlled the town controlled the ability to bring in reinforcements. For the Americans, it was extremely important to take the town, otherwise the Germans could bring additional reinforcements to the beach areas along the town's roads. This task was entrusted to the 82nd Airborne Division.

42 Mikkel Plannthin, Mikkel, *Britain's Victory, Denmark's Freedom* (Stroud: Fonthill Media, 2017), pp.101–104.

Oscar Holst Pedersen was a corporal during the invasion in 320 Glider Field Artillery Battalion of the 82nd Airborne Division. He landed in a glider near Sainte-Mére-Église on the night of D-Day and took part in the fighting in the area behind the Utah Beach. Pedersen was born in Herning on 4 April 1914 and emigrated to the USA in 1938 to work for his brother, who already lived in Iowa. When war broke out, Pedersen volunteered for service and then underwent training in the 82nd Airborne Division. He participated in the campaigns in Africa, Sicily and Italy before taking part in the Normandy invasion. The 320th Artillery Battalion, and Pedersen, landed on parachutes and in 54 fragile gliders, many of which took a devastating hit when they hit the ground when they landed in Normandy. In total, 428 American gliders landed in the Utah sector. The gliders also landed very scattered due to the intense German shelling, and as a result, only two of the guns they brought with them came into action at 09:30 on D-Day – one fired to the south and the other fired to the north. Pedersen and the other troops from the 320th Artillery Battalion fought their way forward to collect the guns. It was not until 8 June that they managed to assemble eight guns together with 325th Glider Infantry Regiment, which then simultaneously bombarded and paved the way for the troops to move inland behind Utah. The troops of the 320th Artillery Battalion continued the subsequent artillery support through Operation Overlord, and the troops were first relieved and returned to England briefly on 11 July 1944. The battalion was later awarded the prestigious Presidential Unit Citation and the French Croix de Guerre with Palms for their efforts in Normandy.[43]

Pedersen escaped unharmed through D-Day and the fighting in Normandy that immediately followed, but on 15 June 1944 he was severely wounded and died three days later, on 18 June, in a field hospital. He was buried in a temporary cemetery near Sainte-Mére-Église. It was not until after the liberation in 1945 that the family in Herning received news of their son's death, and they wanted to bury Oscar Holst Pedersen in his hometown of Herning. However, it would be four years before this funeral took place. An American captain accompanied the hearse all the way to Herning, where Pedersen was laid to rest on 18 June 1949 at Herning Vestre Kirkegård. The coffin was decorated with the American flag, and there were flag bearers from various military departments and the Freedom Council.[44]

Securing the four exit routes from Utah was also of the utmost importance, as this was where the American tanks would break out of the beach area. The American airborne attack was problematic from the start because many of the troops missed their drop zones because of the powerful German anti-aircraft fire, which forced the aircraft off course. The fragile gliders were supposed to land about an hour and a half after the paratroopers, but as they were loaded with the heavy equipment, such as jeeps and guns, many soldiers perished during the landing and were easy targets for German anti-aircraft fire. Much of the original plan for the airborne assault seems to have failed, but due to the many scattered attacks by the paratroopers, it caused great confusion among the German defenders who had difficulty locating where the attacks were coming from. This became a clear advantage for the attacking Allied units.

43 Jørgen Flintholm, *Normandiet og D-Dag – Dengang og nu* (Denmark: Flintholm, 2014), p.201.

44 Arne Mosgaard, *Monumenter, Mindesmærker og Fredede Grave i Herning Kommune* (Herning: Ubirex, 2012), p.4.

Units from the 101st Airborne Division, primarily from 502nd Regiment, 3rd Battalion, secured two of the exit roads from Utah without major resistance. Sainte-Mére-Église and a number of northern approaches were also taken, securing the strategically important traffic hub. Fierce fighting at the La Fiere bridge over the Merderet River raged for some time, but eventually the German defenders surrendered. Chaos, chance and luck characterised much of the airborne assault on D-Day, but despite great challenges, the American paratroopers generally succeeded in completing their tasks.[45]

Another Dane who landed in Normandy on D-Day as a paratrooper was Niels Christensen. He was born on 14 May 1921 and grew up in the small town of Outrup near Varde in West Jutland. He arrived in the USA in November 1937 with his family, where they planned to work and earn money for two years, after which they would return to Denmark. Meanwhile, war broke out and the family felt compelled to stay in the US. When Denmark was occupied on 9 April 1940, Christensen felt he had to do something. He tried several times to enlist in the US Army, but was rejected because he was not a US citizen. Christensen's chance to take his turn in the war came in December 1942, when he finally got the opportunity to join the army. He underwent basic training at Camp Roberts in California before joining the paratroopers and being sent to Fort Benning in Georgia. After completing his training there and receiving his Jump Wings, the status symbol of the paratrooper, he was sent on to Camp Mackall and Fort Bragg to undergo further training. From here, in September 1943, he was sent to England to join the war in Europe. He joined the famous 101st Airborne Division, the Screaming Eagles, which would fight all the way from D-Day to Hitler's Eagle's Nest in Germany. He became part of the 506th Parachute Infantry Regiment, 3rd Battalion, Item Company, which would be dropped behind German lines during the night before D-Day. However, the drop in Normandy turned out to be quite different than planned for Christensen and the other paratroopers who were part of Item Company.

The Allied paratroopers were fully aware of the important task they had been given, and they were also aware of the great dangers of being dropped behind enemy lines. Therefore, the commander of 3rd Battalion, Lieutenant Colonel Robert Wolverton, under whose command was Niels Christensen, gathered his men at the assembly point before they boarded the planes to go to war in Normandy. Here he gave a speech that focused the soldiers on the perilous task ahead:

> God almighty, in a few short hours we will be in battle with the enemy. We do not join battle afraid. We do not ask favors or indulgence but ask that, if You will, use us as Your instrument for the right and an aid in returning peace to the world. We do not know or seek what our fate will be. We ask only this, that if die we must, that we die as men would die, without complaining, without pleading and safe in the feeling that we have done our best for what we believed was right. O Lord, protect our loved ones and be near us in the fire ahead and with us now as we pray to you.[46]

45 Jakob Sørensen, *D-Dag – Operation Overlord 6. Juni 1944* (Copenhagen: People's Press, 2014), pp.110–126.

46 Ian Gardner, *Tonight We Die As Men* (Oxford: Osprey, 2010), pp.113–114.

Chaos and Misdrops at Pointe du Hoc
'I have never been so scared in my life'

C-47 aircraft transported Christensen and the other members of Item Company on their way to their target: Drop Zone D east of the small village of Saint-Côme-du-Mont in the interior beyond Utah Beach. The door to the aircraft was opened over the coast and the strong wind blew much-needed fresh air in to the troops, who were drowsy because they had taken an air sickness pill before boarding. Suddenly, Second Lieutenant Johnston stood up and shouted: "Stand up and strap yourselves in – get ready for equipment check."[47] Christensen followed Johnston's order, stood up and attached himself to the aircraft's static wire, which would ensure that the paratroopers could quickly and efficiently exit the aircraft and land in relative unity. As the aircraft reached the Normandy coastal area, it came under heavy German anti-aircraft fire, which intensified as it was directly over the drop zone. The men were thrown back and forth in the cabin and black clouds of exploding anti-aircraft fire enveloped the aircraft. They grabbed at anything they could to hold on, only to be hit by more anti-aircraft fire, knocking everyone on board to the floor. The troops in the back shouted to the troops in the front to get out as quickly as possible, but at that moment the right engine caught fire and the wing was so badly damaged that it was impossible for the paratroopers to jump.

It was announced that they had missed the drop zone and that the pilot would try to turn around to hit it again, but at that moment the plane began to bank further and further to the right due to the heavy damage caused by the German *Flugabwehrkanone* (a popular term for anti-aircraft artillery). In the event that the troops could not jump, the official orders were issued for the aircraft to turn right and attempt another drop. However, the plane was too badly damaged for the pilot to turn the aircraft round to try again. It was now or never, and the green light indicating that the soldiers had to bail out was switched on.

The damage to the aircraft would have major consequences for the men on board, as Niels Christensen's friend Len Goodgal recalls:

> When we were over the French coast and ready to jump, I could see water below me – everything was quiet. Suddenly all hell broke loose. The plane was thrown around and I thought we had been hit in the tail. PFC [Private First Class] Niels Christensen then told me that the right engine was on fire. First the plane started to dive and then to rise again with the green light on. When we left the aircraft, I stayed with Christensen. My parachute opened and I could see the burning plane plummeting into the sea. As I looked down, I realised I was going into the sea. I dropped my leg bag and as much gear as I could and landed in shallow water just off the beach – I was completely lost. At the same time someone was shouting; it was Private Ray Crouch. We got together and tried to figure out where we were. We later discovered that Christensen and Second Lieutenant Johnston were the only other people to get out of the plane alive.[48]

47 From an article in *World War II*, volume 16, number 2, A Primedia Publication, July 2001, p.35.
48 Ian Gardner, *Tonight We Die As Men* (Oxford: Osprey, 2010), p.165.

15 of their comrades died when the plane crashed into the sea. They did not have time to jump. Of the 45 groups of paratroopers from the 3rd Battalion who were aboard C-47 aircraft, only 8 groups hit their intended drop zone. Despite the low number of soldiers landing in the correct area, it was still the highest number of accurate drops in the entire 101st Airborne Division. The majority of the C-47 transport aircraft came under heavy fire as they approached the Normandy coast, knocking many of the aircraft off course and causing many of the paratroopers to be widely dispersed. They often landed far away from their intended drop zone. In several places, the Germans had flooded fields, which had disastrous consequences for the paratroopers. Many landed in the flooded areas and drowned due to their heavy packs, which could weigh up to 40 or 50kg.[49]

Len Goodgal and Ray Crouch soon realised that they were far from their original target, in fact closer to Omaha Beach than Utah. They landed near the steep cliffs of Pointe du Hoc, where the two paratroopers unknowingly later discovered that a daring attack on the steep cliffs was to be made by the American Rangers. On top of Pointe du Hoc was a German battery that it was believed could hit the troops that landed on both Omaha and Utah Beaches during the invasion. Against all odds, the American Rangers, led by Colonel Rudder, were to make a decisive vertical attack against the German positions.

After Crouch and Goodgal had walked for a few hours during the night, dawn broke and they spotted the first boat taking the American Rangers towards Pointe du Hoc. Crouch and Goodgal waved a white piece of cloth at the boat, but it continued on its way. After wandering for some more time, the two paratroopers arrived at the cliffs where the Rangers were now attacking the German battery. The Rangers were under heavy fire and the Germans were throwing grenades at them from the top of the steep cliffs. Crouch and Goodgal ran to assist the Rangers and began tending to the wounded – they tried to retrieve first aid kits from the boats, but had to give up when they came under fire. At the same time, the American destroyers USS *Satterlee* and USS *Texas* shelled the German bunkers on top of the cliffs. Crouch and Goodgal fought on with the Rangers and finally managed to make it to the top, where they were still being attacked from all sides. Goodgal was ordered by Colonel Rudder to plant a flag in the ground so that they would not be bombarded by their own ships.

225 Rangers from the 2nd Ranger Battalion attacked Pointe du Hoc, which despite an intense initial bombardment was still heavily manned by German defenders when the Americans reached the troop. The Rangers' primary task was to capture six German guns believed to be capable of hitting Omaha and Utah. When the Rangers reached the casemates, they discovered that five of the six guns had already been moved and replaced with telephone poles. The Rangers then moved further inland to establish a roadblock, after which two Rangers on patrol found the remaining five guns located in a field behind Pointe du Hoc. Using thermite grenades (a grenade that does not explode, but melts whatever it comes into contact with), the five guns were neutralised. More German counterattacks came during D-Day and until 8 June, when the Rangers were finally relieved. Of the 225 Rangers that Crouch and Goodgal assisted, only 90 remained to fight on 8 June.[50]

49 Ian Gardner, *Tonight We Die As Men* (Oxford: Osprey, 2010), p.130.
50 Stuart C. Robertson & Dale Booth, *Following in the Footsteps of Heroes: D-Day June 6th 1944*, (Devizes: Sabrestorm, 2014), pp.87–94.

Second Lieutenant Johnston broke his arm when he jumped out of the aircraft and landed between Pointe du Hoc and Omaha, but he later managed to rejoin the rest of the Item Company. When Niels Christensen jumped out of the badly damaged aircraft, however, he found himself alone in the airspace somewhere between Pointe du Hoc and Omaha Beach. Neither Johnston, Goodgal or Crouch were nearby, but Christensen would soon realise that the enemy was not far away. As Christensen jumped out of the C-47, he was caught in the strong slipstream in the airspace over Normandy and lost his leg bag with all the equipment and gear needed in the ongoing invasion. In addition, he also lost his M1 carbine, which undeniably made the situation even more critical in the case that he ran into a German patrol, and this is exactly what happened. Christensen landed in the centre of a German command post near Omaha, and the German soldiers immediately became aware of his presence. With no means of defence, there was nothing to do but surrender. Christensen was now a German prisoner and in the days after D-Day he was transported to St Lô with other American prisoners, where they were assigned to dig up unexploded bombs and grenades. He brought a small notebook with him the night he jumped, and after he was captured, he wrote down his thoughts about the violent experiences on D-Day itself and the first day in German captivity at the town of St Lô:

> I've never been so scared in my life – I prayed a lot. I thought my last hour had come. I prayed that mum knew I was okay. The bombs are falling only 50 feet from where I am – there is nothing left of the city. Wondering when this will all be over and when I can come home.[51]

He was subsequently transferred to a prison camp at Alençon on 13 June and then to Paris on 29 June. In his diary, Christensen describes the severe lack of food for the prisoners, and when they arrived in Paris, a French civilian tried to give the hungry prisoners a piece of bread, but he was discovered by the Germans and shot and killed on the spot. After a month in German captivity in France, Christensen was transported to the German prison camp *Stalag XIIA* near Limburg in Germany aboard a packed troop train, where he was held prisoner until the camp was liberated on 25 March 1945. Despite the camp being liberated after that, German snipers continued to fire at the prisoners, says Christensen. Christensen later returned to the US and became an American citizen in March 1946.[52]

51 Niels Christensen, unpublished diary.
52 Mary Christensen's journal (private collection).

The meeting between Stalin, Roosevelt and Churchill in Tehran in November 1943, where it was decided to focus on the second front. (U.S. Signal Corps photo – Library of Congress)

Gudrun Maersk. (M/S Museet for Søfart)

Nordvest which was renamed *Alan A. Dale.* (Jørgen Linnet)

A section of the Essex Scottish Regiment's first battalion in England, November 1943. Niels Wiesneck is third row from the top, third from the right. (Finn Wiesneck)

DANSK RØDE KORS
CROIX ROUGE DANOISE
AMALIEGADE 18
COPENHAGUE

O. N. R.

Til Røde Kors' internationale Komité, Genève.
Au Comité International de la Croix-Rouge, Genève.

FORESPØRGER — DEMANDEUR

Navn - *nom* Visnek

Fornavn - *prénom* Julius

Adresse Rotterdam Allé
st Magleby.

Meddelelse
(ikke over 25 Ord. Indholdet maa kun vedrøre personlige Familieforhold).

Message à transmettre
(25 mots au maximum, nouvelles de caractère strictement personel et familial).

Kæreste Nils Længes usigeligt efter Brev Ny Lejlighed store Kongensgade Helge aabner egen Forretning Fader Alladin til kongelig Teater alle raske Længes med
Fader Moder

Dato - *date* 14 AUG. 1940

DANSK RØDE KORS ★ CROIX ROUGE DANOISE ★

COMITE INTERNATIONAL CROIX ROUGE

ADRESSAT — DESTINATAIRE

Navn - *nom* Visnek

Fornavn - *prénom* Nils

Adresse M/S "Europa" Ø.K.
Messrs. United Baltic Corporation Ltd.
158, Fenchurch Street.
LONDON, E. C. 3.

Svar paa Bagsiden
(Man bedes skrive tydeligt).

reponse au verso
(Prière d'écrire lisiblement).

- 6 SEPT. 1940

Correspondence was limited for Danish sailors in Allied service. The only form was a very brief Red Cross letter. Here is a greeting to Niels Wiesneck from his father, Julius, dated 14 August 1940. (Finn Wiesneck)

American troops in England in the days leading up to 6 June. (US National Archives)

Andreas Moldt in 1945. (Moldt)

Wiesneck (right) poses in combat uniform with a friend in front of a British Bren Gun Carrier before Exercise Tiger. (Finn Wiesneck)

Andreas Moldt (first left) and part of the Lancaster *ITEM* crew in the period leading up to the Normandy invasion in 1944. (Moldt)

ITEM Lancaster aircraft from 166 Squadron, Number One Group, RAF Bomber Command, in which Moldt was the tail gunner, is being prepared for bombing raids. The square shaft in front of the far bomb bay was used to carry strips of foil to disrupt German radar. To the right is a tube where a camera was placed. *ITEM* was later renamed *IMP*. (Moldt)

2. sektion

Bornholms Tidende

Lørdag den 30. juni 1984 Nr. 149 118. årg.

WEEK-END

En junidag i 1944, man ikke glemmer

Fhv. restauratør John Andreasen, Nexø, deltog som canadisk soldat i invasionen i Normandiet for 40 år siden. - For nogle uger siden gensá han de strande, hvor landgangen fandt sted, og her fortæller han om nogle af de oplevelser, der aldrig slettes af hans hukommelse

Selv 40 år efter glemmer man ikke, hvad der skete, da verdenshistoriens største invasion satte ind den 6. juni 1944, siger fhv. restaurater John Andreasen, Nexø, der deltog i krigen som canadisk soldat.

John Andreasen er nylig vendt hjem efter en rejse til Normandiet, hvor han besøgte stedet, hvor han hin regnfulde junidag gik i land sammen med sine kammerater, der på det tidspunkt i over tre år havde været soldater. Sammen havde de trænet og øvet sig for at kunne gøre en indsats og være med til at få en ende på krigen, der på det tidspunkt havde raset over det meste af verden i godt fem år.

- Hvordan gik det til, at De blev soldat i den canadiske hær?

- Jeg boede i Canada, da krigen brød ud. Jeg er født i Poulsker den 16. september 1910, men allerede i 1928 udvandrede jeg. Jeg var kun 17 år og måtte have speciel tilladelse til at rejse, men det fik jeg og tog af sted. Jeg kom til Lucky Lake, hvor jeg arbejdede ved landbruget. Jeg blev i løbet af få år selvstændig, og jeg havde det godt, da krigen brød ud.

Så skete det, at tyskerne rykkede frem på alle fronter, englænderne måtte trække sig tilbage fra fastlandet og endelig det, at tyskerne havde besat Danmark. Det gjorde indtryk på mig.

Da mine kammerater besluttede at melde sig frivilligt til hæren, gjorde jeg det også. Det var ikke nemt at blive soldat, for fejlede man det mindste, blev man kasseret. Vi var otte, der meldte os samme dag, men kun tre slap igennem. Vi fik nogle dage til at afvikle, hvad vi mente skulle ordnes, inden vi drog i krig og skulle så melde os igen til uddannelse. Jeg solgte alt, hvad jeg havde, min farm og mit kvæg. Jorden ejede jeg ikke, men jeg afhændede alt, hvad jeg ellers havde samlet sammen, så der ikke var noget, der bandt.

Jeg blev taget til luftværnsartilleriet, og efter nogle måneders uddannelse i Canada blev vi sendt til England, hvor uddannelsen fortsatte. Det var i 1941, og inden D-dagen den 6. juni 1944 var der oprettet tre canadiske divisioner.

Træningen var meget hård, men jeg kunne lide det, og selv om vi blev sat ind på Englands sydkyst for at være med i luftforsvaret, fortsatte træningen uafladeligt, så da vi endelig blev sendt af sted, var vi ikke blot professionelle soldater, vi var specialister på vort område allesammen.

Invasionen

Længe før invasionen begyndte, blev der talt og talt om denne dag, hvor vi skulle over og jage tyskerne ud af alle de besatte lande. Noget konkret fik vi ikke at vide. Vi syntes, det tog forfærdelig lang tid, men det var også helt utroligt, hvad der skulle sendes af sted.

Der deltog 702 krigsskibe, 25 flotiller minestrygere, 5.000 transportskibe og 4.000 både, der skulle sejle styrkerne i land fra transportskibene.

Ventetiden blev lang, men endelig kom vi af sted, og min afdeling kom da også i land i Normandiet på selve D-dagen, og det gik fint.

Inden selve landsætningen tog sin begyndelse, var tyskernes kystforsvar blevet bombardret i flere timer. Der deltog nok fly, men de kunne ikke ramme kystbevogtningens reder, for de var gravet ned eller sprængt ind i skrænterne, men flådens kanoner kunne ramme dem, når der blev skudt længe nok og på den rigtige måde. Det lykkedes godt, der hvor vi skulle gå i land, så tabet af mandskab var ikke ret stort, hvad det var flere andre steder, hvor kystforsvaret ikke var blevet ramt og uskadeliggjort. Vi kom i land hen på eftermiddagen, og det foregik uden større uheld for os. Vi mødte ingen tyskere, før vi var flere kilometer inde i landet. Det betød dog ikke, at vi ikke kom i krig, for det gjorde vi i fuldt mål, men ikke på selve D-dagen.

Krig endnu i et helt år

Efterhånden som vi rykkede ind i landet, tog kampene til. Den tyske værnemagt gav ikke op, men forsvarede sig og forsøgte gentagne gange at sætte modangreb ind. I betragtning af, at de havde været i krig i fem år, var det utroligt, hvad de satte ind. Mange af mine kammerater blev dræbt, men tabene hos tyskerne var betydeligt større.

En hel tysk divison med 21.000 mand blev udslettet. Der var 60 mand, der blev taget til fange, men næsten alle andre blev dræbt. Tyskerne havde sat meget store styrker ind, men de blev omkredset og lukket inde i en lomme, der vel var på størrelse med Bornholm. Der var en passage bagud for de tyske styrker, og på begge sider af passagen lå de allierede. De lod tyskerne samle sig og begynde tilbagetrækningen, og fra fra kl 4 til kl. 7 om morgenen blev der ikke løsnet et skud mod dem, de fik uhindret lov at køre mod »udgangen« af lommen. Så sattes et bombardement igang, der praktisk talt udslettede alt levende.

Da vi senere skulle følge efter, blev det nødvendigt at rydde en bane, så vi kunne komme igennem. Der var døde heste og soldater overalt, kilometer efter kilometer.

- Hvordan kunne man slappe af i et sådant inferno?

- Det var sådan, at luftværnskanonen hele tiden var bemandet med halvdelen af mandskabet. Hver gang, vi slog os ned, blev der gravet to huller, et til kanonstillingen og et til mandskabet, hvor de opholdt sig, når de ikke havde tjeneste på kanonen. Vi fulgte 14. feltregiment. Det var vores opgave at holde luften fri for fremmede fly, og det lykkedes helt godt, kan man nok sige.

John Andreasen som canadisk soldat

Der kom mange fly, og vi skød mange af dem ned. Der kom også V-1 bomber, men dem skulle vi ikke skyde efter, men overlade det til luftværnet i England. En V-1 kunne ikke ændre bane, så de var nemme at ramme, og langt størstedelen af dem, der blev sendt af sted, blev skudt ned, før de nåede deres mål.

- Havde De tænkt på, at det nemt kunne komme til at koste Dem livet at være med i krigen?

- Jo, det havde vi sikkert alle, men jeg havde nu den indstilling, at kunne jeg blot komme i land og gøre en indsats en tre-fire dage, var min deltagelse i krigen ikke spildt, men sådan gik det ikke. Jeg klarede mig igennem uden andre mén end at blive døv på det ene øre.

Det værste var, når vi blev angrebet af de tyske styrtbombere. Dem kunne man ikke høre, før de havde smidt bomben, og da var det som regel for sent. Det første vi hørte, var en høj tuden, når de steg næsten lodret til vejrs, men på det tidspunkt havde de smidt deres bombe. En gang var jeg ganske sikker på, at nu var det sket. Så vidt jeg kunne se, kom bomben lige ned mod os, men den ramte alligevel ikke os, men kanonen bagved. Af mandskabet på den anden kanon var der kun en, der nåede at se selve bomben. Vi kunne se, han havde kastet sig ind i beskyttelsesrummet ved siden af kanonen, men bomben ramte, så hans hovede blev revet helt af, og kun nogle skindtrevler holdt det sammen med kroppen. Alle fem, der var ved kanonen, blev dræbt.

Bombet af allierede fly

Det skete også, at vi blev angrebet af vore egne fly. Generalerne havde næppe givet helt rigtige oplysninger om, hvor langt vi var nået frem, og fra luften kunne piloterne ikke afgøre, om det var venner eller fjender, de skød imod, så de kastede bomber mod os.

(Fortsættes side 5)

Kanonstilling på en tysk kirkegård

Stillingerne angrebet af egne fly

FARVE

John Andreasen (front row left) and his platoon in 1945. (Familie Journalen/Karl Ravn)

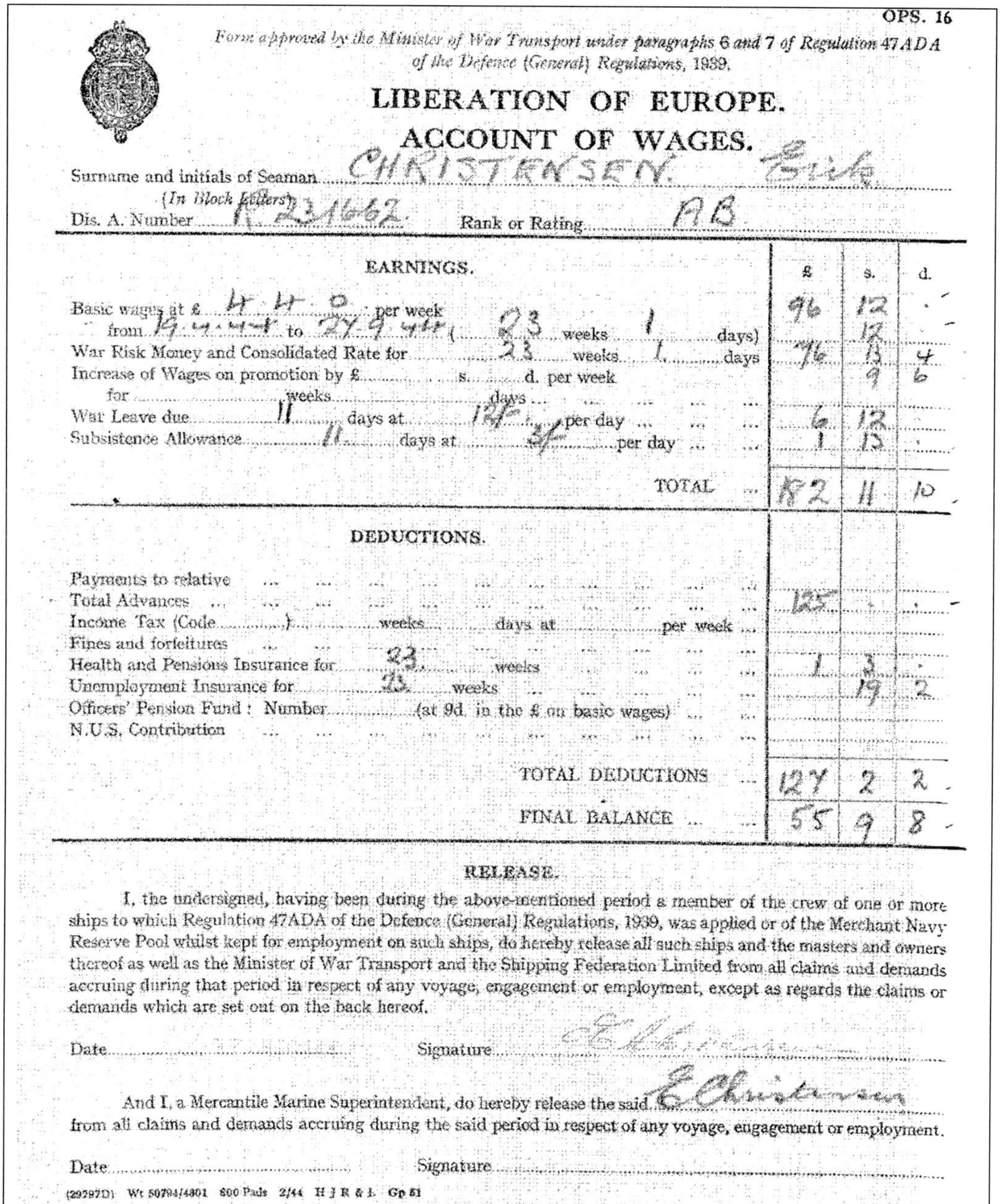

OPS. 16

Form approved by the Minister of War Transport under paragraphs 6 and 7 of Regulation 47ADA of the Defence (General) Regulations, 1939.

LIBERATION OF EUROPE.

ACCOUNT OF WAGES.

Surname and initials of Seaman (In Block Letters) CHRISTENSEN. Erik

Dis. A. Number R231662 Rank or Rating AB

EARNINGS.	£	s.	d.
Basic wages at £ 4 4 0 per week from 19.4.44 to 27.9.44 (23 weeks 1 days)	96	12	–
		12	–
War Risk Money and Consolidated Rate for 23 weeks 1 days	76	13	4
Increase of Wages on promotion by £ s. d. per week for weeks days		9	6
War Leave due 11 days at 12/- per day	6	12	
Subsistence Allowance 11 days at 3/- per day	1	13	–
TOTAL	182	11	10

DEDUCTIONS.	£	s.	d.
Payments to relative			
Total Advances	125	–	–
Income Tax (Code) weeks days at per week			
Fines and forfeitures			
Health and Pensions Insurance for 23 weeks	1	3	–
Unemployment Insurance for 23 weeks		19	2
Officers' Pension Fund: Number (at 9d. in the £ on basic wages)			
N.U.S. Contribution			
TOTAL DEDUCTIONS	127	2	2
FINAL BALANCE	55	9	8

RELEASE.

I, the undersigned, having been during the above-mentioned period a member of the crew of one or more ships to which Regulation 47ADA of the Defence (General) Regulations, 1939, was applied or of the Merchant Navy Reserve Pool whilst kept for employment on such ships, do hereby release all such ships and the masters and owners thereof as well as the Minister of War Transport and the Shipping Federation Limited from all claims and demands accruing during that period in respect of any voyage, engagement or employment, except as regards the claims or demands which are set out on the back hereof.

Date Signature E Christiansen

And I, a Mercantile Marine Superintendent, do hereby release the said E Christiansen from all claims and demands accruing during the said period in respect of any voyage, engagement or employment.

Date Signature

(29797D) Wt 50794/4801 800 Pads 2/44 H J R & L Gp 51

Lønopgørelse for matros Erik Christiansen (ikke Christensen, som inspektøren skrev), FORT ST CROIX.[G]

Pay statement for Seaman Erik Christiansen (not Christensen, as the inspector wrote), who came to Juno aboard *Fort St Croix* in connection with Operation Overlord. The V Articles gave the Danish sailors an extra financial bonus and better working conditions on board the ships, but in return they could now be sent directly to the front in Normandy in 1944. (Tortzen)

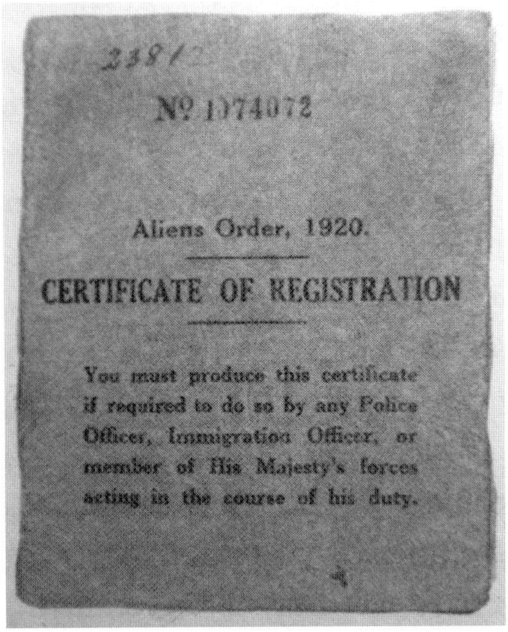

23812

Nº 1074072

Aliens Order, 1920.

CERTIFICATE OF REGISTRATION

You must produce this certificate if required to do so by any Police Officer, Immigration Officer, or member of His Majesty's forces acting in the course of his duty.

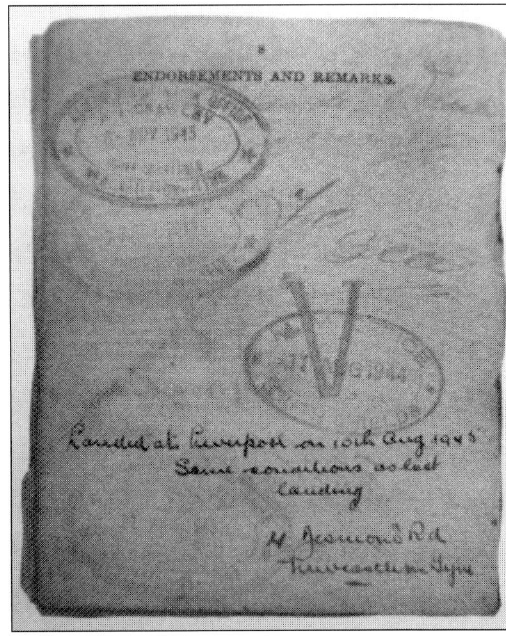

ENDORSEMENTS AND REMARKS.

Landed at Liverpool on 10th Aug 1945
Same conditions as last landing

14 Jesmond Rd
Newcastle on Tyne

As Danish sailors in Allied service were foreigners, they had to carry this type of registration certificate at all times. If they were part of Operation Overlord, they would get a 'V' stamped in their book as proof that they were part of the invasion and thus participated under the terms of the V Articles. The rewards were greater with the 'V' stamped in the book, but so were the dangers. (Tortzen)

American troops during the landing in Excercise Tiger. (Library of Congress's Prints and Photographs division)

Fake invasion ships made of fragile wood were placed on the south coast of England before D-Day. Large columns of vehicles and inflatable tanks were also set-up in several places to give the Germans on the other of the Channel the impression that a major operation was underway. (Imperial War Museum)

Danish ships in convoy heading towards the French coast during Overlord. (M/S The Maritime Museum)

SUPREME HEADQUARTERS
ALLIED EXPEDITIONARY FORCE

Soldiers, Sailors and Airmen of the Allied Expeditionary Force!

You are about to embark upon the Great Crusade, toward which we have striven these many months. The eyes of the world are upon you. The hopes and prayers of liberty-loving people everywhere march with you. In company with our brave Allies and brothers-in-arms on other Fronts, you will bring about the destruction of the German war machine, the elimination of Nazi tyranny over the oppressed peoples of Europe, and security for ourselves in a free world.

Your task will not be an easy one. Your enemy is well trained, well equipped and battle-hardened. He will fight savagely.

But this is the year 1944 ! Much has happened since the Nazi triumphs of 1940-41. The United Nations have inflicted upon the Germans great defeats, in open battle, man-to-man. Our air offensive has seriously reduced their strength in the air and their capacity to wage war on the ground. Our Home Fronts have given us an overwhelming superiority in weapons and munitions of war, and placed at our disposal great reserves of trained fighting men. The tide has turned ! The free men of the world are marching together to Victory !

I have full confidence in your courage, devotion to duty and skill in battle. We will accept nothing less than full Victory !

Good Luck ! And let us all beseech the blessing of Almighty God upon this great and noble undertaking.

Dwight D. Eisenhower

Eisenhower's letter, which was distributed to all troops involved in the Normandy invasion. (Private collection)

Otto Hjalmar Antoft's grave at the Airborne Cemetery in Oosterbeek. (CWGC)

General Eisenhower greets the American paratroopers of the 101st Airborne Division in England before the invasion begins. (US National Archives)

Waco gliders, which were typically used by US troops, take off by means of a tethered wire from a C-47 aircraft. (442nd Fighter Wing archive photo)

The road outside Sainte-Mére-Eglise today. (Private collection)

American paratrooper from 82nd Airborne Division with a German prisoner at Turqueville outside Sainte-Mére-Eglise. (US National Archives)

Niels Christensen in uniform. On his chest is the Parachutist Badge known as Jump Wings, which was a status symbol for every paratrooper. (Mary Christensen)

Niels Christensen (third from left) and his family's arrival in the USA in 1937. (Mary Christensen)

Lieutenant Colonel Robert Wolverton makes a few final adjustments to his parachute before the planes depart for Normandy. Less than 3 hours later, Wolverton was dead. He had a clear sense he would not survive the war, so wrote 21 letters to his newborn son – one letter for each year until he turned 21. (US NARA via Ian Gardner)

101st Airborne Division's 'Screaming Eagle' shoulder patch as worn on Goodgal's left shoulder. (US NARA via Ian Gardner)

Bombers of the 9th Air Force. Air Force bombing Pointe du Hoc in the days leading up to D-Day. (US NARA)

On the morning of 6 June, the 2nd Ranger Battalion has gained a foothold at the top of Pointe du Hoc. To the right and slightly below the Red Cross flag is paratrooper Len Goodgal, who made it out of the 1st Platoon of Item Company's C-47 along with Niels Christensen, Ray Crouch and Lieutenant Johnston before the plane crashed, killing 15 of their comrades. Note the Divisional shoulder patch of 'The Screaming Eagle' on Goodgal's left shoulder, similar to the one worn by Niels Christensen. (US NARA via Ian Gardner)

The bomb craters are clearly visible from the air. 2nd Ranger Battalion subsequently began the assault on the steep cliffs at Pointe du Hoc on D-Day. (US NARA)

German bunker at Pointe de Hoc showing damage from Allied bombs or shelling. (Private collection)

The German defenders on top of Pointe du Hoc had removed five out of six guns and replaced them with telegraph poles because of the fear of Allied bombardment. The fears were well founded as Pointe du Hoc was strategically carpet bombed on D-Day. The effects of the bombardment can still be seen today. (Private collection)

HEADQUARTERS 506TH PARACHUTE INFANTRY
APO 472, United States Army

GENERAL ORDER)
:
NUMBER.....12)

REGRADED UNCLASSIFIED
ORDER SEC ARMY BY TAG/ ________
POSTED RAC__________BY ______

15 June 1944

Under the provisions of Circular 186, WD, dated 11 May 1944, The COMBAT INFANTRYMAN BADGE is awarded the following named Officers and Enlisted men for exemplary conduct in action against the enemy.

1. OFFICERS

Lt. Col.	Chase, Charles H.	1st Lt.	Heehan, Thomas
Lt. Col.	Strayer, Robert L.	1st Lt.	McFadden, Frank J.
Lt. Col.	Turner, William L.	1st Lt.	Mehosky, Edward S.
Lt. Col.	Wolverton, Robert L	1st Lt.	Miller, Melvin M
Major	Buechner, Carl A,Jr	1st Lt.	Hinton, Herber L.
Major	Foster, Franklin E	1st Lt.	Morton, James G .
Major	Grant, George S.	1st Lt.	Nixon, Lewis
Major	Hannah, Harold W.	1st Lt.	Nye, James F.
Major	Horton, Oliver M	1st Lt.	Peacock, Thomas A.
Captain	Cox, Lloyd J.	1st Lt.	Pyne, William E.
Captain	Davis, Melvin O.	1st Lt.	Reid, William E.
Captain	Gross, Jerre S.	1st Lt.	Reeder, John H.
Captain	Harwick, Robert F	1st Lt.	Roblyer, Delos A.
Captain	Hester, Clarence	1st Lt.	Stokes, George A.
Captain	Howell, Eli H.	1st Lt.	Sweeney, Patrick J.
Captain	McKnight, John T.	1st Lt.	Tuck, Andrew E III
Captain	Moon, Robert S	1st Lt.	Tye, Ronnie, V, Jr.
Captain	Mulvey, Thomas P	1st Lt.	Viertel, Herbert R
Captain	Patch, Lloyd E	1st Lt.	Wilson, William V
Captain	Peters , Edward A	1st Lt.	Winters, Richard D.

Cpl.	Stallings, Marvin H.	Pvt.	Fernandez, George V.
Cpl.	Zobrosky, Stanley	Pvt.	Finder, Edwin
T/5.	Kristie, Gene	Pvt.	Galbraith, William P.
T/5.	Millican, James E.	Pvt.	Gavrock, Lonnie L.
T/5.	Riley, Leslie B.	Pvt.	Goodgal, Leonard S.
T/5.	Vanderpool, Orville.	Pvt.	Hopper, Willie H.
Pfc.	Ambisco, Gilbert	Pvt.	Hawkins, Jesse M.
Pfc.	Barrios, Manuel M.	Pvt.	Heavenridge, Robert J.
Pfc.	Boggs, John	Pvt.	Hoffman, Raymond D.
Pfc.	Brown, Ellis E.	Pvt.	Hogue, Dewey H. Jr.
Pfc.	Brown, Jake L.	Pvt.	Jackson, Thomas E.
Pfc.	Burg, Harry L. Jr.	Pvt.	Kangas, Robert W.
Pfc.	Calhoon, Richard L.	Pvt.	Karalunas, George J.
Pfc.	Carney, Warren K.	Pvt.	Kinzy, Robert C.
Pfc.	Carnes, Jack E.	Pvt.	Koch, Paul J.
Pfc.	Christensen, Niels N.	Pvt.	Lillard, Harold W.
Pfc.	Cook, James P.	Pvt.	Lowell, Norman W.
Pfc.	Copeland, Allen P.	Pvt.	Lujan, Frank
Pfc.	Cress, Frank A.	Pvt.	Maczuga, Frank J.
Pfc.	Dziepak, Theodore E.	Pvt.	McMillan, George R.
Pfc.	Halverson, Donald B.	Pvt.	Mezoy Roy
Pfc.	Harrington, William	Pvt.	Morgan, David D.
Pfc.	Hedric, Max D.	Pvt.	O'Christie, Jerry F.
Pfc.	Hill, Lester R.	Pvt.	Penner, Robert J.
Pfc.	Hinson, Bryant L.	Pvt.	Phillips, Howard
Pfc.	Houk, John J.	Pvt.	Powers, Raymond L.
Pfc.	Hove, Marion H.	Pvt.	Rainwater, Bernie B.
Pfc.	Johnson, Harold A.	Pvt.	Ranney, Myron N.
Pfc.	Kelly, Gerard P.	Pvt.	Somerville, Warren A.
Pfc.	Kenfield, George E.	Pvt.	Stedman, Harold T.
Pfc.	Kittia, John J.	Pvt.	Swanson, Francis H.
Pfc.	Lane, Lawrence F.	Pvt.	Swann, Bernard M.
Pfc.	Lukasavage, Walter J.	Pvt.	Tobias, Earl P.
Pfc.	Madona, Joseph P.	Pvt.	Tucker, Claud L.

Pfc.	Lukasavage, Walter J.	Pvt.	Tobias, Earl P.
Pfc.	Madona, Joseph P.	Pvt.	Tucker, Claud L.
Pfc.	Nagy, John J.	Pvt.	Weber, Paul J.
Pfc.	Newell, George D. Jr	Pvt.	Weirich, Glen L.
Pfc.	Olson, William E.	Pvt.	Westhuis, Andy H.
Pfc.	Pinkston, Paul S.	Pvt.	Widman, Earl
Pfc.	Poynter, Alvin	Pvt.	Wines, Ge[illegible]ld J.

8486

RESTRICTED

16. Continued Company "I"

Pvt.	Wright, John A.	Pvt.	Wright, Clarence M.
Pvt.	Young, Robert L. Jr.	Pvt.	Zapalac, George G.

Pvt. Cosner, Glen H.

By order of Colonel SINK:

MAX T. PETROFF
Captain, 506th Parachute Infantry
Ass't Adjutant.

OFFICIAL:

MAX T. PETROFF
Captain, 506th Parachute Infantry
Ass't Adjutant.

Previous page and right: On 15 June 1944, the Combat Infantryman Badge was awarded to paratroopers who had participated in the Normandy invasion. Niels Christensen was among them, even though he was a prisoner of the Germans at the time. (US National Archives)

Then: the town of Sainte Marie du Mont behind Utah. Many American paratroopers were dropped in the area to secure the approaches from the beaches so the US 4th Infantry Division could advance from Utah. (US NARA / Private)

Now: the town of Sainte Marie du Mont behind Utah. Many American paratroopers were dropped in the area to secure the approaches from the beaches so the US 4th Infantry Division could advance from Utah. (US NARA / Private)

Men from 3rd Battalion, 506th Parachute Infantry Regiment, aboard a C-47 aircraft during training in England. The American paratroopers could have 40–50kg of equipment strapped to their bodies. The fear of landing in water on D-Day was great, as the heavy packs would prove fatal to the paratroopers if they landed in the flooded areas of Normandy. (Michel De Trez via Ian Gardner)

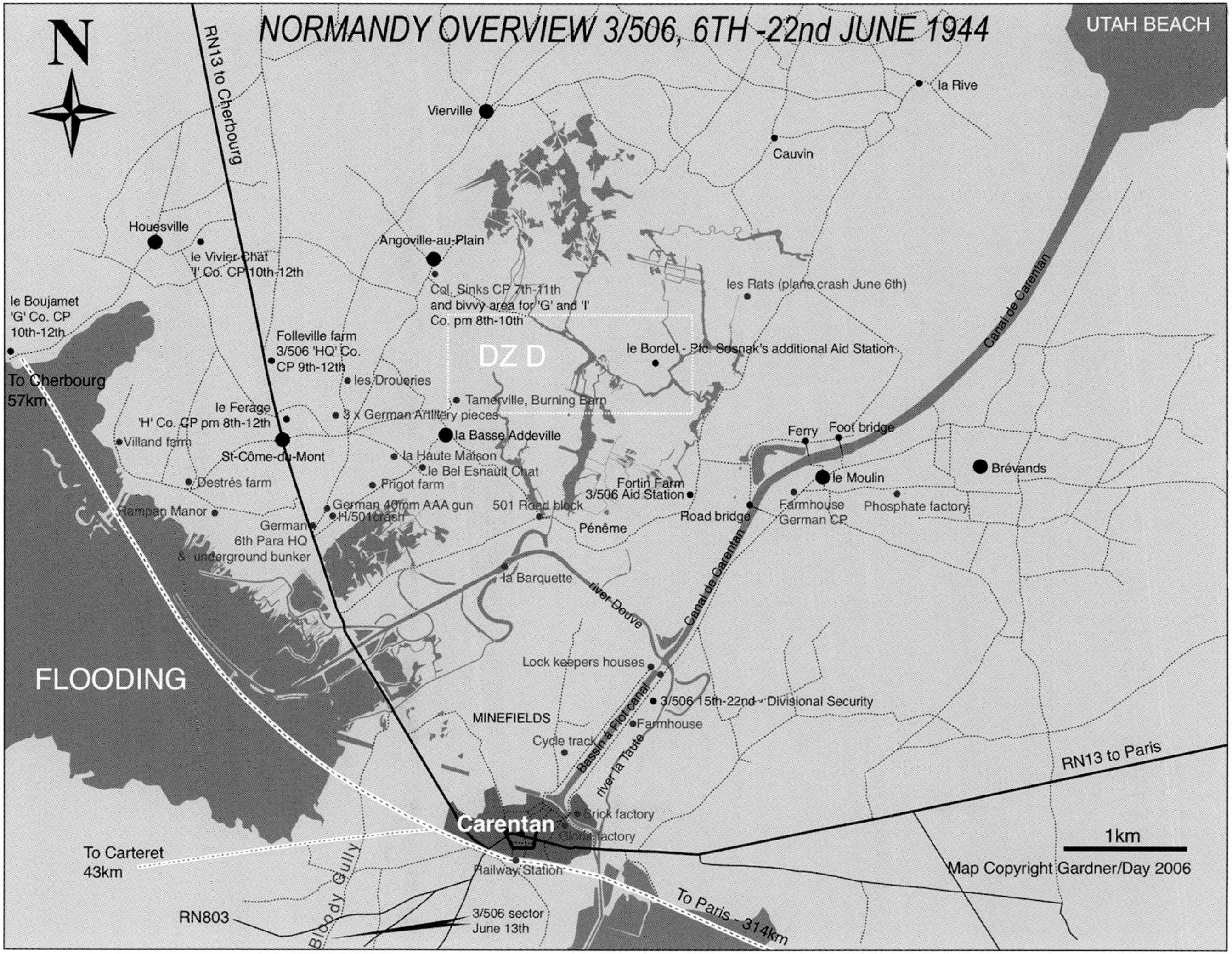

Landing Zone D, where Niels Christensen and the rest of the 3rd Battalion, 506th Parachute Infantry Regiment, were to be dropped. Due to heavy German fire from anti-aircraft guns, Niels Christensen landed northeast of the drop zone, close to Omaha and Pointe du Hoc. (Gardner & Day)

Part 3

Day of Days – D-Day

11,590 fighters and bombers began the invasion by bombing the five beach sectors and German bunkers along the coast and inland. The aim was to break down the section of Hitler's Atlantic Wall in Normandy so that Allied soldiers could more easily take the coastal area and open the second front. Hitler ordered the construction of the Atlantic Wall, which consisted of a belt of bunkers from the North Sea to the Franco-Spanish border, to resist an Allied seaborne invasion. The Atlantic Wall, which Organisation *Todt* was responsible for building, was put to the test during the Operation Overlord. German propaganda about the unbreakable defence of the Atlantic Wall suffered a massive defeat of its credibility when the Allies managed to land and gain a foothold on the coast on D-Day. Despite the Atlantic Wall being well-established and well-armed in Normandy, there was a significant weakness in the German defence: the troops. At many of the beach sectors, the German defence consisted of depleted German regiments from the Eastern Front, elderly soldiers and teenagers who could in no way be compared to Hitler's elite troops. However, in places along the coast and inland in Normandy there were highly battle-hardened units, including elite SS armoured divisions and the infamous German paratroopers of *6. Fallschirmjägerdivision*. The Allies had never been able to mount a successful invasion against an elite, trained defence force positioned in concrete bunkers, including gun emplacements, which were also designed to withstand bombing attacks. In addition, the coast of Normandy was heavily mined, as was the case on the west coast of Jutland. Between the Allies at sea and the German bunkers in the dunes of northern France, six million mines were placed.[1]

Jens A. Nørgaard, B-26 Marauder Pilot

The Danish-American, Major Jens A. Nørgaard, participated in the initial bombing raids over the Utah coastal area aboard the B-26 Marauder bomber *Mary Jo*, which had been named after Nørgaard's wife. *Mary Jo* was part of the 495th Squadron of the 344th Bomb Group, part of the 9th Air Force. Nørgaard was born on the former Danish island of St Croix, after which his Danish-born parents moved to the USA. The month of June 1944 was extraordinarily eventful for Nørgaard, as he not only had to participate in the invasion of

1 Antony Beevor, *D-Dag: Kampen om Normandiet* (Copenhagen: Lindhardt & Ringhof, 2009), pp.96–194.

Normandy on D-Day, but two days before the invasion began, he became a father, and the day after the invasion he was promoted to lieutenant colonel.

Nørgaard played a very prominent role during the B-26 bombing raids in the early morning hours of D-Day, as he was formation leader aboard the lead B-26 bomber that was to begin the bombardment of the Utah sector. The 344th Bomb Group, which Nørgaard led, was chosen to lead the raid because of their previous exploits and in particular because of their precision bombing. The 344th was therefore chosen to lead Bomb Groups 387th, 397th, 394th, 323rd and 386th during the attack on the Utah Beach coastline. Nørgaard was to be the lead pilot for a formation of more than 400 B-26 bombers. The first aircraft was scheduled to begin dropping bombs at 06.05 a.m. on 6 June and the last in the formation was to have dropped its bombs at 06.25 a.m., or H-hour minus 5. Characteristic of the day before D-Day, Nørgaard had difficulty orientating himself above the dense and dark clouds. He turned to his navigator, Lou Offenberg, to see if he could locate the target. Offenberg promptly replied: "I have not the faintest idea where it is."[2] At that moment, the heavy clouds disappeared for a while and Nørgaard's formation leader aircraft could see the targets. The bomb groups attacked the German positions with great efficiency, and the bombing raid was a success for Nørgaard and the rest of 344th Bomb Group. The B-26s hit their targets with great precision, with only 1 aircraft shot down out of 56.[3] In July 1945, Nørgaard was awarded the French Croix de Guerre with palm for his 'exceptional participation in the war, which was particularly evident during the operations in the liberation of France.' He also received the Distinguished Flying Cross and the Air Medal with Oak Leaf Clusters.[4]

Thorkil Jensen, B-17 Flying Fortress Navigator

Thorkil Jensen was born in Vejle, Denmark, and came to the USA with his family in 1923 at the age of 4. He grew up in Stillwater, Minnesota. His parents spoke Danish at home, and so did Thorkil at first. However, it was not long before he started responding in English, as his two younger brothers had not learnt Danish.

When the war broke out, Thorkil was actually still a Danish citizen because his parents had not registered him as an American citizen, as they were not sure if they would remain in the country. It was not until 1955 that Thorkil became a US citizen. When the attack on Pearl Harbor took place in December 1941, Thorkil was 22 years old and felt that at some point he should enlist.

However, this step was not without its problems, precisely because Thorkil was not yet an American citizen. He wanted to join the navy, but when he tried to enlist, he received the following message from the recruiting officer: 'You can't enlist here, you are not even a citizen of this country.' This took a toll on Thorkil, as he fully felt like an American. He then tried to join the air force, but that would also prove to be difficult. Eventually, however, he managed to get in after he submitted an application explaining why he wanted to join the service.

2 Mary Christensen's journal (private collection), p.16.

3 Lambert Austin: *344th Bomb Group m "Silver Streaks": History & Remembrances World War II*, (St Petersburg, Fl: Southern Heritage, 1996).

4 From archives of the Museum of Danish America.

Thorkil did not mince his words and said how much he loved the USA. He then succeeded in joining the air force where, after completing his training, he became a navigator aboard a B-17 bomber in the 8th Division Air Force, 91st Bomb Group, 324th Squadron. In 1944, the crew flew from Nebraska in the B-17 aircraft, made a stopover in Iceland, and were then scheduled to land in Scotland, but were unable to do so due to bad weather. They therefore continued to Wales. Thorkil's first mission was a bombing raid over Berlin, and he subsequently flew several missions near Schweinfurt. Thorkil and the rest of the crew made it through their missions unscathed, but one of Thorkil's friends aboard another B-17 was not so lucky:

> I had a friend who flew on another aircraft and on a mission over Schweinfurt they flew directly into anti-aircraft fire. They were completely pulverised. You also knew there would be losses when we didn't have fighter escort, because we didn't hit many enemy aircraft from our B-17s.[5]

During Operation Overlord, Thorkil and the other hundreds of B-17 bombers that would take part in the early bombing raids on D-Day were fully focused on the dangers associated with this mission:

> On D-Day we flew in a parallel line at 10,000 feet to support the invasion. The altitude itself made a big difference for us, as you could normally fly up to 25,000 feet, where you had a good chance of getting away unscathed from fighters and anti-aircraft fire, and then the Germans had to be pretty sharp to get us. But when you're at 10,000 feet and they hit you, the plane can be cut in half, and one half can suddenly see the other half whizzing past. I really hated the enemy fighters more than flak, because it always seemed like flak was going to hit you. Many of our guys were wearing flak jackets anyway. Fighters, on the other hand, could do a lot more damage, I felt. But several of our men were hit by German flak.

Thorkil Jensen flew two missions on D-Day itself, and he flew a total of 30 missions throughout 1944 and 1945. He received several medals, including the Air Medal, the Victory Medal, and a Presidential Unit citation.

Danes in the Royal Air Force

The Danes in the two Norwegian, 331 and 332, Squadrons of the Royal Air Force were tasked with providing fighter cover for shipping and defending the area around Isigny. Their primary purpose was to keep the German bombers away from the area, as the Allies expected the Luftwaffe to launch a counter-attack once they realised the invasion was a reality. However, the Luftwaffe never launched the anticipated counter-attack, and the Allied air forces were thus dominant throughout D-Day. The Allies had 171 squadrons in

5 The following quotes are from Veterans History Project interview with Thorkil Jensen <http://memory.loc.gov/diglib/vhp/bib/loc.natlib.afc2001001.9466>.

the air during the day in defence of the invasion area. Along the entire Western Front, the Germans had only 500 aircraft at their disposal, of which 5 approaching the invasion area were shot down. By contrast, 113 Allied aircraft were shot down, mainly by German flak.[6]

Lieutenant Colonel, and operation planner, Kaj Birksted was responsible for the planning of all daytime fighter operations for the two Norwegian squadrons; Group Captain John Cunningham was responsible for the night-time operations. Birksted was the only foreigner at staff level, but Birksted's important task as a planner was entrusted to him largely due to his exploits previously in the war. Since his promotion to Wing Commander, he had led his squadrons on 71 offensive missions, personally destroying 5 German aircraft and damaging more. Despite Birksted's administrative role on D-Day, he personally conducted early morning overflights of the invasion beaches as feedback on the invasion was slow in coming. He set off for Normandy in a Spitfire to assess the situation, and at the time the fighting along the beaches was at its peak and he had a good view of the brutal battle.[7]

Jørgen Kjeldbæk was a Spitfire pilot in the 501 Squadron. He made two flights on D-Day – the first from four to six o'clock in the morning. He later recorded in his logbook: 'Low cover over assault area Operation Neptune. Patrol uneventful. Landed Hawkinge.'[8] He also flew a flight in the evening of D-Day from 18:00–20:00, where he once again recorded in his logbook: 'Low cover patrol over assault beaches.' Despite Kjeldbæk's notes about undramatic flights on D-Day, the reality – especially for the troops on the beaches – was quite different. Kjeldbæk made a total of 11 flights in connection with Operation Overlord.

Kjeld Rønhof participated in four Spitfire missions in connection with Operation Overlord. The first was on the morning of D-Day over Omaha. From the cockpit, he could see the scale of the invasion from the start in England all the way to the Normandy coast and the brutal fighting that took place on Omaha:

> Below us we saw the largest collection of ships I had ever seen. It was probably the largest collection of ships the world had ever seen. We went out to sea until we could just make out the Cherbourg Peninsula. Here we turned 20 degrees to port and soon after we were over our assigned patrol area, which was the American sector over Utah and Omaha. We split up into three formations with red, blue and yellow sections separately. From my patrol line, which was mainly over Omaha, I could see a lot of activity. Everything from large warships to the smallest landing craft were here. Small boats were darting in and out to keep track of this anthill. Time and again, the heavy battleships and cruisers were enveloped in huge clouds of smoke, where you could see the red-yellow muzzle flames from the huge guns. The sea rose to foam around the warships due to the recoil from the heavy armour. A few seconds later, huge explosions could be seen far inland where the heavy shells were hitting. Across the beach, a steady stream of soldiers were being landed by landing craft, darting back and forth like little ferries.[9]

---

6 Susanne Zima Feierskov, *Med vinger og våben* (Copenhagen: Gyldendal, 2011), p.222.

7 Susanne Zima Feierskov, *Med vinger og våben* (Copenhagen: Gyldendal, 2011), pp.223–225.

8 Taken from Thomas Oldrup, *Danske Søfolk ved D-Dag – en Vigtig Indsats for Danmark (Helsingør: Museet for Søfarts årbog: Søfolk i Krig – nedslag i den maritime historie, 2014)*, p.187.

9 Kjeld Rønhof, *Vi fløj for Friheden* (Copenhagen: Four Stripes,1991), pp.105–106.

> As we approached the invasion, we started to soften up the hinterland there... And there was a civilian population that had been told to stay away. Because we were shooting at everything and everyone. I violated a regulation when I fired at the same target twice in a row. You were only supposed to fire at the target once and then move on to the next one. But I grazed a German lorry, but then turned round to finish it off completely. It was horrible to witness because I could see these strange black long things along the coast that I thought were dead fish. I decided to fly closer to investigate as there were no German airmen coming to meet us. As I approached the sea surface I realised it [the black line] was human. There were thousands of bodies floating around down there.[10]

The Arrival of The Fleet

Half an hour after the bombers had made their attack on the German coastal fortifications, the warships began their bombardment. The six oldest battleships involved in the bombardment were three American and three British. The USS *Nevada* was the only battleship to survive the Japanese attack on Pearl Harbor and was now part of Operation Overlord. Also with the fleet here were the USS *Arkansas,* USS *Texas* and the three British battleships; HMS *Warspite,* HMS *Ramillies* and HMS *Rodney. Arkansas* was built way back in 1912 and *Warspite* took part in the Battle of Jutland in 1916. *Rodney* was the youngest of the six ships, built in 1927.

When the naval bombardment began on the morning of D-Day, the Germans experienced overwhelming firepower from the Allied warships. Troops and personnel aboard the transport ships and landing craft could feel the intensity and force of the bombardment as shells flew overhead. *Texas* and *Arkansas* fired approximately 600 shells at the German bunkers on top of the cliffs at Pointe du Hoc.

The coastal area and off the five beach sectors were home to 68 destroyers, whose primary task was to fire on the German bunkers and thereby give covering fire for the land troops that would soon storm the beaches. Several German batteries concentrated their fire on the destroyers. Other destroyers were attacked and hit by German E-Boats near Sword, and the attack resulted in the Norwegian *Svenner* breaking in half and sinking. This was the only Allied ship to be sunk as a direct result of German naval activity on D-Day. The dane Christian Bror Nejrup was aboard *Svenner* and perished along with 30 others from the ship. The wreck is still located off the coast of Sword. The ship's anchor was salvaged in 2003 and is today a memorial near Hermanville-sur-Mer.

Other destroyers were sunk by the German gun batteries and mines on D-Day. Despite the heavy damage Allied destroyers caused to the German gun bunkers, it proved difficult at times to destroy the German guns because of their solid reinforced concrete casemates. However, when the destroyers' heavy shells hit the bunkers, it often had a massive effect on the German crew inside. The fierce attacks could cause fainting and even death from the tremors and air pressure of the Allied shells falling on and around the bunkers. Others

10 Interview with Kjeld Rønhof in the DR programme 'D-Dag Den Længste Dag', rebroadcast June 2004.

were deafened by the continual extremely loud explosions. Despite the shock effect of the Allied fire, the majority of the German guns were able to return fire and resume firing on the destroyers after the bombardment. Throughout D-Day, the large battleships would duel directly with the German coastal batteries both on the beaches and in the Normandy hinterland. Major German batteries were involved, such as the Crisbeq Battery at St Marcouf behind Utah – one of 16 major German positions in Normandy, where four 210mm guns placed in concrete casemates were ready to open fire on the battleships. In the Utah sector alone, there were 110 German guns ranging in size from 75 to 170mm calibre.[11]

The Danish Ships

Of the 6,939 maritime vessels involved in Operation Neptune and Operation Overlord, 860 were exclusively intended for transport. 31 of these 860 were Danish ships, corresponding to 3.6 percent of the total transport fleet. Of these 31 Danish ships, 24 sailed with the Dannebrog hoisted. On board the 31 ships were more than 800 Danish seamen. The purpose of the ships was to transport troops and vital supplies to the invasion coast. Approximately one in 20 of the Allied sailors was Danish. It is also worth mentioning that four Danish-manned minesweepers participated under the Dannebrog in the Royal Navy in the period immediately following Operation Overlord. The importance of being able to sail with the Dannebrog flying over the ships during the invasion was crucial. Having been seen as pro-German and disloyal to the Allies, Danish sailors now had the opportunity to represent their country alongside the Allied forces. On 25 December 1943, the sailors had regained the right to sail under the Dannebrog. This was a great gift from the British Merchant Navy, and it was largely due to the efforts of the war sailors, as many of them had already paid the highest price – their lives.[12] By December 1943, 66 of the 145 Danish ships under British administration had already been destroyed and 422 Danish sailors had died. Furthermore, 21 other Danish ships under other Allied merchant fleets had been sunk during the same period, resulting in a further 73 fatalities.[13]

Danish Sailors

The change from the flag of the British Merchant Navy, The Red Duster, to the Dannebrog, did not mean any change in conditions for Danish sailors.

The first Danish ships to participate in the invasion set sail in the afternoon of the same day, 6 June. The invasion was in full swing and there was fierce fighting along the Normandy coast. The majority of the ships transporting troops and supplies to Normandy consisted

11 Jakob Sørensen, *D-Dag – Operation Overlord 6. Juni 1944* (Copenhagen: People's Press, 2014), pp.140–144.

12 Erik Kragelund, *Overlord – Den Danske Deltagelse i Invasionen i Normandiet i 1944* (Copenhagen: Radius, 2013), pp.1–9.

13 The following is based on the research of Erik Kragelund, former chairman of the War Sailors Association.

of flat-bottomed coastal steamers designed to unload close to shore. Furthermore, these steamers were very functional during the invasion as they could enter smaller harbours where the larger ships could not dock. The flat-bottomed steamers also had another advantage, as they were able to utilise the tidal differences, which are large along the Normandy coast. Many of the landing sectors where the invasion was to take place, especially at Omaha, had no harbours, so the flat-bottomed steamers were used. These were able to sail right up to the beach at high tide and unload troops and equipment. Then, at low tide, the tide would lower the ship so that it was almost settled on the seabed. This meant that lorries could drive directly to the ships and pick up supplies. The ships would then wait, sometimes up to a week, for the high tide to bring them off again. This was a particularly effective method in the weeks after D-Day, when there was less shelling.

On D-Day itself, there was a need for faster ways to unload the ships' cargo, as the heavy fire from the German guns meant that the ships could not sail all the way to the beach areas. Therefore, the so-called 'Ducks' (DUKW) were used. These were amphibious vehicles that could sail up to the side of the transport ships, and via the ship's crane, parts of the cargo could be unloaded into the amphibious vehicles. These could then sail directly onto the beach and drive the supplies to a warehouse at the beach area. Jørgen Linnet was on board the ship *Alan A. Dale*, which arrived in Omaha on 10 June, and he clearly remembers how the Ducks were used:

> There were no harbour areas. Everything was loaded into amphibious boats that were constantly going back and forth on the coast. They were there 24 hours a day to get as much military material as possible to the troops inland. It was also important to get some airfields built over there as soon as possible, as they probably didn't want to go back with their Spitfires et cetera so they could save on fuel and make better use of their air force. It was always more of a challenge to load on the open sea than at a harbour.
>
> The plans had a lot to say about how the unloading would take place. When the weather is fine, it's no problem, but when it's windy, you have to be careful not to unload anything into an amphibious boat and tip it over. After all, it was very small boats that picked up the gear.[14]

On D-Day and in the days that followed, these types of unloading missions could last up to 30 hours, during which the cargo ships would be relatively exposed. The Allied warships constantly sent shells over the heads of the ships to keep the German gun positions ashore at bay. This created harsh working conditions for the Danish warships, and at the same time, the first ships to arrive on the coast witnessed the gruesome fighting that had already taken place in the early morning hours of D-Day and in some places was still going on behind the beaches. There were dead soldiers and destroyed vehicles and equipment along the coast. Radiotelegraphist Hans Mathiasen from Fanø arrived on Omaha in the evening of D-Day aboard the Danish-manned ship *Empire Beatrice* and clearly remembers the great pressure the sailors were under:

14 Quote from an interview with Jørgen Linnet, February 2016.

> Everything was about getting supplies of all kinds and troops ashore in the fastest possible time so that the captured areas could be expanded and depots built for the great breakthrough that lay ahead, and they worked day and night, without regard to enemy attacks or falling splinters from anti-aircraft guns and with all conceivable invasion craft and discharge methods.[15]

The more than 800 Danish sailors who were part of the transport fleet in Operation Overlord were vital to the invasion. During the first six days of the invasion, the transport fleet landed 326,000 men in Normandy. A figure equivalent to the current combined population of the Danish cities of Esbjerg and Aarhus. In addition, 100,000 tons of equipment and 54,000 vehicles were transported to the coastal area. The transport ships were crucial for the invasion itself and for keeping the attacks ongoing while it was happening.[16] It is also worth mentioning that between the Danish uprising on 29 August 1943 and the liberation of Denmark in 1945, the navy's leadership, against protocol and on their own initiative, attempted to send Danish naval officers to service in the British Royal Navy. Experienced commanders and lieutenant commanders were preferred, as they could be important for the rebuilding of the Danish Navy after the war. The Royal Navy was eagerly looking for well-trained younger officers. As a result, several Danish naval officers joined the invasion based on this type of recruitment. Lieutenant Commander Henrik Rømeling was on board the monitor HMS *Erebus* and Lieutenant Commander Niels F. Lange was on board LST *1S8* (Landing Ship Transport). Lieutenant Commander Find Haugsted participated in convoy duty from England to the invasion area on board HMS *Campbell*. Lieutenant Commander Eigil Wern also participated as a diving and salvage expert in the subsequent clearing of the invasion beaches of the many dangerous objects that were still off the coast.[17]

The Five Landing Sectors: Utah

Utah was the most isolated of the five landing sectors. Located in the far west and physically separated from the nearest sector, Omaha, by the Vire River, the capture of the Utah exit roads was of utmost importance as they could connect the two sectors. To secure these, the American 82nd and 101st Airborne Divisions were deployed. The Airborne Divisions were dropped in the area behind Utah. At low tide, the American troops landing on Utah had to cross close to 400 metres of open terrain to reach relative safety at the German-built tank wall on the dunes. There were three attack sectors on Utah itself: Tare Green, Uncle Red, and Victor. In the dunes, the Germans had built bunkers and emplaced guns, and in the hinterland they had flooded kilometres of the areas that many American paratroopers had already become fatally familiar with.

15 N. M. Kromann, *Fanø Sømænd i Storm og Stille* (Fanø: Kromann, 1960), p.218.

16 Erik Kragelund, *Overlord – Den Danske Deltagelse i Invasionen i Normandiet i 1944* (Copenhagen: Radius, 2013), pp.31–32.

17 Hans Christian Bjerg, Svend Kieler, Søren Laub: *For Flaget og flåden – om marines personel og dets Virke 1943-45* (Copenhagen: Søværnet, 1995), pp.190–201.

The American 4th Infantry Division, under the command of General Raymond Barton, led the attack on Utah. Of these, elements of the 8th Regiment and the 1st Engineer Special Brigade made up the first attack wave on the morning of D-Day. The German defence consisted of the *Infanterieregiment 919* of *Infanteridivision 709*, which was a mixed unit of all ages but mostly German. Some were Austrians and other veterans of the Eastern Front who had been wounded and were no longer fully fit for combat. In addition, there were elements of the *Infanteridivision 243*, which would be able to act in a more mobile manner in the event of an attack. Like many other places in Normandy, the Atlantic rampart at Utah was not complete and was still under construction on 6 June 1944. 865 ships made up Task Force U, which targeted Utah.

Tens of thousands of anxious sailors and just as many seasick soldiers, who had been at sea for nearly 60 hours, finally approached the coast off Utah at 3 a.m. in the morning. The soldiers slowly began climbing down the nets placed along the sides of the troopships to board the smaller Higgins landing craft (LCVP) that would take them onto the beach itself for the initial assault. 30 men could be aboard each of the landing craft, which were designed to sail directly onto the beach; here, a front ramp would drop down and the soldiers could storm the area as quickly as possible. At 4.30 a.m, the order was given to begin the attack. The small landing craft had to travel almost 13 kilometres on the stormy sea before they reached Utah. One landing craft hit a sea mine and went down in the dark sea. Another had engine trouble and drifted helplessly in the big waves. What remained were 20 landing craft with around 600 men. The naval and aerial bombardments began at 6 a.m. with the intention of causing as much damage to the German bunkers on the beach as possible. 32 Sherman DD (Duplex Drive) tanks, which could float and drive at sea and then drive directly onto the beach, were also sent out: 4 of these went down in the rough sea. Shortly after the tanks were launched, the 20 landing craft arrived on the beach at 6.30 a.m., but the strong current had driven the boats far off of their original target on Utah – almost a mile south of their original planned location. The seemingly enormous disaster of being landed far from the original target would, however, prove to be an advantage for the troops.

The ramp of the landing craft hit the cold water and the American soldiers jumped out and immediately began to climb the almost 400 metres to the German-built tank wall where they could take cover. All the way to the beach, they encountered sporadic fire from the German troops positioned inside the dune area. Along with the first wave of soldiers was 56-year-old US Brigadier General Theodore Roosevelt Junior – son of former President Roosevelt.

The Brigadier General quickly grasped the situation and despite the troops being far from their target, Roosevelt uttered the laconic phrase: "We'll start the war from right here!" On 12 July 1944, a month after D-Day, Roosevelt died of cardiac arrest and was awarded the American Medal of Honor. Because the initial bombing raids, primarily from the B-26 bombers led by Jens Nørgaard among others, had been so effective, Roosevelt managed to lead a group of men directly behind the German defences to locate one of the four exit routes from the beach. Roosevelt spotted a house with a red roof, which according to his intelligence should have been located further south. He made a quick decision and ordered all incoming troops from the sea to this sector to continue the invasion from this point. The decision was of utmost importance as the American troops could now attack the other German fortifications along the coast from the rear, probably saving many lives.[18]

ITEM Lancaster gunner Andreas Moldt did not have long to rest after the initial bombing raid behind Utah on the night of 5/6 June. On D-Day, it was 'ops on' again, another order to attack an area near the coast was given, and the crew on board were once again quickly in the air. This time, however, the aircraft were met with stronger resistance from the Luftwaffe. 6–7 minutes before the aircraft reached its target, Moldt spotted a dark spot to the left and quickly warned the pilot that there was something near them. The spot quickly disappeared from Moldt's field of vision, but the pilot warned him to keep an extra close eye out for enemy fighters. At the same time, the navigator reported that the target was in sight, and the bomb bay doors opened shortly afterwards. That same moment, Moldt once again spotted a foreign object in the distance:

> Both index fingers rest on the two triggers and I give the turret a few small jerks to feel the situation... Suddenly I see two small bright spots! I have no doubt and immediately pull the triggers without having time to use the sights. I have to aim the first volley at the tracer bullets. He fires at the same time; I see the flames from his two 20mm cannons and two machine guns. All my tracer bullets disappear into him and after 4 or 5 seconds I stop for a moment. I feel the skipper start a corkscrew manoeuvre, but when I see the German pull up a little, I know he's no longer aiming at us, so I shout to the skipper to go steady again. The German did what I didn't expect: at a distance of only 50–60 metres, he pulls up with his nose straight at us, and at this distance I can't actually miss. He gets two volleys in the right wing root. Where his petrol tanks are, and I see flames coming out. Every fifth bullet is a tracer and every fifth is armour piercing. I had now realised that the attacker was an ME 410 with two aft-facing machine guns, so that area got a long burst. Then he disappeared down the left wing and on fire.[19]

With the outer part of the beach taken, it was now the task of the 4th Infantry Division to push the Germans further inland behind the beach and thereby make contact with the American paratroopers who were already deep behind the beach area. At 10 o'clock 12th Regiment of the 4th Infantry Division landed on Utah from landing craft. There was still sporadic shelling from German guns located further inland in the area behind the beach. Henning Møller from Frederikshavn was part of the 12th Regiment. As the exit roads were secured at the beach, bottlenecks quickly developed, meaning that the infantry from the 12th and 22nd regiments could not move exclusively via the roads, as this would delay the advance. Henning Møller was thus forced to wade through the flooded marshlands behind the beach. A scenario with soldiers moving slowly through a marshland would normally have disastrous consequences due to German artillery. Soldiers in open areas are usually easy targets, but because of the initial air strikes and the presence of paratroopers, the German

18 Stuart C. Robertson & Dale Booth, Dale, *Following in the Footsteps of Heroes: D-Day June 6th 1944*, (Devizes: Sabrestorm, 2014), pp.72–81.

19 Andreas P. Moldt, *Natbomber: Slaget om Europa som en Dansker Oplevede det i Invasionssommeren 1944* (Copenhagen: Gyldendal, 1985), pp.63–64.

artillery did not pose a major threat. Henning Møller and the rest of the 12th Regiment would cross through the area unhindered. The 4th Infantry Division later participated further in Operation Overlord, when they helped take Cherbourg on 25 June. Møller also took part in intense fighting at Periers of 6–12 July, where the 4th Infantry Division broke through the German left flank and managed to push the enemy back to Avranches. Henning Møller was killed on 18 July 1944, probably during the advance towards Avranches. He is buried today at the American Cemetery at Cambridge, England; he received the Purple Heart medal for his sacrifice.[20]

Danish sailor Thorald Nielsen arrived on Utah after the initial attacks of the morning of D-Day aboard the Danish DFDS ship *Tomsk*. Nielsen had already experienced being shipwrecked several times and torpedoed by German E-Boats since signing up for Allied service in 1940. However, he signed up for another tour of duty when he signed the V Articles to join the invasion force for Normandy. *Tomsk* transported American soldiers and vehicles to Utah and was greatly affected by the logistical challenges associated with the invasion. The thousands of freighters that had to unload in a limited area plus the lack of harbour facilities meant that *Tomsk* had to wait up to seven days off Utah, despite arriving in the sector on D-Day itself. Thorald Nielsen clearly remembers the intense wait:

> We walked quietly onto the coast, all the way to the beach, which was codenamed Utah. Of course there was a lot of shooting, but we were almost like front row spectators. I wasn't really that frightened. It was almost anticlimactic, but we were not actually allowed to land the vehicles. We spent almost seven days waiting for that order, and dissatisfaction quickly spread among the American soldiers and not least their platoon leader, who was all worked up to go to fight the Germans. Now they sat there and could not vent their frustrations. Next to us were the large battleships, spasmodically bombarding the coast with shells, and our trouser legs were fluttering from the pressure wave. Finally, the order to land came, and when we sailed out again, our fresh water supply had dwindled considerably. We had to refuel and we were on our way to a small tanker, which we had to walk alongside. In front of us was a small landing craft, but suddenly it disappeared in a big bubble. It must have been a mine. We wondered if we would have activated it too if we had sailed ahead.[21]

By early afternoon on D-Day, the 4th Infantry Division had landed almost 8,000 men without much resistance. By late afternoon, it had pushed through to the locations of the paratroopers from 101st Airborne Division.

The transport ships landed more than 24,000 soldiers and 1,700 vehicles in the Utah sector on D-Day, of which 197 soldiers from the 4th Infantry Division were subsequently reported killed, wounded or missing. The paratroopers had done an effective initial job of securing escape routes and destroying the German guns inland. If you add the paratroopers' casualty figures to the casualties in the actual area of Utah Beach, the statistics show that in addition

20 Frederikshavn During the Occupation 1985: p.126.
21 Claus Arboe-Rasmussen & Bent Sørensen, *De befriede os* (Copenhagen: Folk & Sikkerhed, 2005), p.81.

to the 197 from the 4th Infantry Division, 2,400 men were killed, wounded or captured. However, the attack on Utah was still considered a success. The American troops in the Omaha sector would fare differently.[22]

The Five Landing Sectors: Omaha

Omaha was the second of the two American sectors and, unlike Utah, the site of the most brutal fighting on 6 June. Many of the initial Allied manoeuvres to disable the German defences failed at Omaha. Several of the Danes involved also witnessed this first-hand. What made Omaha special were the high cliffs where the German positions were located. These caused enormous problems for the American soldiers from the 1st and 29th Infantry Divisions, who had to take the beach. The approximately 12,000 soldiers from *Infanteridivision 352* and *Infanteridivision 439 Ost-Batallion*, who manned guns and machine guns on the cliffs and in concrete bunkers, were in extremely advantageous defence positions. The Germans were ready all along the Omaha line and their guns, mortars, anti-tank guns and machine gun barrels were aimed at the American soldiers on the landing craft that they could see in the distance. The capture of Omaha was essential, as it was the only place between the Vire estuary and Arromanches where a real beach existed. The rest of the area was characterised by steep slopes and cliffs, as at Pointe du Hoc.

The colour of the sand on Omaha Beach is still more golden than the other landing beaches, and the American troops landing in the Omaha sector were greeted with the same golden colour on D-Day. A stretch of more than 300 metres of golden sand had to be traversed by the American troops to reach the dunes. The only place the troops could take cover was by the German Spanish horsemen and Rommel's 'asparagus stakes' with mines on the top. The bomb craters on the beach that the initial bomber raid was supposed to have created to give the ground troops more opportunities to take cover were nonexistent.

The bombers had hit next to the beach. Located directly behind Omaha, there were four major arterial roads and one minor road leading from west to east to the three villages of Vierville-sur-Mer, Saint-Laurent-sur-Mer and Colleville-sur-Mer. It was clear to the Allies, as well as to the Germans, at Omaha that whoever controlled these roads controlled the entrance to the rest of Normandy.[23]

Omaha, like the other landing beaches, was divided into eight smaller sectors: Charlie, Dog Green, Dog White, Dog Red, Easy Green, Easy Red, Fox Green and Fox Red. The first wave to attack the western side of Omaha was from the 116th Infantry Regiment of the 29th Infantry Division, supported by a company of the 2nd Ranger Battalion. The first wave of attacks on the eastern side consisted of troops from the experienced 1st Infantry Division, including the 16th Regiment. Initially, 32 DD tanks were to be launched to attack and support the ground troops. The plan was then for engineer troops, supported by the tanks and naval warships, to clear the beach of German obstacles, paving the way for the rest of the combat troops. The attack on Omaha opened at 05:50 on the morning of 6 June with

22 Stuart C. Robertson & Dale Booth, *Following in the Footsteps of Heroes: D-Day June 6th 1944*, (Devizes: Sabrestorm, 2014), pp.80–81.

23 Antony Beevor, *D-Dag: Kampen om Normandiet* (Copenhagen: Lindhardt & Ringhof, 2009), pp.72–82.

the planned bombardment by naval ships. The navy stationed at Omaha had the two battleships, USS *Texas* and USS *Arkansas*, as well as one British and two French cruisers, eleven destroyers and numerous other specialised ships, including those carrying important engineering vehicles to break through the beach area. The 32 specially constructed DD tanks of the 741st Tank Battalion were launched six kilometres from the beach, but the stormy weather and high waves proved disastrous for the heavy amphibious tanks. One by one, the DD tanks and their crews went down in the high waves and sank in the sea off Omaha. Only 5 of the 32 tanks made it to the beach. The tanks, which would have given the American troops a major advantage in the attack, were now gone and the American troops had to attack the beach without optimal tank support and without the air and naval bombardments having caused major damage to the German positions. The problems continued when the smaller landing craft filled with soldiers were ordered to head for the beach. They were positioned about 16 kilometres from land, but many of these boats also went down in the high waves. Some of the smaller DUKW were heavily loaded with equipment and guns and sank like stones to the seabed.[24]

Arthur Larsen, 1st Infantry Division
'You don't have time to see what's in the water'

The attack continued despite the loss of men and tanks, and the remaining landing craft continued towards the beach. On board one of these was the Dane, Arthur Larsen. Larsen, from Frederikshavn, was one of the Danish sailors who was serving in the Danish Navy at the time of the Danish occupation and later had the opportunity to enlist in the American Army. As fate would have it, Larsen became part of the 1st Infantry Division, which participated in the landing on Omaha. Larsen joined the army after the attack on Pearl Harbor on 7 December 1941 and went to a training camp in South Carolina for six months before being shipped to Africa and later taking part in the invasion of Sicily during Operation Husky on 10 July 1943. After that, time was spent training and practising for what was to be the 1st Infantry Division's greatest test to date: the invasion of Normandy. As Arthur Larsen recalls:

> You know you're in it and you can't get out, so you just have to keep up… And then it went from there. You had to crawl down the side of the ship in a net and into the landing craft, and then we set off towards land.[25]

Arthur Larsen was in one of the first attacks on Omaha. There was confusion and chaos everywhere and it soon became clear that he had to react quickly and instinctively:

24 Jakob Sørensen, *D-Dag – Operation Overlord 6. Juni 1944* (Copenhagen: People's Press, 2014), pp.168–189.

25 This and the following are quoted from Arthur Larsen's account on the DR radio programme 'Den Store Landgang' by Poul S. Poulsen, 6 June 1969.

> You don't have time to look left and right – you just have to move forward and get up as quickly as possible, and then of course get up to our company. But then you get split up many times, someone gets lost, and then you get put back together again. You don't think about it too much, you just see it, and you probably think about yourself too. You just have to get there; you don't have time to see what's in the water. The main thing is to get ashore and move on. We had to have our weapons ready, but there was pretty tough resistance. Very tough resistance to begin with… And there were many more casualties on the beach. Because their [the Germans'] weapons were set up for crossfire. It wasn't easy to get through. But after about 12 hours, you could start moving slowly. And get up into the dunes. And then it was a real battle when we got up… And we got our tanks and our anti-tanks ashore, and then we started driving.

Larsen participated in direct attacks on the German positions on D-Day. Attacks that resulted in many American soldiers being killed. He clearly remembers how heavily fortified these bunkers were and how they had to be taken:

> You can't attack a bunker; you actually have to bombard it. Sometimes you can, if there are air gaps between the defences – you attack with flamethrowers to burn them up in there. We also used flamethrowers south of the line to get them out. It was mostly young men and old men sitting in there.

In the initial assault wave on Omaha, 9 companies attacked, and of these, almost three entire companies were wiped out before they even reached the beach. Arthur Larsen's company was also hit hard on D-Day and during the Normandy invasion in general.

The company was split up, people were injured and evacuated, and many were killed:

> We were scattered to the winds. We were actually only 7 (after the invasion was over), but then we got reinforced with others. Some get lost, some get shot, and some get picked up of other companies. You replenish all the time. We were actually 275 men and there were only 7 left.

It soon became clear to the American commanders that things were very bad on the beach in the western assault sector of Omaha. The advance across the 300 metre stretch from the water's edge to the first dunes took up to 45 minutes. Two-thirds of 2nd Ranger battalion was killed or wounded on the beach. Another company of the Ranger battalion lost one in four men during the attack.

The attack on the eastern flank of Omaha, where Arthur Larsen landed, was no different to the western flank. The Germans' machine guns opened fire the moment the front ramp of the landing craft went down, and most of the American soldiers who arrived in the first wave were killed or seriously wounded immediately. Miraculously, a few platoons managed to escape the heavy fire and take cover on the dunes without major casualties, but generally, even on the eastern flank of Omaha, numerous bodies began to accumulate at the water's edge and numerous wounded lay on the beach. There was neither time nor opportunity to pick up the wounded, as new troops were constantly being brought onto the beach. The wounded and dead piled up at the water's edge, and the landing craft had no other option than to sail directly between and through them to get more troops to the beach as quickly as possible. In the areas where the Germans had a direct line of sight and the opportunity to fire on the landing craft, the American troops suffered the most casualties. Soaked soldiers moving slowly with heavy packs were easy targets for the German machine gunners in the dunes and bunkers. The situation was chaotic and critical, most especially at Vierville and Saint-Laurent-sur-Mer due to the Germans' ideal positions to fire on the landing craft. The American soldiers who made it across the beach and took cover at the sea wall were typically hit by German mortars that had already fired into this position. This had fatal consequences if they did not advance as quickly as possible from there as well. The American engineer troops had also landed in the wrong places on the beach, which meant that the German obstacles could not be blown up and the escape routes to the hinterland could not be opened immediately.[26]

Svend A. Petersen, USS *Augusta*
Front Row with The Flagship

Aboard the flagship USS *Augusta,* the Dane, Svend A. Petersen, found himself off the Omaha sector. Petersen was born in Denmark in 1916, where he spent his childhood before the family moved to the US.[27] While the USS *Augusta* provided fire support off Omaha, Petersen could watch the terrifying scenario on the beach. The troops were pinned down on the shore, unable to move forward, and bodies were piling up. However, the navy managed to provide so much fire support that the German defenders were forced to remain in their positions. This meant that where the German positions needed assistance, they could not receive it, as the Germans could not move between their own positions because of the heavy bombardment. The American troops on the beach could then slowly advance and attack the individual German positions on the dunes.

On board *Augusta*, Lieutenant General Omar Bradley could also watch the battle unfold. Bradley had overall responsibility for the two American attacks. As the attack progressed on the beach, it became increasingly clear to him that the success of the attack was in jeopardy. More and more reports of resistance too strong to move off the beach reached *Augusta.* At 8.45 a.m., Bradley received word that none of the troops had yet managed to break through the German defences, and elsewhere the troops had been forced to withdraw. By midday, the reports to *Augusta* were equally grim and it became clear to Bradley that the attack was in danger of ending in disaster. He considered at this point whether to recall all troops and send them to support the attacks in either the Utah or Gold sectors. However, he knew that evacuating the troops would result in even more casualties, as a withdrawal would draw the already vulnerable soldiers away from their cover at the German obstacles on the beach. The situation was critical in every way, but before Bradley was forced to make a final decision on the attack, a crucial message arrived at *Augusta.* At 11.37 a.m. it was

26 Jakob Sørensen, *D-Dag – Operation Overlord 6. Juni 1944* (Copenhagen: People's Press, 2014), pp.180–189.
27 Archives of the Museum of Danish America.

reported that there was a major breakthrough at the breakout road at Les Moulins. The Germans had left the positions and Easy Green sector was open.

The troops were thus now able to slowly move away from the sector and move further behind the dunes. Considerations of retreat were forgotten, and Bradley continued to press the attack.[28]

The first minor breakthrough on Omaha occurred at 7.30 a.m. when a group of commanders from the 116th Regiment assembled a small force to make an attack on a German position. The group managed to penetrate about 200 metres inland at Les Moulins, where they held their ground for a while, but were pushed back relatively quickly. At around 9 o'clock, the 3rd Battalion of the 116th Regiment managed to fight its way through a German position, and elsewhere smaller groups of soldiers also managed to break through the German defences and began to defeat several German positions. With each position taken, the German defences slowly began to break down. Finally, the decisive breakthrough came at Easy Green sector. The American troops were exhausted, physically and mentally. They had seen their comrades wounded, killed and dying on the beach, where the golden sand was now more blood red than ever. The troops advanced across the dunes and tried to push the Germans further back, but the offensive only reached a few kilometres inland. Exhaustion was total after the fierce fighting, and instead, the American soldiers dug in and held their ground at Vierville and St Laurent.[29]

One of the engineers who helped clear the beach of its many obstacles was Poul Egon Pedersen. Together with the other engineers from the 360th Army Corps, Pedersen arrived on Omaha in the second wave during the intense shelling that characterised the landing here. After the initial delays caused by the heavy fighting, the engineers slowly but efficiently began clearing the sector of the many German obstacles that were in the way of the Allied advance. By late afternoon on D-Day, the area was passable for the many vehicles that now began to stream to the beach from the transport ships.

Pedersen was born on 3 January 1922 in Isenvad south of Ikast in Jutland. In 1929, the family emigrated to the USA and arrived in New York aboard the SS *United States*, after which they moved to Chicago and opened a Danish boarding house. Pedersen graduated from 8th grade in 1936 and started technical school in Chicago. He had always been fascinated by aeroplanes, so when he was drafted into the army in 1943, he tried to join the air force but was rejected. Instead, he joined the Engineer Corps. He underwent basic training in Maryland and when the order came to move to Europe, the engineers were sent to Scotland and then Manchester, where he contracted a severe case of pneumonia, from which he almost died. When Pedersen recovered, he was ordered to Wales. Here he helped plan much of the engineering logistics for the landing at Omaha. After D-Day, he fought at St Lô, Brest, and helped blow up a submarine base near Marseille before finally taking part in the liberation of Paris.

After the Normandy campaign, Pedersen took part in the Battle of the Bulge in December 1944, where he was wounded in the neck by shrapnel from a German tank. After recovering,

28 Jakob Sørensen, *D-Dag – Operation Overlord 6. Juni 1944* (Copenhagen: People's Press, 2014), pp.185–189.

29 Jakob Sørensen, *D-Dag – Operation Overlord 6. Juni 1944* (Copenhagen: People's Press, 2014), pp.189–191.

he was once again assigned to the engineers and helped build pontoon bridges wherever the Germans had destroyed them during their retreat. During the war, he was asked several times if he wanted to be a sergeant, but he refused time and time again, as he did not want other people's lives in his hands. After the war, Pedersen trained as an engineer and held several prominent positions, including helping to develop jet engines for fighter planes and also the so-called 'stealth technology' for B-2 bombers. Pedersen died in February 2007 in Chicago.

Dane Tage Pedersen, 1340th Engineer Combat Battalion

Another engineer who landed on Omaha on D-Day was Dane Tage Pedersen, who was part of Company C, 1340th Engineer Combat Battalion, US Army. Pedersen was part of the Allied front line from D-Day all the way to Germany in 1945, where his rank at the time was sergeant.

Pedersen was born on 4 March 1919 in Randers, Denmark. At the age of 17, he had already experienced war when he volunteered to fight in the Spanish Civil War. He enlisted in the US Army on September 11, 1943. He underwent a few months of training in America and was then sent over to England for more intensive training in preparation for the Normandy invasion. After that, they just waited for the order to begin the invasion, as Pedersen recalls:

> We had so many dry runs that when we finally crossed the Channel for real, many of us thought it was just another one of our exercises, but we soon found out that this time it was for real. And it was for real. We landed on Omaha Beach and it was tough. At St. Lo it was pretty bad again, but from there we did pretty well until we got to the Siegfried Line and Hürtgen Forest. In Hürtgen we were only 19 men out of about 120 who came back after four days in the first line. We crossed the Rhine with the 9th Armored Division and with them mostly through Germany. It went so fast and many times everything was in a big mess, God knows how many times we were surrounded.[30]

Pedersen was originally a war sailor in the Danish merchant navy. He was one of those caught outside the German blockade on 9 April 1940. At the time, Pedersen's ship was on its way to Africa, but went to Ireland instead. Here he took a Norwegian boat to America, where he helped organise the Scandinavian Seamens Club. Shortly after, he went to sea again in American and Panama boats and was torpedoed for the first time in the fall of 1940, where he was in the lifeboat for a few hours before being picked up.

Shortly after, he set sail again for the Mediterranean, Crete, Tobruk, Alexandria, Haifa, et cetera. When Japan bombed Pearl Harbor on 7 December 1941, Pedersen was on his way to the Soviet Union with supplies. On the way home, they sailed to England, as the route to Iceland was too dangerous at the time due to German submarines. 'Along the way we saw hundreds of floating mines,' Pedersen recalls. They then went to Ireland for a vacation and then back to England, where they were loaded with explosives and ammunition for the Mediterranean.

30 Correspondence from Tage Pedersen's private letters (Torben Vildner Pedersen).

The return journey went all the way around South Africa. Here their ship was torpedoed between Madagascar and South Africa. The weather was terrible and they lost two crew members. During the torpedoing, the wooden deck exploded and Pedersen got a splinter in his eye. They were subsequently in the lifeboats for 11 days, so the eye became infected. He had to be hospitalised in Port Elizabeth, where he stayed for three months. From there he returned to New York, where he enlisted in the US Army.

During the campaign in Belgium, Pedersen was wounded and spent three weeks in a field hospital before returning to duty.

When liberation came in 1945, he was in Czechoslovakia, but there was still fighting against the Germans, who would not surrender. He returned briefly to Denmark in 1945 and received an Honorable discharge from the US Army on 26 March 1946.

After the war, he reflected on cruel experiences he had witnessed:

> I've experienced more than I like to think about. I have always been on the front line with the armour, and I have a lot of scary memories that I will try to forget as soon as possible.

Tage Pedersen died at sea after the war while fishing off New Foundland.

Danish Sailors at Omaha

The majority of the Danish transport ships had Omaha as their destination. Soldiers, vehicles, weapons, ammunition and supplies were needed for a successful landing. The first Danish ship to officially arrive in Omaha on the evening of D-Day was S/S *Aarø*. Like many of the other Danish merchant ships, the ship was ideal for an operation of this magnitude. Because of their flat-bottomed design, they were ideal for taking troops and equipment directly onto the beach and then waiting for the tide to bring them off again. With the fierce fighting going on along the coast, it was typically not possible for the ships to unload in this way, but *Aarø* succeeded. On other Danish ships, the amphibious vehicles were used and the troops climbed aboard via nets along the sides of the ships. *Aarø* arrived of Omaha in the middle of an air raid, so the crew quickly manned the ship's anti-aircraft guns to fire on the German aircraft. Amidst the chaos that still reigned into the evening of D-Day at Omaha, it was not easy to navigate to the exact destination at which to unload, and as First Officer Richard Kragelund on board *Aarø* recalls:

> On Omaha Beach, where *Aarø* was going in, things got very rough. We could hear it out at sea. I had the greatest difficulty finding out exactly where on the beach we should enter. The simple fact was that the Royal Air Force had bombed the entire hinterland during the night and then switched to bombing the entire invasion area on the beach until the first landing troops arrived. So there wasn't much for me to navigate by... We sailed up onto the beach and waited for the water to drop... When it did, we unloaded both personnel and vehicles. It went quite easily, it was well-rehearsed.[31]

31 Christian Tortzen, *Kampen på Havet* (Copenhagen: Information, 2011), p.197.

The ship's anti-aircraft guns were called into action several times during the first few nights. *Aarø* made four trips across the English Channel – both to Omaha and Utah – with much-needed supplies for the troops on the front lines.

Erik Egebak from Vrå in Vendsyssel was aboard the American Liberty ship *Joseph Pulitzer*, arriving in Omaha in the late afternoon of D-Day. The plan for unloading the ship's cargo was ready, but nothing could prepare Egebak for the sight of Omaha:

> Everyone knows today that there was no harbour to run into, so troops and equipment had to be landed directly onto the beach. In other words, we had to run as far in towards land as we could possibly get to, and then unload our soldiers and equipment, which were then ready for combat, ready to go into battle as soon as they came up on the beach... And we did that... And at least the first time, it was tough going, I thought. Firstly, there was an infernal racket with noise and explosions and God knows what else. At the same time, there was a line of large warships lined up on the coast. Big battleships, all the big ships they could muster, firing low over the beach. There was such a continuous curtain of fire over our heads – hitting the dunes and the beach. It was really hard going.[32]

But it was not only inland that there was heavy shelling. Allied destroyers and cruisers were constantly shelling the German positions in the hinterland, and the German guns further inland behind the dunes were also trying to neutralise the ships off the coast. *Erik Egebak* witnessed this from the front row:

> Initially it was the landing craft that ran in that suffered a lot of damage. But I think by the time we got over there, they had turned their fire more towards the troops going ashore. There were a couple of individual ships that were sunk, but one of them was sunk by a bomber. The other big ship that was sunk right next to us, I never found out what it was sunk by. It was certainly a troop transport ship that was carrying several thousand soldiers who were going to be put ashore... And then suddenly this big ship tipped over on its side, and people swarmed over to this side, where they stood there hoping to be taken off. Some thought it was a submarine that had sneaked in, others that it was a mine, but the ship sank anyway. Fortunately, they had managed to land most of their troops.[33]

Captain Axel Mathiasen aboard the Danish coastal steamer S/S *Avance* arrived off Omaha early in the morning of 7 June and then made several trips with supplies to Normandy. 'It looked like the sky was going to crack,' Mathiasen later described on his arrival.[34] *Avance* landed a small artillery battalion in less than an hour. One of the crew members aboard the ship also described what it was like to be part of a war situation of this intensity: 'We

32 Quoted from Cicerone ApS and Nexus Communication's interview with Erik Egebak and archive material in connection with the production of the documentary 'The War Sailors'.

33 Quoted from Cicerone ApS and Nexus Communication's interview with Erik Egebak and archive material in connection with the production of the documentary 'The War Sailors'.

34 Christian Tortzen, *Kampen på Havet* (Copenhagen: Information, 2011), p.198.

soon got used to all the firing of guns of all calibres, the buzzing of airmen, volley fire from machine guns, noise and roaring all around, so terrible that it sounded worse than 10 working shipyards.'[35]

J. P. Sørensen was on board *Gudrun Mærsk* and arrived off Omaha on 7 June in the early morning. It was still a dangerous place to be, as he recalls:

> I clearly remember an aeroplane – a big bomber that was hit by the Germans, and you could see it starting to bring its nose down. You could count the crew jumping out – six men jumped out. The worst part of it all was that the aeroplane crashed, so it looked like it came down right on top of our heads. It went down maybe 30 metres from the side of the ship into the sea with a big bang – it caused such strong waves that we were rocking back and forth in the water. Then we could see everything that happened on land – it was an inferno… It was a really bad place. A lot of people lost their lives there.[36]

Gudrun Maersk was carrying 3,500 tons of petrol in 20 litre cans. The danger of sailing with such an explosive cargo and sailing directly to one of the most dangerous sectors during the Normandy invasion certainly left its mark on the ship's crew. Henrik Bødker Knudsen from Frederikshavn was, like J. P. Sørensen, on board *Gudrun Mærsk* and clearly remembers the explosive cargo and the subsequent trip to Omaha:

> 24 hours after D-Day began, we were anchored in the newly established harbour and unloaded petrol into amphibious boats, which sailed onto the beach and piled it up, where other vehicles gradually removed it… While we were unloading, we could follow the whole spectacle. There was a steady stream of landing craft coming in over the beach with tanks and military vehicles of all kinds… In the first days we could see and hear the front on land. At night it looked as if a curtain of tracer bullets had been hung up and remained there for several days. There must have been huge amounts of ammunition being used, and that was only within our small section.[37]

Captain Folmer Clausen was born in Silkeborg, but lived most of his life on Fanø. He sailed out in 1938 and first returned in 1946. Captain Clausen was on board the Danish ship *Lillian*, which arrived off Omaha on the evening of D-Day with equipment and important maps of Normandy for the officers:

> We entered the so-called Omaha sector, which was under American control. We brought various equipment for the troops who were now charging towards Hitler's giant fortress. Among other things, we had several tons of general staff cards. We dropped anchor some distance from the coast. It was a magnificent sight to see

35 Christian Tortzen, *Kampen på Havet* (Copenhagen: Information, 2011), p.198.

36 J. P. Sørensen interviewed by Ulrik Brandt. Recorded at Bombebøssen in Christianshavn on 9 August 2005.

37 Henrik Bødker Knudsen, *Krigssejler* (Copenhagen: Frihedsmuseets Venners Forlag, 1992), pp.99–100.

> the hundreds of vessels spread out over the sea as far as the eye could see. On the shore, things were rough, meaning that the Germans had already been pushed some distance inland, where they had become stuck. The Allied warships' heavy guns repeatedly intervened in the battle by sending a shower of giant shells – each weighing 8 to 100kg – down over the German lines. The spectacle was deafening, and to make matters worse, occasionally a few German airmen would turn up, and then we got a practical demonstration of what the word 'blanket of fire' meant. There must have been thousands of guns firing.[38]

The Danish sailor V. Bostrup, who was aboard the ship *Fanø*, entered Omaha sector on the night of 7 June and clearly remembers the great activity in the sector:

> We saw a German plane crash into the water some distance from us, heard two others being hit and felt shrapnel flying down from them – it was *Fanø*'s two 40mm anti-aircraft guns that gave the airmen that reception! The crew consisted of American gunners, but the *Fanø*'s crew also served at the guns.[39]

In the nights that followed, Bostrup experienced similar scenarios, wearing a steel helmet and lifejacket and feeling the attack first-hand:

> Suddenly I heard a screeching noise and felt a jolt down my back – I gasped – then my lifejacket rattled off and fell to the deck! I quickly turned round, bent down to grab the vest and saw that a piece of shrapnel from a grenade had hit it. A chill ran down my spine when I saw that the shrapnel, which was about 130mm long and torn at one end as if it were two knife blades stuck together, had actually cut my thick waistcoat off and penetrated 30mm into the tyre. It weighed 250 grams. I must have almost been sent for!

Holger Jensen arrived on Omaha the night after D-Day between 6 and 7 June as a marine inspector. Although the horrific sight of destruction and death was a harrowing experience, the need for cooperation meant he had to concentrate on the task he had been assigned to complete:

> You had to kind of step to the side to avoid stepping on bodies or parts of bodies and limbs… I guess the first thing you notice is all the fire, the rounds, machine guns and tracer bullets. When you're in the middle of so much horror, I don't know if everything stops, you don't think about it, you just think, this is your job, you do it as long as you can. If one person fails in that game, he can be responsible for the death of a lot of his comrades. A group like that, it's a team. Each man has his function that he must not fail. There's only one way to fail, and that's if you get shot or otherwise put out of the game.[40]

38 Report from the Mitfanoe.dk archive.

39 This and the following are quoted from Sven Arvid Birkeland, *Sænket af tyskerne – Danske krigssejlere i 2. Verdenskrig* (Copenhagen: Gyldendal, 2012), pp.361–362.

40 With the following this is quoted from Holger Jensen's account for the DR radio programme 'Den store Landgang' by Poul S. Poulsen, 6 June 1969.

Shortly after Holger Jensen arrived on Omaha, he had the opportunity to inspect the area near Vierville-sur-Mer and walk around the German positions where brutal fighting had taken place less than 24 hours ago:

> There was one gun emplacement in particular that I went to look at. It had caused the death of a lot of men because they hadn't been able to hit it. The aircraft and battleships couldn't do anything about it, so the Germans had sat in there and fired until an American soldier came along and got a hand grenade through the firing slit where the barrel of the 88mm cannon stuck out. Then he got some [more] hand grenades in there…

Holger Jensen was given a particularly important task in the period after D-Day in relation to the logistics of the extensive shipping traffic that was now on its way to Omaha and to the two later artificial floating harbours, one of which was established at Omaha. He was subsequently given full command of the Normandy harbours and later over a third – the port of Rouen. At one point, he was responsible for the logistics of 10,000 American soldiers in Normandy. Holger Jensen achieved the rank of lieutenant colonel and was decorated with orders from both the United States and the United Kingdom.

By the evening of D-Day, Omaha was secured, but the beach was a wasteland of dead soldiers and smashed vehicles in flames. The beachhead gradually filled up with wounded soldiers and more soldiers and vehicles arriving on the beach in preparation for D-Day+1. The management of logistics on the beach was now paramount. 34,000 men were landed and the engineer troops made an extraordinary effort to remove the many obstacles. German snipers were still present in the area, and this particularly affected the American soldiers who were working to open the exit routes away from the beach. By evening, 13 passable routes had been opened and tons of supplies had been landed from the freighters. One of the reasons Omaha has subsequently been referred to as 'Bloody Omaha' is largely due to the number of American soldiers killed. By the end of D-Day, the Americans had suffered more than 2,000 dead, wounded or missing. At the same time, around 1,200 German soldiers had died.[41]

Danish-Americans in the 743rd Tank Battalion

Einar Sørensen arrived on Omaha on 7 June together with 743rd Tank Battalion. The battalion's role during the Normandy invasion was to support the infantry and push the offensive further inland. Sørensen was a Danish emigrant. As part of an exchange programme, he came to the USA in 1927 at the age of 18, specifically Nebraska, where he later found work as a farmer. When news of the attack on Pearl Harbor broke on 7 December 1941, Sørensen enlisted in the army to take his turn. Sørensen's role in the battalion was to service tanks and transport supplies, such as fuel and ammunition, back and forth between the front lines so that the advancing tanks did not run out of either. He also provided support during the offensive after D-Day by operating a heavy machine gun placed on top of the lorry.

41 Antony Beevor, *D-Day: The Battle for Normandy*, (London: Viking, 2009), p.135.

During one of the trips between the front lines, Sørensen's lorry and the other supply vehicles and tanks came under heavy fire from German artillery. A fuel canister in the back of Sørensen's truck was hit and exploded, causing the petrol to engulf the entire truck in flames. As there was a risk that the other fuel cans on the truck would explode, endangering other vehicles and tanks nearby, Sørensen remained in the driver's seat to drive the burning truck to a safe distance from the others. Sørensen reached safety and, mindful of the much-needed tank ammunition in the bed of the lorry, he began extinguishing the fire with a fire extinguisher. He managed to control some of the fire and saved the remaining ammunition before the lorry exploded. For his action, he received the prestigious Silver Star Medal.

743rd Tank Battalion was chosen to be one of the three assault battalions that would land among the first attack waves on D-Day. These would primarily act as support for the 116th Regiment of the 29th Infantry Division's attack on the Omaha, *Dog Green* and *Dog White sectors.* Carl E. Nielsen was also part of the 743rd Tank Battalion, Company C, and landed on Omaha on D-Day as a radio operator in a tank. Born in Denmark in 1914, he emigrated with his family to the United States and enlisted on 23 July 1943 in California. The B and C companies were to handle the new armoured invention, the DD tanks. These tanks were an invention that would make it easier to attack with amphibious tanks from the sea. An inflatable belt would be stretched over the tank, which could then drive directly down a ramp on a ship off the coast and sail onto the beach to attack the enemy directly from the sea. The plan for the amphibious tanks was to give the attacking forces an advantage, but on the other part of Omaha, the *Easy Red* sector, the DD tank landing from 741. Tank Battalion went anything but well. As previously mentioned, the tanks were landed from the ships almost six kilometres from the beach, which resulted in the tanks being unable to handle the high waves and sinking to the bottom. 27 out of 32 DD tanks sank as a result, and most crew members drowned. B and C Companies of the 743rd Tank Battalion, where Carl E. Nielsen was part of C Company, had a strong-willed captain named Ned Eldar, who realised that the high waves could be fatal for the companies' 16 DD tanks. Therefore, he ordered the tanks to be landed directly on the beach via LCT (Landing Craft Tank) landing craft instead. The LCTs arrived on the beach at approximately 6.40 in the morning, about 15 minutes later than planned. Although the 743rd Tank Battalion had more success in landing the tanks than their colleagues from the 741st Tank Battalion. The 743rd Tank Battalion still had great difficulty getting off the beach as they had no infantry support to locate the German targets further inland. In addition, the tide was rising so fast that they had little room to manoeuvre.

On 14 June, the 743rd Tank Battalion, including Einar Sørensen and Carl E. Nielsen, were assigned to the 30th Infantry Division after having been assigned to and assisted both 29th Infantry Division, 1st Infantry Division, 5th Ranger Battalion and 3rd Armoured Division. 743rd Tank Battalion was attached to the 30th Infantry Division for the rest of the war. They engaged in heavy fighting at the Vire River, Mortain and were mistakenly hit by Allied bombers at St Lô. Later they took part in the offensive in France, Belgium, Holland and Germany. Carl E. Nielsen later lost his life and was included in the casualty statistics in connection with an offensive at Fronhoven in Germany on 22 November 1944. He was posthumously awarded the Purple Heart medal.[42]

42 Wayne C. Robinson & Norman E. Hamilton, *Move Out, Verify: The Combat Story of the 743rd Tank Battalion* (United States Army, 1945), pp.32–34.

The Five Landing Sectors: Gold

The centre of the five landing beaches was Gold. The area stretches almost 16 kilometres from the idyllic fishing village of Port-en-Bessin and to the town of Ver-sur-Mer. The coastal area consists largely of steep slopes and cliffs, which made landing in the western part of the Gold sector impossible. However, this was possible in the eastern sector of between the towns of Asnelles and Ver-sur-Mer. The capture of the western sector of Gold was also of utmost importance, as there was a German gun battery at Longues-sur-Mer that had to be neutralised before the British and American sectors could be linked. As with the other landing sectors, Gold was also divided into four smaller attack sectors: How, Item, Jig and King.

Characteristic of the Gold sector is that despite the fact that the sector is historically generally more overlooked than the other sectors, there were more established German positions than at Omaha. 17 defence positions were located on Gold compared to the 15 at Omaha. Around 2,000 German soldiers from the *Infanteriedivision 352* and *Infanteriedivision 716* defended Gold. In addition, *Infanterieregiment 726*, commanded by *Colonel* Korfe, was located in the town of Bayeux. These units were responsible for the area between Le Hamel and the border up to the Omaha sector. Furthermore, the *Osttruppenbatallion 441* from *Infanteriedivision 716* was deployed in the area of Ver-sur-Mer and a reserve unit further inland consisting of troops from the 3. Battalion, *Infanterieregiment 916*, *Infanteriedivision 352*. Finally, there was a mobile reserve in the area behind the coast in the form of *Kampfgruppe Meyer*, which included 2,700 men from *Infanterieregiment 915*, and from two battalions from *Infanteriedivision 352*. As was the case with the other beach sectors, the Atlantic rampart was not completed at Gold, and despite the large German presence in the area, there were still not enough soldiers to establish a complete and effective defence. Over the years, the fighting on the Eastern Front had had a major impact on the defence of Western Europe, as more and more German troops were ordered east. *Infanterieregiment 915* had moved towards Carentan in the Utah sector on the night of 6 June when they were ordered to attack a company of paratroopers. Several hours later, the German regiment arrived, only to find that there were no paratroopers. They had been misled by the Operation Bodyguard. *Infanterieregiment 915* was now far from Gold and Bayeux, and this greatly weakened the mobile defence on the beaches at Gold.[43]

The British attackers on Gold were some of the most experienced troops in all of the landing sectors on D-Day. The British 50th Division entered the fighting in Belgium and France as early as 1940. They were evacuated at Dunkirk and subsequently took part in the campaigns in North Africa and Sicily. The commander of 50th Division, General Graham, who had previously commanded the 56th Division at Salerno, however was the only Allied soldier who had previously commanded an amphibious assault. The plan of attack was similar to the plan on Omaha. After the initial bombardment, launched at 05:10 by the air force and navy, the DD tanks were to be deployed first, then specialised tanks and engineer troops were to be landed to clear any German beach obstacles in the sector, with troops and

43 Stuart C. Robertson & Dale Booth, *Following in the Footsteps of Heroes: D-Day June 6th 1944*, (Devizes: Sabrestorm, 2014), pp.206–214.

artillery to be landed next. At 07:25 on 6 June, the first landing craft were from Task Force G with British troops from 50th Division at the Jig and King sectors on Gold. At each sector, two battalions attacked together and a third was in reserve.

Troops from No. 47 Commando also attacked the strategically important harbour town of Port-en-Bessin. The overall plan was that as soon as Gold was captured, the troops would be organised as quickly as possible and then begin the offensive against the larger objective, the city of Caen.[44]

50th Division was not only up against the Germans manning the *Atlantic Wall*, but the elements of nature were also a major obstacle. High and low tides were crucial to the success of the D-Day attacks. The higher the tide, the less space the Allied troops had to deploy equipment and troops. Time was therefore a decisive factor in terms of getting more troops into position before the tide rose again. The 231st Malta Brigade attacked Jig sector while 69th Brigade attacked King sector. The British forces broke through the German lines relatively quickly despite strong German resistance and continued the attack towards Bayeux. At the village of La Rivière in King sector, 69th Brigade met resistance from two of the infamous German 88mm guns, with the British tanks in particular suffering heavy losses. At Jig sector, the troops were soon met with heavy resistance from *Infanteriedivision 716*, which had more or less fortified the small village of Le Hamel.

The attacks on the western side of Gold were made by the 1st Battalion, the Hampshire Regiment, the objectives of the various companies being to take parts of Le Hamel, Arromanches and Cabane. At the latter was a strong artillery position. The attack would then continue towards the villages of Asnelles and Ryes to take the roads into the harbour town of Arromanches.

The capture of Le Hamel was crucial for further inland movement. However, the German positions in the area did not take as much damage during the initial bombing raids as on other beach sectors. Therefore, the task of the engineers and the specialist tanks was more important than ever, as they were now responsible for clearing the beach obstacles and, most importantly, securing the area from mines. This was particularly successful for the 1st Dorsets and the 1st Hampshires, who took the village of Les Roquettes, despite the fact that this was not actually 1st Hampshires' objective. It turned out to be an advantage that the 1st Hampshires had landed in the wrong place and thus avoided attacking a heavily defended gun position at Le Hamel, as originally planned. 1st Hampshires' landing at Les Roquettes therefore most likely meant that their losses were significantly lower than if they had landed where planned.

However, it also meant that Le Hamel was far from secure and that the position could cause major damage to the next waves of British troops that landed in the area. With the help of specialist armour, such as the Churchill AVRE tanks, they managed to break through the German positions at the village and the infantry could then attack the German positions with less risk of being hit by German mortars and guns.[45]

By the afternoon of D-Day, the biggest threats to the defence of Gold had been defeated. Thousands of soldiers and vehicles were already being landed, but the task was far from over.

44 Ken Ford, *D-Day 1944 (4): Gold and Juno Beaches* (Oxford: Osprey, 2002), pp.40–45.

45 Jakob Sørensen, *D-Dag – Operation Overlord 6. Juni 1944* (Copenhagen: People's Press, 2014), pp.214–221.

The attack had gone relatively smoothly, despite heavy resistance at Le Hamel, but it was a different story for the British No.47 Commando who were to take the smaller harbour town of Port-en-Bessin. Even before the troops had landed, three of the landing craft carrying the soldiers were sunk. However, several survivors made it ashore and fought their way to the rest of the troops. Where the remaining British commandos landed near Le Hamel, there was still more resistance from the Germans. The German troops put up fierce resistance to the British soldiers near the exit road to Port-en-Bessin, resulting in 40 men being killed or wounded before they could advance towards the objective. The commandos then had to march 15 kilometres from the landing at Gold before arriving in the town. They passed the German battery at Longues-sur-Mer, which continued to fire on the Allied warships at sea, causing them major problems due to the range of the guns. However, the commandos had orders to continue towards Port-en-Bessin – orders which they followed. The commandos arrived in the small town late at night on the 7th, and then gathered forces to attack the German positions early in the morning. Here they encountered a well-prepared German defence that would not abandon the town, but after sustained attacks, the commandos managed to capture the small port town. Half of the force was killed or badly wounded, but the town was taken.[46]

The central part of Gold was secured on D-Day and troops and supplies began pouring onto the beach. The next objective was to secure the beachhead towards Omaha and then reach the larger and strategically important town of Bayeux. The landing at Gold was largely successful despite the strong resistance, especially at Le Hamel. The German armoured reserves of *Kampfgruppe Meyer* were far away from Gold due to the intelligence of the presence of American paratroopers behind Utah, and the plan to use the armoured reserves for counterattacks was thus not realised in Gold sector. On the other hand, *Kampfgruppe Meyer* made it back to Bayeux before the British troops reached the area, and they managed to form a defence around the town that slowed the British advance until 7 June. However, the British attack was highly effective and the stubborn defence of the German panzer reserves resulted in only 90 out of 2,700 men of *Kampfgruppe Meyer* being able to fight on as 7 June drew to a close.

Despite the success of the landing at Gold on 6 June, around 1,000 British soldiers from 50th Division were killed and wounded. A figure that could have been significantly higher if the British specialist tanks had not been so effective and even more so if the German armoured reserves had not been as far from the beach as they were on D-Day.

Most importantly, 25,000 British soldiers had been landed on the beach and were ready to continue the offensive.[47]

46 Jakob Sørensen, *D-Dag – Operation Overlord 6. Juni 1944* (Copenhagen: People's Press, 2014), pp.221–222.

47 Jakob Sørensen, *D-Dag – Operation Overlord 6. Juni 1944* (Copenhagen: People's Press, 2014), pp.224–225.

Niels Wiesneck, Essex Scottish Regiment
'The invasion had started by this time...'

One of the former Danish sailors who arrived as part of the replacement troop convoys at Gold on 7 June, was Niels Wiesneck. He was now a soldier and part of the Canadian Essex Scottish Regiment, but which would not, itself, take part in the fighting in Normandy until about a month after D-Day.

In 1942, the Allies had, as previously described, attempted to conducted a raid at Dieppe – Operation Jubilee. An action that failed completely, with the result that the Allies were thrown back into the sea by the Germans. One of the leading regiments during the Dieppe raid was the Essex Scottish Regiment, which Wiesneck had not joined at the time. The regiment had suffered catastrophic losses during the raid, so it was a vengeful regiment that was finally allowed to fight the Germans again in Normandy. In the week leading up to 6 June, Wiesneck was placed in a closed camp somewhere in England with his regiment. Everyone knew an invasion was imminent and was eager to get going. What happened was that Wiesneck became unwell, developed a fever and eventually fainted. He was picked up by ambulance and transported out of the restricted area to the nearest hospital. Something as trivial as inflammation in a tooth had turned into inflammation in his jaw and head, and he had the tooth operated on at the hospital. After some time in hospital he was taken back to the same closed camp, but by this time the invasion had already begun, his regiment had been transferred to another camp and Wiesneck was separated from the Essex Scottish Regiment. He was then attached to a replacement company and sent to Normandy on 7 June, despite the fact that the Canadian Essex Scottish Regiment had not yet received orders to leave at this point. He arrived at Gold, which was actually a British sector:

> By this time the invasion had started and I was sent over there, so I was there on the second day with this replacement company. I arrived at the beach off something called Bayeux. We got ashore fairly dry and had to spend the night in various bomb craters.[48]

Wiesneck participated in various patrols in the area as well as daily chores with the replacement company:

> The next day we were sent out on reconnaissance – still with the status of a reserve company. That's how the first few weeks went. Finally, I was authorised to transfer [back] to my old regiment at Essex Scottish.

The Essex Scottish Regiment only arrived in Normandy on 5 July, and only then was Wiesneck allowed to transfer back to his regiment. The regiment missed D-Day and the initial fighting in Normandy, but Wiesneck with the rest of the regiment would find that the Germans still had the will to fight in Operation Overlord's later stages.

48 The following quotes come from Kystmuseet Bangsbo Arkiv's material about Niels Wiesneck, where a taped interview is available.

The Five Landing Sectors: Juno

Juno is almost 10 kilometres of coastline, but the initial attacks at the sector on D-Day took place within a stretch of only about 5 kilometres. Troops from the Canadian 3rd Infantry Division carried out the attacks on the beach areas, with heavy fighting taking place at the villages of St-Aubin-sur-Mer, Bernières-sur-Mer and Courselles-sur-Mer. Juno, like the other beaches, was also divided into smaller sectors: Mike and Nan – comprising Mike Green, Mike Red, Nan Green, Nan White and Nan Red. The Canadian assault force faced a German defence, with bunkers located among the idyllic cafés, hotels and beach houses on the seafront. Allied aerial reconnaissance had therefore not had optimal conditions, as the German defences were not clearly visible from the air, in comparison to the sectors where the bunkers were not in a populated area.

The German defences consisted of 15 large and 9 medium batteries and several lines of defence, supplemented by guns ranging from 50mm to 88mm plus machine gun nests, armoured trenches, minefields and mortar positions focused on the beach area. The German troops at Juno were primarily soldiers from *Infanteriedivision 716*, about a third of whom were Eastern Front veterans, they were well prepared, but the troops were outnumbered, of mixed quality and so were their weapons. The area behind Juno consisted of wide open fields with small wooded areas, which allowed the Canadian attackers to advance quickly from the beach area, but also made the troops very vulnerable to German artillery. With this scenario in mind, the Germans had built defence positions in the smaller villages on the road to Caen. In addition, the largest German radar station in Normandy was located nearby at Dòuvres-la-Delivrande. *Infanteriedivision 716* also had problems with transport, which for the most part could only be done by horse or bicycle – or it was on foot. The attacking Canadians were extremely vengeful after the failed raid at Dieppe two years earlier. They had volunteered to go to war and now they finally had the chance to return to French soil. The Canadian troops were thus undoubtedly mentally prepared to avoid being thrown back into the sea, as had happened at Dieppe, at all costs.[49]

The Canadian attack on Juno was scheduled to begin at 07:45, making it the last attack to begin out of the five beach sectors on D-Day. The Royal Navy began the intensive bombardment of the sector at 06:00 and continued constantly for the next two hours. The bombardment was carried out by 12 cruisers, 11 destroyers and the two old British battleships *Warspite* and *Ramillies*. The 38cm guns of the two battleships meant that the ships could also be used to fire on targets at Sword, Juno and Gold. 15,000 Canadian and 8,000 British soldiers from three brigades were responsible for attacking the sector and breaking through the Atlantic Wall at Juno. 7th and 8th Brigades of the Canadian 3rd Infantry Division attacked in the morning, and the 9th Brigade from the Division was deployed in the late afternoon to continue the offensive inland. Surprisingly few German guns returned the navy's fire when it began early in the morning, and this was most likely due to the heavy smoke from the Allied bombardment, which made it impossible for the Germans to spot their targets at sea.

49 Stuart C. Robertson & Dale Booth, *Following in the Footsteps of Heroes: D-Day June 6th 1944*, (Devizes: Sabrestorm, 2014), pp.182–185.

As with the other landing beaches, wind and weather were also a major factor in the Juno landing. The high seas and stormy weather prompted the commanders at Juno to make a crucial decision: the 28 amphibious tanks planned for the landing were not to be landed off the coast, as had happened so disastrously at Omaha. It was feared that the DD tanks would capsize in the high seas. Therefore, they were landed closer to the beach. However, this meant that the landing had to be postponed by 10 minutes because the tanks could not act as support for the infantry storming the beach. Therefore, the landing craft with the infantry on board waited impatiently for the tanks to arrive. Several of the newly developed Allied tanks, such as the 'Crocodile', which had a flamethrower mounted instead of a machine gun in the hull, began landing on Juno. The landing also included the efficient Priest tanks with 105mm guns mounted on them. Shortly afterwards, the engineer troops followed to clear the water and beach edges of German obstacles so that the landing craft could sail directly onto the beach. Despite being 10 minutes behind schedule, the fleet stopped its bombardment at 07.30, which was according to the original schedule. Five minutes after the bombardment had ceased, the troops were supposed to attack. Instead, they arrived 15 minutes later than planned, and as the bombardment had stopped in the meantime, this allowed the German defenders to crawl out of their protective bunkers and man their guns and machine guns. The Canadian and British troops with tank support began the planned attack but on their way into the beach, they received less fire than expected from the German guns – mainly due to the intense initial bombardment from the Allied air force and navy – but by no means all German positions were neutralised. In fact, only 14 percent were destroyed during the bombardment. The bombs had typically hit further inland than directly on the intended German positions, and when the landing craft were a few hundred metres from the beach, sporadic German mortar fire began to hit the landing troops.

The time interval between the end of the naval bombardment and the arrival of the troops on the beach meant that the German troops were ready and able to follow the landing craft as they made their way inland. However, they did not open fire, but waited for the landing craft to reach the water's edge and for the ramps to fall, the moment when the troops were at their most vulnerable. When the first wave of landing craft reached the beach and the ramps dropped into the wet sand, the Canadian and British troops poured out. At the same moment, German machine gun nests and soldiers with small arms opened fire on their enemy. The first Allied soldiers encountered a wall of bullets and grenades as they stormed towards the German positions. The casualties were heavy – so heavy that the first wave casualties can be compared to the losses on Omaha.

The Americans lost 1 in 19 at Omaha on D-Day. On Juno, 1 in 18 was lost. The Canadian Royal Regina Rifles suffered the worst, with almost half of Delta Company's men killed before they even reached the beach.

It soon became clear to the Canadian troops that the beach area meant certain death, and the objective was now clear: get out of the fatal beach area and over the dykes to reach the flat countryside and continue the offensive. The Crocodile tanks were crucial to breaking through the German positions and the troops quickly followed to take the neighbouring villages. The German positions at the towns of Courseulles and Benières were largely undamaged, but despite 65 casualties, troops from the Queen's Own Regiment managed to take the towns. The village of St Aubin was also taken relatively quickly as the specialist tanks shelled the German bunkers. Shortly afterwards, around 50 German soldiers surrendered to the

Canadian troops. About the same number of wounded and dead Germans were left behind after the tank attack.[50]

Danish Sailors at Juno
'We were ready to jump over the side'

About an hour after the first landing craft hit Juno and the first attack wave went ashore, the smaller DUKWs began bringing supplies onto the beach. These picked up the supplies from the cargo ships off the coast, where several Danish ships and sailors were on board. One of these was Hans Juelsdorf, who joined the Danish Merchant Navy in 1934 when he was just 16 years old. When Denmark was occupied on 9 April 1940, he was on board the Danish ship S/S *Diana* in Newcastle, after which he quickly signed up for Allied service and sailed under the flag of the British Merchant Navy until liberation in 1945. Juelsdorf experienced being attacked by a German Focke-Wulf 'Condor' bomber in the North Atlantic in 1941. The third bomb hit the ship, which subsequently went down – one man died and several were badly injured and had to be rescued along with the rest of the crew. Holger Jensen was on board *Diana* during the attack and its subsequent sinking. On D-Day, Juelsdorf was second mate aboard the DFDS steamship *Brynhild*, which was to land 50 soldiers and tons of supplies including 1,000 cans of fuel on Juno. He recalled arriving on Juno on D-Day:

> We had been told that we weren't going on a picnic, and it was true. We went all the way to the beach to unload, and there was a big fight on land. [51]

Brynhild, as one of the few Danish ships, made supply trips to two different landing sectors. After discharging at Juno, it sailed back to England to pick up supplies and then returned to Normandy, but this time to Sword. *Brynhild* made a total of five trips to Normandy with supplies.

Another Danish ship that arrived at Juno was the large and modern *Fort St Croix*. In the days leading up to D-Day, the ship was docked at Tilbury in England with hundreds of Canadian soldiers travelling to Juno. The ship was ready to sail when the message that the invasion had been postponed due to stormy weather reached the telegraph operator. On the morning of 7 June, the crew was told to sail for Normandy and Juno Beach. One of the sailors on board was Dane Erik Christiansen:

> Even though I had been on 24-04 watch [the shift covering the night], I was still curious to see the Normandy coast. When we got there, we were 1 kilometre from the coast and there was a lot of smoke. Some big cruisers were inside of us and they were firing at targets inland. The Germans weren't firing at the ships out to sea because they only knew the distance to the beach. So we could see how they

50 Jakob Sørensen, *D-Dag – Operation Overlord 6. Juni 1944* (Copenhagen: People's Press, 2014), pp.231–239.

51 The following quotes come from an interview journalist, author and editor Jakob Andersen conducted with Hans Juelsdorf in Normandy in 1994.

> were shelling the shore. We were basically safe out to sea. We were able to unload our equipment. We had 60 ton booms where we had to unload into the battens. I think they were called Landing Craft Tank. We unloaded and were over there for a whole day and then went back home to Tilbury. We were 27 times back and forth. We slept with our life belts on and had personal papers inside our chests. We were ready to jump over the side. We had heard about the Germans with their torpedoes that went for the sound of screws. It left its mark on you.[52]

Fort St Croix was fired upon by German guns on the trips to Normandy, but was not hit. The unloading of the ship at Juno took 30 hours, during which the anxious Danish sailors were never far away from the ship's anti-aircraft guns, which had to be used several times during the unloading, as the sailor Kaj recalls:

> The memory of our dear old Tivoli's colourful fireworks faded. And here and there a German aeroplane would go down in the water or on land. We were credited for shooting one of them down, but whether it was true or not, we were not able to confirm.[53]

Georg Unger, who was also on board *Fort St Croix,* described the sight of the invasion fleet and his experiences on D-Day in his diary:

> As far as the eye can see it is full of ships, there must be about 5,000 in total. A number of them are warships, firing incessantly overland. The Germans were here about 5 miles away. Otherwise the country looked cosy with woods and fields. From where we were, we could see two small towns with church towers rising up. It looked quite homely, you wanted to go for a walk ashore .... In the afternoon and at night we have alarms all the time. We don't get much sleep; we have to get up every moment. We can still hear German machines in the air, and there is much shooting, but we see nothing of the enemy, we are covered with smoke all the time. The next morning we are discharged again and go straight back to England.[54]

Viggo Hans Nielsen arrived at Juno on board *Thyra III* on D-Day itself:

> We sailed as far in as possible in the morning to Juno and unloaded the soldiers. They had to wade ashore, there were no other options at the time. We were very far out and where the Germans could hit us. Several German airmen tried to attack us, but they were quickly shot down.[55]

52 Quoted from the DR documentary film 'Støt Står den Danske Sømænd', directed by Lars Grarup and produced by Jørgen Melgaard in 1985.
53 Christian Tortzen, *Søfolk og Skibe 1939–1945, bind 4* (Copenhagen: Lindhardt & Ringhof, 1985), p.422.
54 Christian Tortzen, *Søfolk og Skibe 1939–1945, bind 4* (Copenhagen: Lindhardt & Ringhof, 1985), p.420.
55 The following quotes are from an interview with Viggo Hans Nielsen conducted by Kjeld Sasbye on 16 February 1984.

The actual unloading of the troops from *Thyra III* was problematic from the start, as the DUKWs did not come out to *Thyra III* as planned. Therefore, the soldiers on board had to fight their way to the beach in water up to their necks. As was typically problematic for the other Danish ships, Nielsen and the rest of the crew on board *Thyra III* also experienced the dilemmas with the tides, which meant that the crew had a lot of time at Juno:

> We waited for the tide to be right so that the ship was almost on the bottom. Then the vehicles were unloaded. Then we had to wait for the high tide to return so we could sail out again. It was almost 24 hours before the high tide came again, so the second mate and I went for a short walk on the beach next to the ship. There was a house on fire and there was a German sniper who had been killed. We went to the trenches and looked, and there were anti-aircraft guns still firing. When the tide was right, we tried to sail out again, but we got stuck. So an old paddle steamer pulled us free and we sailed back to England… And then it was back at shuttle speed with supplies.

The Danish doctor on a Norwegian destroyer *Kjeld Seyer-Hansen* was possibly the only Danish doctor to take part in the Normandy invasion. He was aboard the Norwegian destroyer *Glaisdale* along with several unnamed Danes who were part of Task Force J that went in to Juno on D-Day. Seyer-Hansen went to the Faroe Islands in 1938 as a newly qualified doctor, and at the outbreak of war he was first reserve doctor at Thorshavn Hospital. At the end of 1943, he enlisted as a naval doctor in the Free Norwegian Forces, as he felt that his skills would most likely be more useful here. He subsequently joined the destroyer *Stord*, but shortly before the invasion he was transferred to the destroyer *Glaisdale*. At the same time, Seyer-Hansen's wife in the Faroe Islands mistakenly received a letter stating that her husband had died on board *Stord*. Flags flew at half-mast in many places around Thorshavn, but Seyer-Hansen's wife, Kamma, refused to believe that he was dead. It was not until late 1944 that the family at home was informed that he was still alive. The British-built *Glaisdale* joined the Free Norwegian Forces in 1941 and supported dozens of convoys in the period leading up to D-Day. *Glaisdale* escorted convoy J10 to the Canadian sector Juno. The ship's role was to participate in the bombardment of the Nan sector of Juno in the early morning of D-Day. Seyer-Hansen's surgical skills were put to good use as the many casualties among the first waves of attacks on Juno began to trickle in.

On 10 June, *Glaisdale* came under fire from German E-Boats laying mines off the coast of Normandy, but the Norwegian destroyer managed to chase the German boats away. On 23 June, *Glaisdale* encountered an acoustic mine off the coast of Normandy. There were no injuries or casualties, but the explosion damaged the ship's engines. However, it was able to stay afloat and, albeit with limited engine power, return to Portsmouth, where it was taken out of service for repairs. Seyer-Hansen was then officially away from the front, but subsequently served at the naval hospital in Edinburgh.[56]

56 Information from various newspaper clippings from Randbøl Lokalhistoriske Arkiv, 19 August 1979.

John Andreasen, 69th Light Anti-Aircraft Battery, 4th Light Anti-Aircraft Regiment, 3rd Canadian Division
'Dead bodies were everywhere – both our own and Germans, and some civilians'

The German defence at Juno was effective and the delay between the Allied bombardment ending and the arrival of troops on the beach on the morning of D-Day gave the Germans a clear advantage. 90 of the 306 landing craft involved in the landing were damaged or destroyed at Juno.

The delay in the attack also posed another problem: 10 minutes later, the characteristic Normandy tide rose, further obscuring the German mines in the water. This undoubtedly made it even more difficult for the landing craft to manoeuvre between the German obstacles, and just as undoubtedly increased the losses in both men and material. Around 20,000 soldiers and 900 tanks and vehicles were landed on Juno on D-Day, but the area was still marked by casualties due to German snipers in the evening. The Danish anti-aircraft gunner in Canadian service, John Andreasen, landed on Juno in the late afternoon of D-Day with the remaining anti-aircraft regiments while there was still an overwhelming amount of activity and many dangers ahead.

> The section where our division was to land was called Juno… We were told that our ship would try to land us in the afternoon, because the infantry and artillery and tanks were going in first, but we had plenty of time, I thought, I wanted to be an eyewitness as much as being in the middle of the battle. There were still a hundred boats in front of us and at our sides. The first ones were now starting to sail back empty, they were going back to England for more soldiers and equipment. Our landing craft was close to a large English warship, it had 8 x 10-inch guns in its turrets. It was lying broadside to the shore and firing continuously, each shell it sent over land weighed 1,000kg. There were fires almost everywhere and a lot of German shells landed on the beach and in the water, occasionally a car or cannon was hit and blew up. There was a boat that sailed into a small estuary to our left, and when it disappeared behind a warehouse it must have hit a mine, because we heard a bang and pieces of the boat appeared above the building. Our aircraft flew continuously along the beach and every time they found a suitable target, they dived and opened fire with their machine guns.

As John Andreasen approached Juno, the reality of what lay ahead became more and more apparent as the devastation on the beach got closer and closer:

> In the middle of the afternoon we started sailing in [towards the shore], and the captain shouted over the loudspeaker that all hands should be away from the vehicles[57] and guns so as not to get stuck, he wanted to see if he could give us a dry landing. The ship accelerated the engines, but it came to a sudden stop when we hit

57 Andreasen actually uses the Danish word for "car" throughout as a slang term for vehicles but his meaning is clear and I have translated as "vehicle" to make this clear.

> a sandbar, here we sat with about a metre and a half of water in front of the ship, but the tide was too far out. We had to get the chains off our vehicles, we were on the top deck, so we should have a good landing. There were still a lot of German shells landing in the water around us, so we wanted to get off the ship as quickly as possible. It didn't look good on the beach, vehicles and landing craft had been hit by artillery and had caught fire; the fire had burnt out but you could still see smoke and sparks coming off of it. Materials were floating everywhere. We hurried to drive behind some houses that looked more or less intact, otherwise it looked awful, most houses were shot to pieces. There were gliders everywhere, one lying over a house, another with its nose buried deep in a wall. There were dead bodies everywhere, both our own and Germans, and a few civilians. I saw a Frenchman standing with a three-year-old child in his arms looking at a small house that was completely in ruins.

Andreasen's regiment was then ordered to move further inland. The goal was to push the Germans back as far as possible on D-Day to take the nearest towns between the beach and the larger city of Caen. However, the final objective, Caen, turned out to be much harder to take than expected:

> Our infantry advanced that day all the way to the outskirts of Caen, but had to retreat again to about 6 to 8 kilometres from the city. The town where we landed was called Courseulles. We stopped behind the houses and we tore all the fibrous, waterproof material off the vehicle exhausts and gun barrels. When we were done with that, we drove on and along a very bad road. We sat on pins tenterhooks looking in all directions, the gun was loaded, as were all of our rifles and machine guns. We did not know what we were going to encounter.[58]

After D-Day, it was estimated that 914 Canadian and 243 British soldiers were killed or wounded. The majority of casualties on Juno occurred within the first hour of the landing.

The objectives of the sector were achieved in the first few hours, but fierce fighting continued behind the coastal area until late in the evening. In the west of the sector, the Canadians reached 10 kilometres inland and met with British troops at Creully. The next waves of troops poured out on the landing craft from the transport ships, but the German mines on the beach were still a great danger to the men going ashore and to the dense traffic now in the sector. Revenge for Dieppe was well underway for the Canadian troops. The next objective lay 14 kilometres inland: the capture of the large city of Caen.[59]

For a nation with a population of only 11,500,000, Canadian participation in the Normandy invasion was unrivalled. Canadian troops were part of the front throughout Operation Overlord, and almost every Allied combat force involved Canadian participation. The navy, air force, infantry, minesweepers, paratroopers, engineers and tank crews all included Canadian volunteers. What made them unique was the fact that they *were*

58 John Andreasen, unpublished diary, pp.35–36.

59 Jakob Sørensen, *D-Dag – Operation Overlord 6. Juni 1944* (Copenhagen: People's Press, 2014), pp.234–235.

volunteers; British and US forces were a mix of conscripts and volunteers, but all Canadians involved in the invasion chose to participate of their own will. This was perhaps especially remarkable considering that less than 30 years earlier, Canada had lost almost an entire generation during World War I.[60]

The Five Landing Sectors: Sword

The easternmost sector of the five landing beaches, Sword, stretched for more than eight kilometres from the outskirts of Langrune-sur-Mer in the west to the port town of Ouistreham in the east. However, the D-Day attack would take place on the much narrower stretch between Lion-sur-Mer and Ouistreham. More than 12 kilometres inland lies the city of Caen, which was an important strategic city for the Allies to take. The idyllic coastal villages of Sword had been one of the most popular holiday destinations in the region before the war. However, by the time D-Day arrived, the idyllic coastal towns had disappeared as the towns were heavily transformed with German concrete positions placed all along the coastline. Sword was divided by the Allies into four attack sectors: Oboe, Peter, Queen and Roger, to be attacked by the British 3rd Division. Unlike Gold and Juno, Sword was to be attacked by just one brigade and not two brigades attacking in unison.

The attack was to be more narrow and focused, as the first of the brigades' breakthrough would pave the way for the reserve brigades. The plan was then for the British troops to link up with the paratroops that had been dropped at Bénouville and together they would advance towards Caen.

The German defence consisted of troops from *Infanteriedivision 716*, primarily located in concrete positions along the beach sector, but a large number of German defensive positions were also located in the area behind the beach and towards Caen. The Germans were fully aware of the need to reinforce the area behind the beach if the Allies were to succeed in breaking through the beach area. Caen was vital to the Germans and the continued strategic battle in the event of an Allied invasion. Even more important than the German positions on the road to Caen was the presence of the *Panzerdivision 21* in the area. This was to counter-attack in the sector if the Allies broke through the beach positions, thereby stopping the Allies before they reached Caen.

The German positions along the coast were tactically and effectively positioned, and the two batteries at Merville and Le Havre in particular could do significant damage to the Allied troops that landed on the beach on D-Day. However, after heavy fighting, the Merville battery had already been captured by British paratroopers from 9th Battalion of 3rd Airborne Brigade, who neutralised the four heavy German guns early in the morning of D-Day. Due to the Allied smoke screen at Sword, the battery at Le Havre was unable to effectively use the heavy guns against the British troops, but instead attacked the battleship HMS *Warspite*, although without damaging the ship. Sword itself, however, had a reinforced German defence consisting of mines, trenches and machine gun nests;

60 Stuart C. Robertson & Dale Booth, *Following in the Footsteps of Heroes: D-Day June 6th 1944*, (Devizes: Sabrestorm, 2014), p.185.

additionally, the feared 88mm guns and mortar positions were placed on the ridge behind the beach.

The British attack on Sword was executed very similarly to the landings on Gold and Juno. However, the Sword landing was much more effective than on the other two beaches. The objective was twofold for the British 3rd Division. First, and primarily, the beach area was to be taken, and then (very ambitiously) Caen was to be captured. After the bombers had dropped their loads on the German positions, the fleet began its bombardment at sunrise on D-Day. Two battleships, one battlecruiser, five cruisers and thirteen destroyers took part in the bombardment. Among these was the Norwegian *Svenner*, which was sunk on D-Day and in which the Dane Christian Bror Nejrup was killed. At 06:15, the first of the 31 DD tanks began sailing towards the coast in high seas. The tanks approached the beach and quickly drew fire from the German positions. The naval bombardment had not yet ceased, and this had consequences for the DD tanks, which were hit by rockets from naval ships, causing two tanks to sink. At 07:20, the first of the tanks rolled onto the beach along with men from the Royal Marines, who began clearing the beach of obstacles and mines. The German 88mm guns on the ridges behind the beach were very effective, although the fire on Sword was not as heavy as on Omaha or on Juno, but it was heavier than on Gold and Utah.

The 8th Infantry Brigade continued the attack on Sword in the Queen sector after the DD tanks were landed. Subsequently, the two British Commandos, Nos 4 and 10, attacked Ouistreham. No.10 Commando included 177 vengeful Frenchmen who were keen to liberate their homeland. In addition, 41 Commando attacked Lion-sur-Mer and subsequently linked up with the Canadian troops at Juno. The German troops at the forward positions on the beach slowly began to fire on the troops going ashore, and the German obstacles on the beach caused the British troops great problems. There were also German snipers positioned at the front line and these were very effective against the British soldiers slowly coming ashore.[61]

Eric Arnold Aage Kiaer, No.3 Commando

No.3 Commando took part in the disastrous raid at Dieppe in 1942, and it was therefore a vengeful regiment that was now back on French soil. No.3 Commando arrived in the second wave at Sword and, after landing at La Bréche, was to link up with the British 6th Airborne Division on the eastern flank of Sword. Eric Arnold Aage Kiaer participated in the landing as a member of No.3 Commando.

Born in London to Danish parents, Kiaer enlisted for British service when war broke out. In April 1940, shortly after the occupation of Denmark, Kiaer began training as an officer. He was commissioned as a second lieutenant in the Royal Fusiliers and shortly thereafter transferred to the newly established commandos. He was subsequently promoted to lieutenant and was sent to North Africa with No.1 Commando in 1942, where he took part in the Allied landings during Operation Torch. In November 1942, Kiaer was captured by the

61 Jakob Sørensen, *D-Dag – Operation Overlord 6. Juni 1944* (Copenhagen: People's Press, 2014), pp.239–245.

Germans and transported to an Italian prison camp. He attempted to escape from the prison camp, but was recaptured shortly afterwards. Kiaer refused to remain in captivity and made another escape attempt in late 1943, which almost succeeded. Together with another group of escaped prisoners, Kiaer walked 1,000 kilometres south across the Apennines in Italy in 6 weeks to reach the Allied lines.

However, luck was not in his, and the rest of the group's, favour as they were captured by the Germans shortly before they reached the Allied lines. Kiaer was now placed in another prison camp, but just 12 hours after the group was back in the camp, he organised another large-scale escape attempt. This time, the group managed to reach the Allied lines.

Kiaer subsequently returned to England and volunteered for service with No.3 Commando, which was to take part in the Normandy invasion. Intensive training for the invasion began, and at the same time Kiaer was recommended by the commander of the 1st Special Service Brigade, Lord Lovat, for one of the highest British military decorations, the Military Cross, based on his repeated escape attempts in Italy.

Kiaer landed on Sword, specifically Red Beach, with No.3 Commando at 09:05 on D-Day. There were strong German defences in the sector and this was Kiaer's undoing. Three of the landing craft carrying the soldiers were hit by German shells before they reached the beach and casualties were high. Lovat later described the Kiaer incident: 'Eric Kiaer was killed before we reached the dunes. Wounded and half drowned during the landing, dragged down by the heavy rucksack, he was picked up and dragged across the sand.'[62] Eric Arnold Aage Kiaer died of his wounds at Sword on D-Day, aged just 25, and was later buried in the war cemetery at Bayeux in Normandy. Kiaer's younger brother, Leslie Herbert Sonne Kiaer, was a platoon leader in a parachute regiment and met the same fate as his brother during the fighting at Arnhem during Operation Market Garden in September 1944. Leslie Kiaer is buried at the war cemetery at Oosterbeek.

Despite losses in No.3 Commando, the soldiers continued towards their objective and subsequently reached the (now) Pegasus Bridge, which led across the Caen Canal, where they met up with the glider troops of the Ox & Bucks Light Infantry who had taken the bridge in the early morning hours of D-Day. The British troops were effective in their attack on Sword. Just a few hours after the landing, the line between Ouistreham and Le Bréche was secured and a battalion of the 2nd South Lancashires moved to the bridge and then the Regiment advanced towards Hermanville-sur-Mer. However, the logistical chaos on Sword soon became a challenging factor. Troops, equipment and vehicles were rapidly piling up on the beach and the tide was rising fast, while German guns continued to fire sporadically at the beach. The engineer troops and specialist armour worked at double speed and finally managed to open up the area behind the beach, despite the fact that a small section between Sword and Juno Beaches was still in German hands.[63]

62 Lord Lovat, *March Past: A Memoir* (London: Weidenfeld & Nicholson, 1978), p.211.

63 Lord Lovat, *March Past: A Memoir* (London: Weidenfeld & Nicholson, 1978), pp.296–342.

The B-26 Marauder bomber *Mary Jo* on exercise in England. (The Pima Air and Space Museum)

The crew aboard the B-26 Marauder bomber *Mary Jo*. Pilot Major Jens A. Nørgaard in the centre of the back row. Nørgaard would later achieve the rank of Lieutenant Colonel. (Karl Leach)

Above: Thorkil Jensen married his wife while on leave in Minnesota in 1942. (Veterans History Project)
Right: Kaj Birksted in 1945. (Freedom Museum)

Flight Lieutenant *Jørgen Kjeldbæk on a Spitfire Mk. VB in the period leading* up to D-Day. Invasion stripes were painted on the wings to make it easier to identify friend from foe. (Freedom Museum)

The Norwegian 331 and 332 Spitfire squadrons, of which Kjeld Rønhof and Kaj Birksted were a part. Both took part in D-Day and the Normandy invasion. The photo shows 331 Squadron at Catterick, in spring 1942. (Tvedte)

The Dane Christian Bror Nejrup died onboard the Norwegian destroyer *Svenner* on D-Day. (The Naval Museum)

Above: The anchor from *Svenner*, which today serves as a memorial. (Normandywarguide.com)
Above right: Hans Mathiasen became a captain at the end of the war. (Kromann)
Right: Danish gunner wearing helmet and life jacket on board *Avance* during Operation Overlord. (M/S The Maritime Museum)

Aalborg Stiftstidende

B - Udgave

178. Aargang — Tirsdag den 6. Juni 1944 — Numer 152

Invasion indledet i Frankrig

Landsætning af Faldskærms-tropper i Normandiet

Amfibie-Operation mellem Floderne Seine og Vie

BERLIN, TIRSDAG, RB

DEN LÆNGE VENTEDE INVASION fra Englændernes og Amerikanernes Side er i Dag i de tidlige Morgentimer begyndt ved Nedsætning af Luftlandingstropper i Omraadet ved Seine-Mundingen. Le Havres Havn bliver i Øjeblikket heftigt bombarderet. Søstridskræfter fra den tyske Krigsmarine er foran Kysten i Kamp med fjendtlige Landgangsfartøjer.

Faldskærmstropper søger at erobre Flyvepladser

BERLIN, TIRSDAG, RB.

»INTERNATIONALE INFORMATION« meddeler: I de første Morgentimer den 6. Juni begyndte efter al Sandsynlighed Englændernes og Amerikanernes ventede Angreb paa de europæiske Vestkyster. I Omraadet mellem Seines Munding og Østkysten af Normandiet blev der iagttaget talrige Landgangsbaade og andre lette Krigsfartøjer.

Samtidig berettes det, at paa Nordspidsen af den normanniske Halvø springer engelsk-amerikanske Tropper ud fra talrige Flyvemaskiner. Deres Opgave er sandsynligvis at sætte sig i Besiddelse af nogle Flyvepladser for at skaffe Plads til den yderligere Landsættelse af Tropper.

Voldsomt Angreb paa Calais og Dunkerque

BERLIN, TIRSDAG, RB.

Samtidig med, at Invasionen i de tidlige Morgentimer i Dag begyndte med Nedsætning af Luftlandingstropper i Omraadet ved Seines Munding, angreb stærke Formationer af Bombemaskiner Omraaderne ved Calais og Dunkerque. Det tyske Luftforsvar traadte straks i Aktivitet.

Paa disse Steder er der endnu ikke blevet landsat fjendtlige Tropper.

Tyngdepunkterne er i hele Normandiet

Store Skaar slaaet i den første britiske Faldskærmsjæger-Division

BERLIN, TIRSDAG, RB.

»INTERNATIONALE Information« meddeler: De kombinerede Landgangsoperationer, som Amerikanerne og Englænderne i de tidlige Morgentimer i Dag begyndte mod den europæiske Vestkyst fra Søen og ad Luftvejen, omfatter hele Kystafsnittet mellem Le Havre og Cherbourg.

Medens Tyngdepunktet for Luftlandingsangrebene ligger i hele Normandiets Omraade og ved de vigtigste Flodmundinger i Seine-Bugten, er der mellem Seine-Mundingen og Vie-Flodens Udmunding i Atlanterhavet over en bred Front blevet sat en Amfibie-Operation ind i stor Stil, i hvilken foruden talrige Landgangsfartøjer af de mest forskellige Typer ogsaa lette, allierede Søstridskræfter deltager i betydeligt Omfang.

Udfor Seines Munding er der blevet observeret 6 svære Krigsskibsenheder og 20 Torpedojagere, med hvilke de tyske Kystbatterier har optaget Kampen. Betydelige Dele af Faldskærmsformationerne, som skulde gennemføre det første Angreb paa Vesteuropa ved Masseudspring ved Flodmudninger og paa de vigtigste Flyvepladser paa den normanniske Halvø, er allerede i Mellemtiden blevet revet op.

Ifølge de foreløbige Meldinger kan der regnes med, at der er blevet slaaet store Skaar i den 1. britiske Faldskærmsjæger-Division.

Stort Krigsskib i Brand

BERLIN, TIRSDAG, RB.

Det lynhurtigt indsatte Forsvar fra de tyske Sikringsformationers Side mod de engelske og amerikanske Faldskærmstropper, som i Ly af kunstig Taage og dækket af stærk Artilleri-ild blev landsat ved Seine-Bugten, har allerede kunnet opvise sine første Resultater. Talrige Luftlandingsenheder er allerede blevet tilintetgjort. Et stort Krigsskib kom i Brand i Seine-Bugten efter en Artilleritræffer.

Kort over den vestlige Del af Frankrig med de Steder, hvor Invasionen er sat ind

Spændingen omkring Dagen »D« udløst

De Allieredes Indmarch i Rom Signal til Invasionens Begyndelse

BERLIN, TIRSDAG, STB

DEN LÆNGE VENTEDE Invasion i Vesteuropa har taget sin Begyndelse i de tidligere Morgentimer i Dag, meddeles det fra kompetent militær Side i Berlin. Paa den franske Kanalkyst mellem Seineflodens Munding og Normandiets Østkyst observerede de tyske Vagtposter ved Atlanterhavsvolden ved Daggry store Mængder allierede Landgangsbaade, der eskorteret af lette britiske Krigsfartøjer nærmede sig Kysten.

Indmarchen i Rom Signalet

Dermed skulde altsaa Spændingen omkring den ubestemte Dag »D« være kommet til Udløsning, og det synes, som de Allieredes Indmarch i Rom har været Signalet til Invasionens Begyndelse.

Forbitret Kamp ved Kysten

Udfor den franske Kanalkyst foregaar en forbitret Kamp mellem Enheder af den tyske Krigsmarine og Invasionsflaaden. Yderligere Rapporter meddeler, at stærke allierede Bombeformationer foruden le Havre angriber Omraaderne omkring Calais og Dunkerque. Det tyske Luftforsvar har taget Kampen op mod Angriberne. Allierede Landgangsoperationer i dette Omraade er derimod hidtil ikke rapporteret.

Saavidt man paa nuværende Tidspunkt kan skønne, drejer de Landgangsoperationer, som tidligt i Morges er blevet indledet mod den franske Kanalkyst, sig om den virkelige Optakt til Invasionen, erklærer de tyske Militæreksperter. De Operationer, som er i Gang, er af langt større og omfattende Karakter end alle hidtidige Commandoraid mod europæiske Kystomraader.

Stiger i Voldsomhed fra Time til Time

Kampene trukket ind i Landet til Egnen omkring Caen

AF EINAR PRAVITZ

BERLIN, TIRSDAG (Metro Press)

INVASIONSSLAGET paa og ved Normandiets Kyst — præcis de samme Egne, som for snart 1000 Aar siden dannede Udgangspunkt for Historiens sidste store Landgangsaktion tvers over Kanalen, Vilhelm Erobrerens Landgang i England — vokser fra Time til Time i Voldsomhed og Omfang, fremgaar det af de tyske Rapporter, som uafbrudt strømmer ind fra den ny Krigsskueplads.

Angrebet begyndte kort efter Midnat

Aktionen forfølger et dobbelt Maal

BERLIN, TIRSDAG, RB.

»INTERNATIONALE Information« meddeler: Saavel den terrænmæssige Udstrækning som Antallet af indsatte Tropper viser, at Englændernes og Amerikanernes Angreb mod Seine-Bugten og Normandiet er en Operation i stor Stil. Dens Omfang gaar langt ud over Grænserne for et »Commandoraid«, og uden Tvivl betegner Operationen Invasionens første Fase.

Aktionen forfølger aabenbart et dobbelt Maal. I første Række vil de Allieredes Overkommando benytte de to Flodmundinger mellem Le Havre og Cherbourg til her i Ly af faste Brohoveder at kunne landsætte yderligere Angrebsformationer med svære Vaaben. Derfor nedsættes de engelske og de amerikanske Faldskærmsformationer i dette Omraade.

Montgomery Øverstbefalende

LONDON via Bern, TIRSDAG RB.

General Montgomery er Øverstbefalende for de Tropper, som foretager Invasionen, og som omfatter britiske, kanadiske og amerikanske Styrker.

Front page of *Aalborg Stiftstidende*'s for 6 June 1944: 'Invasion initiated in France'. (Nordjyske Historiske Avisarkiv)

DUKWs (D is the designation for a vehicle designed in 1942, U means "utility (amphibious)", K refers to all-wheel drive and W describes two rear axles with traction). The 'Duck', as it was nicknamed, was an important tool for carrying supplies during the invasion. (M/S Museet for Søfart)

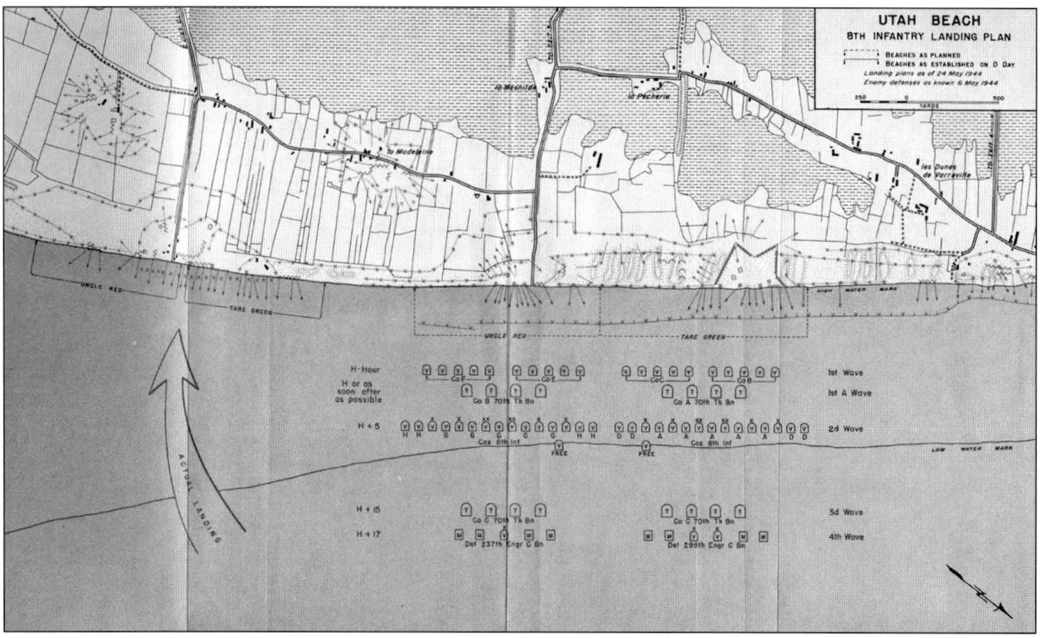

Map of the Utah invasion sector. (US National Archives)

Despite the initial attack being over on 6 June, the sea was still dangerous for ships, as seen here when the American ship *AM-125* sank en route to Utah after hitting a mine on 7 June. (US National Archives)

Utah on D-Day when Brigadier General Roosevelt led all troops to the 'house with the red roof', which still stands on Utah beach today. (US National Archives / Private)

Utah beach today with the 'house with the red roof'. (US National Archives / Private)

The tank wall on Utah beach today. (Private collection)

American soldiers from the 8th Infantry Regiment of the 4th Infantry Division rest at the tank wall on Utah on 6 June. Parts of the wall can still be found on Utah beach today. (US National Archives)

The Danish DFDS ship, *Tomsk*, arrived in Utah on D-Day, but had to wait seven days to unload soldiers and vehicles due to logistical challenges and tidal differences. (M/S Maritime Museum)

Andreas Moldt aboard the Lancaster bomber *ITEM*. The aft turret had four Browning machine guns. (Moldt)

Henning Møller from Frederikshavn landed on Utah on D-Day with the 12th Infantry Regiment of the 4th Infantry Division. (Kystmuseet Bangsbo Arkiv)

Thorald Nielsen was on board *Tomsk* on D-Day and had a clear view of the major operation on Utah. He had also previously sailed aboard the Danish ship S/S *Avance*, which was also part of the invasion force. (Claus Arboe-Rasmussen)

American Medics treat wounded in the Utah Sector on the morning of D-Day. (US National Archives)

The damage from the D-Day fighting in the Utah sector is still visible on the German bunkers today. (Private collection)

American soldiers take cover in a Higgins landing craft near Omaha. (US National Archives)

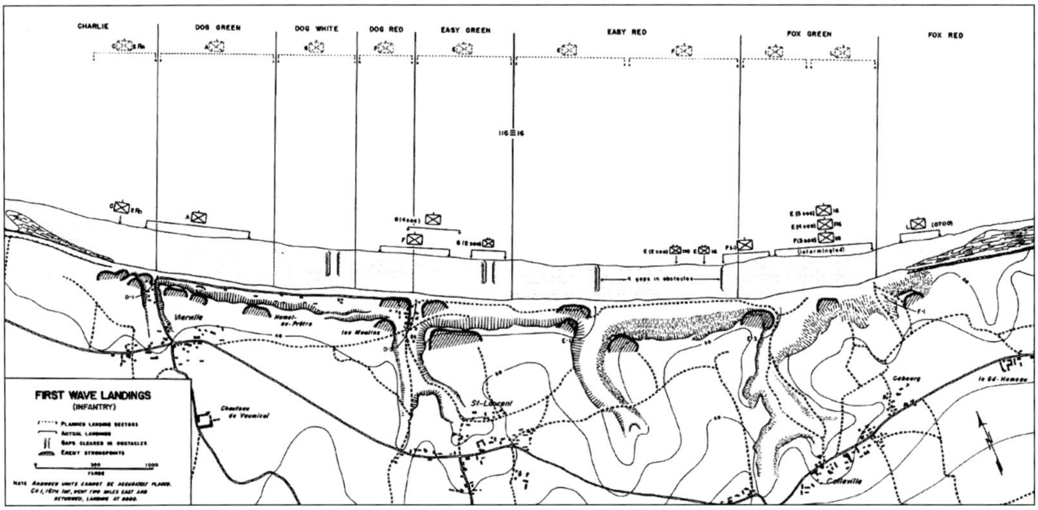

Plan for the D-Day attack in the Omaha sector. (US National Archives)

Contemporary photo of Omaha on a rainy and foggy June day. (Private collection)

American troops on their way to Omaha. (US National Archives)

American troops travelling towards Omaha. (US National Archives)

The view from the area behind Omaha. The Germans had ideal opportunities to establish a strong defence in the hilly landscape. (Private collection)

USS *Augusta* lies off the coast of Omaha on D-Day. At the same time, Higgins landing craft are bringing troops to the beach. (US NARA)

Above: Svend A. Petersen was on board *Augusta* on D-Day. (US NARA)
Right: Svend A. Pedersen photographed in France during the summer of 1944. (Carl Steffensen)

Above: Poul Egon Pedersen stands by the sign for the Danish boarding house that the family ran in Chicago. (Carl Steffensen)
Right: Poul Egon Pedersen sitting facing the camera on Omaha late in the afternoon on D-Day. (Carl Steffensen)

S/S *Aarø* was taken over by the Ministry of War Transport in 1940. The ship participated in the invasion of Normandy on 6 June 1944 and made four voyages to the area with troops and equipment. *Aarø* was wrecked on 6 October off Omaha after a collision with the Norwegian S/S *Lysland*. (Freedom Museum)

Soldiers and vehicles aboard a ship bound for Omaha on D-Day. (US National Archives)

American troops land on the beach in the Omaha sector on D-Day. (US National Archives)

Wounded soldiers of the 3rd Battalion, 16th Regiment of 1st Infantry Division, receive cigarettes and food after the attack on Omaha. (US National Archives)

Holger Jensen. (Jørgen Aarlo Jensen)

Holger Jensen picked up this knife from a leg floating in the water near Omaha and brought it home to Denmark after the war. (Freedom Museum)

The binoculars that Holger Jensen used as a marine inspector at Omaha. (Freedom Museum)

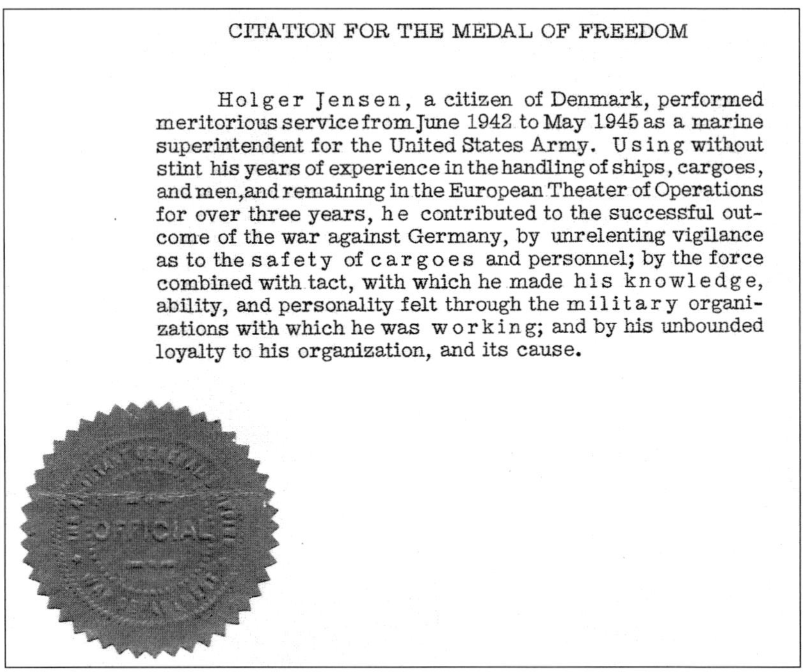

CITATION FOR THE MEDAL OF FREEDOM

Holger Jensen, a citizen of Denmark, performed meritorious service from June 1942 to May 1945 as a marine superintendent for the United States Army. Using without stint his years of experience in the handling of ships, cargoes, and men, and remaining in the European Theater of Operations for over three years, he contributed to the successful outcome of the war against Germany, by unrelenting vigilance as to the safety of cargoes and personnel; by the force combined with tact, with which he made his knowledge, ability, and personality felt through the military organizations with which he was working; and by his unbounded loyalty to his organization, and its cause.

OFFICIAL

Holger Jensen achieved the rank of Lieutenant Colonel and was decorated with several orders from the USA and England, including the Medal of Freedom. (Jørgen Aarlo Jensen)

The Omaha sector (Easy Red sector) at St Laurent-sur-Mer in the days after D-Day. The German position WN65, where there is still a German gun today, was extremely favourable for the defence of the sector. (US NARA)

The Omaha sector (Easy Red sector) at St Laurent-sur-Mer today. (Private collection)

Omaha (Dog Green sector) at Vierville-sur-Mer on 6 June 1944. Today, a memorial to the US National Guard is placed on top of the German WN72 position, where the 88mm gun caused many American casualties on D-Day. The gun is located in the bunker to this day. (US NARA)

Omaha (Dog Green sector) at Vierville-sur-Mer today. Clearly visible is the memorial to the US National Guard placed on top of this German position, where the 88mm gun caused many American casualties on D-Day, the gun remains in the bunker to this day. (Private collection)

Einar Sørensen receives The Silver Star from Major General Leland S. Hobbs in January 1945 for his action with the burning lorry during the artillery attack in Normandy. (Kris Harsh)

Carl E. Nielsen's burial place at the American cemetery in Margraten. (Fields of Honour database)

DD tank with inflatable skirts used in the Omaha landings. (Imperial War Museum)

British commandos from the 47 Royal Marine Commando run ashore at the Jig Green sector on Gold on D-Day, 6 June. (Imperial War Museum)

British purpose-built tanks, such as the Churchill AVRE tank with a petard mortar, were crucial in breaking through the German positions at Gold. One of these stands today at Graye-sur-Mer. (Private collection)

The German battery at Longues-sur-Mer, which the British 47 Commando passed on their way to Port-en-Bessin, was located between Omaha and Gold and was bombarded with 1,500 tons of bombs from Allied aircraft in the run-up to D-Day. Throughout D-Day, the battery was bombarded by Allied warships, the USS *Arkansas* and the French cruiser *Georges Leygues*. The battery returned fire on the warships causing HMS *Bulolo* to retreat out to sea. 3 of the battery's 4 guns were neutralised by the cruisers HMS *Ajax* and HMS *Argonaut* during the day, while the last one continued to fire on the ships until 19:00. The 184 men of the battery then surrendered to the 231st Brigade. During D-Day, the battery fired 170 shells. The guns still remain in the casemates to this day. (Private collection)

Spoils of war were common for soldiers from both sides of the war. Niels Wiesneck brought many items home to Denmark after the war, such as this Nazi flag. (Finn Wiesneck)

Niels Wiesneck in Canadian uniform during training in England. (Finn Wiesneck)

Viggo Hans Nielsen in 1945. (Lis Nielsen)

Tanks of the 7th Armoured Division heading inland behind Gold on 7 June 1944. (Imperial War Museum)

Canadian soldiers storm Juno on D-Day. (Library and Archives Canada)

Troops of the 9th Canadian Infantry Brigade land at Bernières-sur-Mer in the Juno sector on D-Day. (Library and Archives Canada)

Hans Juelsdorf returned to Normandy in 1994 for the 50th anniversary of D-Day. Here he and two other veterans were honoured by the Mayor of Bayeux, Pierre Vastier with the words: "We thank you. For your courage. For your hardship. For your valour. For giving us our freedom." Juelsdorf also received a medal from the French Regional Council in 1994 and a personal letter and diploma from French President Mitterand thanking him for his efforts. (Jakob Andersen)

HNoMS (His Norwegian Majesty's Ship) *Glaisdale* off the coast of Normandy in June 1944. (Navy Photos Collection)

Wounded Canadian soldiers from the Queens Own Rifles await evacuation at Bernières-sur-Mer in the Juno sector. (Library and Archives Canada)

The same location on Bernières-sur-Mer in the Juno sector today. (Private collection)

German prisoners march along Juno at Bernières-sur-Mer in the late afternoon of D-Day on their way to be transported to a prison camp in England. (Library and Archives Canada)

The same stretch of Juno beach at Bernières-sur-Mer today. The house has been repaired and is today a family home. (Private collection)

John Andreasen (left) and a friend standing with an abandoned Nazi flag in the period after D-Day. (Bornholm Island Archive)

Canadian troops use an anti-aircraft gun on the afternoon on D-Day. This Bofors gun is similar to the one John Andreasen was trained to operate. (Library and Archives Canada)

Wounded and exhausted British soldiers land at Sword on D-Day. (Imperial War Museum)

British commandos, including Eric Kiaer, of the 1st Special Service Brigade under the command of Lord Lovat land at Sword on D-Day. (Imperial War Museum)

Eric Arnold Aage Kiaer. (Commandoveterans.org)

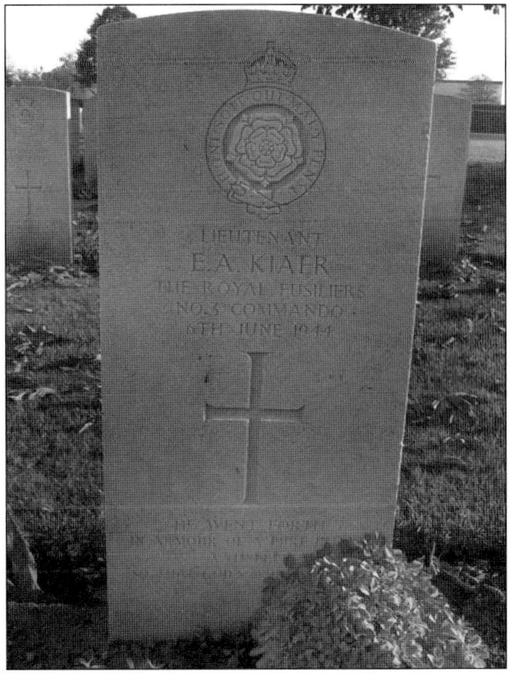

The inscription on Eric Arnold Aage Kiaer's gravestone at the British military cemetery at Bayeux: "He went forth in armour of a pure intent and fell so that God's work be done." (Commandoveterans.org)

Above: Evald Brinck in British uniform (Evald Brinck)
Right: British troops from 5th Parachute Brigade examine invasion dollars at RAF Fairford on 3 June 1944 in the days leading up to D-Day. (Imperial War Museum)

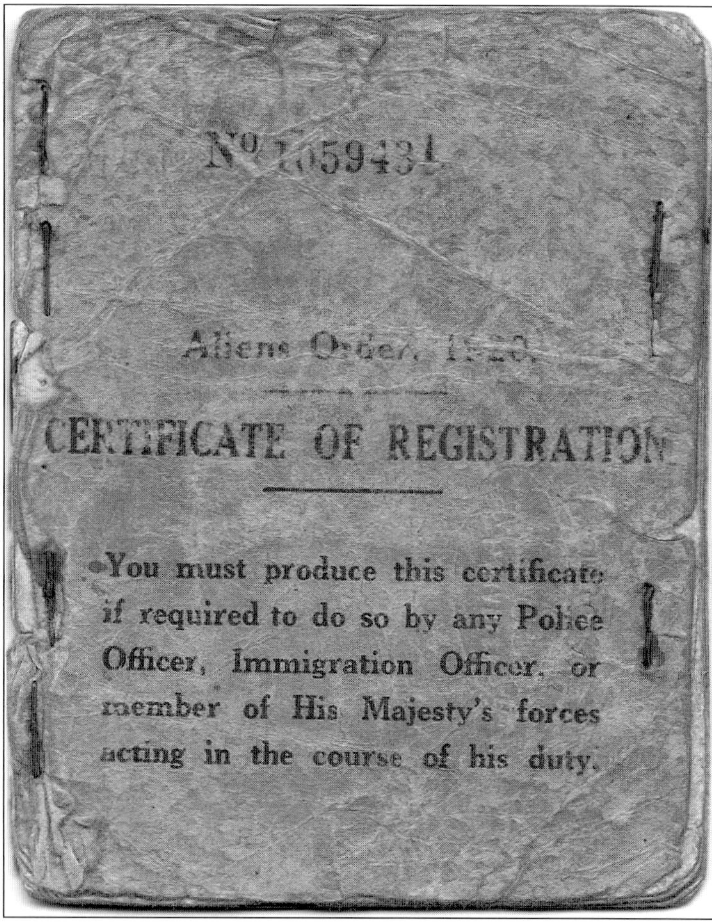

Karl Adolph Goth's shipping papers. (Simon Bang)

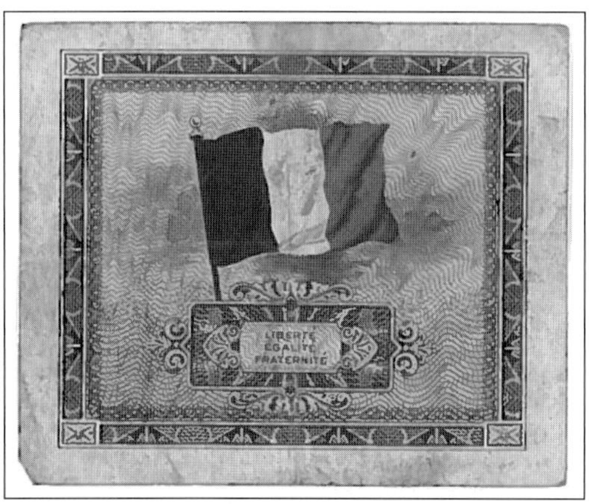

Left: Niels Wiesneck who ended up in Canadian service and participated in Operation Overlord with The Essex Scottish Regiment also received invasion dollars and brought them home to Denmark after the war. (Finn Wiesneck)

British troops attacking Sword, Queen White on D-Day. (Imperial War Museum)

Photograph of a standing Emil Blytgen-Petersen, who was a member of the Danish Council in London and editor of *Frit Danmark* – The Free Danes' magazine in London, on board a DUKW (amphibious vehicle). The Danish sailors assisted the Norwegian steamship S/S *Lysaker V* with unloading off the coast of Normandy during the invasion in 1944. (M/S Museet for Søfart)

FRIT DANMARK

3. Aarg. Nr.3 | Udgivet af en Kreds af Danske | Juni 1944

INVASIONEN OG DET DANSKE FOLK

"Vesteuropas Folk! Troppestyrker af de allierede Styrkers Ekspeditionshær gik i Morges i Land paa den franske Kyst. Denne Landgang er et Led i de Forenede Nationers fælles Plan, som er lagt sammen med vor store russiske Allierede, og som tager Sigte paa at befri Europa. Jeg bringer Dem alle dette Budskab: Selvom dette indledende Angreb ikke har fundet Sted i Deres eget Land, saa er Befrielsens Time dog nær. - Alle Patrioter, Mænd og Kvinder, unge og gamle har en Indsats at gøre, naar den endelige Sejr skal vindes. Til Medlemmerne af Modstandsbevægelserne, hvadenten de faar Deres Meddelelser hjemmefra eller udefra, siger jeg: Følg de Instruktioner, De har faaet. Til Patrioter, som ikke tilhører organiserede Modstandsgrupper siger jeg: Udsæt ikke Deres Liv for unødig Fare, men fortsæt Deres passive Modstand, indtil jeg giver Dem Signalet til Rejsning og til Kamp mod Fjenden. Den Dag vil komme, hvor jeg faar Brug for Deres samlede Styrke. Indtil den Dag paalægger jeg Dem den haarde Opgave at udvise Disciplin og Tilbageholdenhed."

Med disse Ord indledtes det Budskab, som General EISENHOWER paa Invasionsdagen udsendte til Folkene i det undertrykte Europa. Gennem Krigens Aar har vi lært, at intet er de allierede Nationers politiske og militære Ledere mere fremmed end at udtale store Ord og forhastet Optimisme. Derfor virker General Eisenhowers Sætning: BEFRIELSENS TIME ER NÆR med saa stor Styrke paa os. Vi ved, det er mer end et Haab der finder Udtryk, - det er et Løfte, som vi trygt kan forlade os paa. Overalt i Europa, i Danmark som i de Lande, der endnu haardere end vi har følt Nazismens Tryk, betyder Invasionen i Frankrig en kraftig moralsk Stimulans til at fortsætte og udvide Kampen. Men det er værd ogsaa at lægge Vægt paa den Advarsel, der ligger i den Øverstkommanderendes Budskab: Hverken den organiserede Modstandsbevægelse eller den store Befolkning bør handle paa egen Haand. Man skal følge de Instruktioner, der udsendes af Frihedskampens hjemlige Ledelse og den allierede Overkommando.

I Frankrig kæmper i Dag de engelske og amerikanske Tropper for at udvide det Fodfæste, de allerede saa sikkert har erobret. Men samtidig er Signalet givet til de franske Patrioter, der i stadig stigende Skala falder Tyskerne i Ryggen. Jernbanelinjer afbrydes, Broer sprænges i Luften, tyske Garnisoner angribes, og adskillige Steder besættes hele Byer og Egne af Partisanerne.

I Danmark skærpes Sabotagen mod krigsvigtige tyske Industrier, og Transportmidler destrueres. Men endnu er det for tidligt at lade Kampen træde over i Partisankrigens Fase. Ordren hertil vil først blive givet af de Allieredes Overkommando og Danmarks Frihedsraad i Forening, naar Tiden er inde.

Det er aldeles nødvendigt, at vi alle viser den Beherskelse, det kræver, ikke straks at sætte alle Kræfter ind for at svække og fordrive vor Fjende. Men dette betyder ikke, at vi skal ligge paa den lade Side. Alle, der har meldt sig til de organiserede danske Frihedsstyrker, skal forberede sig paa deres Opgaver og skabe saa stærk en Hær som overhovedet muligt. Og hver eneste Dansker, der af Hjertet ønsker sit Lands Befrielse, skal gøre op med sig selv, hvorledes han kan yde sin Indsats.

Thi den Dag, der kaldes, skal det ikke blot være selve Modstandsbevægelsens Medlemmer, der sætter Liver i Vove for at bekæmpe vore Undertrykkere.

Det skal være hele Folket, der kæmper for sin Frihed.

FRIT DANMARK

OGSAA DE KAN YDE HJÆLP TIL FRIHEDSKÆMPERNE OG DE ALLIEREDE TROPPER !

Despite the fact that Blytgen-Petersen could not be physically present on D-Day, it was extremely important for 'Free Denmark' to describe the invasion so that the morale of the Danish people could be maintained and the hope of Denmark's liberation was still preserved. (Freedom Museum)

The Danish ship S/S *Alf* in German harbour before the war. (M/S Maritime Museum)

Omaha beach after D-Day. Barrage balloons hover over the transport ships, from which vehicles and soldiers pour out to continue the offensive in Normandy. (US National Archives)

Attack and Counter-Attack

By the early morning of D-Day, Sword Beach was in British hands and under the control of the 3rd Division. The further advance and link up with the airborne troops in the eastern sector then took place and everything went largely according to plan.

The commandos continued towards their objective, *Stützpunktgruppe Riva Bella* defence area, where they met up with the British airborne troops east of the Caen Canal. The reserve battalion of the 1st Suffolks followed the British commandos to the outskirts of Colleville-Montgomery around midday and linked up with the commandos. They continued the attack, cleared the German positions, given the code names Morris and Hillman by the British, and then continued towards the ridge at Hillman, known as Point 61. However, the ridge would be anything but easy to take and the direct reason why the British failed to take Caen on D-Day. Before this time, there had been no reports of *Panzerdivision 21* in the area. The position at Hillman was well known to British intelligence, but they had not been able to determine exactly how many Germans were garrisoning the position. The heavily fortified facility, which was connected by trenches and underground tunnels, was actually manned by more than 400 men. The 1st Suffolks attacked it at 13:10 after an initial naval bombardment off Sword, sparking an inferno of a firefight as the British troops attempted to breach barbed wire barrages and minefields near the position. The British mortars and tanks did no damage to the German troops in the underground tunnels, and a stalemate of sorts ensued as the British soldiers began to fall in droves, unable break through the German defences. The stand-off lasted over an hour and it soon became clear to the division commander, General Rennie, that the objective of reaching Caen on D-Day was far from being achievable. Instead, it was decided that the 1st Norfolks would pass around the German position despite heavy fire from German machine guns. At the same time, reports came in that the *Panzerdivision 21* was heading towards the area. The stalemate at Hillman continued until 16:00, when small groups of British engineers and soldiers had crawled and fought their way through the German minefields and bursts of machine gun fire. Little by little, the British troops overcame the various defences in the German compound and the fighting continued for another hour before the Hillman position was in British hands. This only happened after the troops had thrown grenades into the air vents of the bunkers, which caused the majority of the German troops to surrender. However, a number of German soldiers, including the commander of *Infanteridivision 736*, *Colonel* Krug, remained in the underground bunkers and only surrendered the next day at seven o'clock in the morning.

The Hillman position was on the road to Caen, and with this location, the Germans' tactic of trying to delay the Allied attack during a possible invasion by placing positions behind the beach had paid off.[64]

In the western part of Sword, a link-up between Sword and Juno had failed because *Panzerdivision 21* had attacked in this area. The *division* had already made small attacks during the night of D-Day and captured large groups of British paratroopers of the 6th Airborne Division. Thereafter, the *division* remained in a holding position, and the reports

64 Stuart C. Robertson & Dale Booth, *Following in the Footsteps of Heroes: D-Day June 6th 1944*, (Devizes: Sabrestorm, 2014), pp.169–174.

that the landing at Sword was underway prompted the commander, *General* Feuchtinger, to await further counter-attack orders. The *division* was repeatedly attacked by groups of British paratroopers before the *division* commanders took the decision to attack the force that had landed at the River Orne. The commander of the *Panzerdivision 21*'s *Regiment 22*, *Colonel* Oppeln, was ordered to break off the counter-attack here and move his men back to the outskirts towards Caen to counter-attack in the coastal area between Juno and Sword. Without much resistance, *Panzergrenadierregiment 192* consequently reached the coast at around 8 p.m. on the evening of D-Day. However, *Panzerdivision 21* lagged a little behind, as the tanks found it difficult to advance quickly in the Normandy countryside. Meanwhile, the Canadian and British troops had observed the arrival of both the *Panzergrenadierregiment* and the *Panzerdivision* in the area, and at a distance of two kilometres, the Allied guns and tanks began attacking the armoured column. There were losses on both sides and a large part of the German tanks were lost. Furthermore, American and British aircraft attacked the German tanks and *Colonel* Oppeln made a tactical withdrawal to minimise losses. Only a small number of German tanks had reached the *Infanteridivision 716* at the front line at Lion-sur-Mer, and around 70 German tanks were destroyed or damaged.[65]

As D-Day drew to a close, the Allies had gained a foothold on the beaches in all five beach sectors. Utah, Gold, Juno and Sword were all successful, though not without major losses, but by no means as difficult to take as was the case on Omaha. The objective of reaching Caen in the Sword sector on D-Day had failed – German resistance had been too strong and had impeded the advance. 29,000 British soldiers had landed at Sword on D-Day, and 630 were dead or wounded. The sector was secured, but there were still significant dangers in the following days. By the end of D-Day, the British were five kilometres north of Caen. At the same time, *SS Panzerdivision 12* was heading towards the city from the south to defend it: the Battle of Caen would be decisive for the further development of the Normandy invasion.[66]

Hans Juelsdorf arrived on Juno aboard *Fort St Croix* on D-Day and spent four days in the sector unloading supplies. *Fort St Croix* then returned to England to pick up more supplies and then sailed to Sword. Although it was almost a week before Juelsdorf returned, there was still danger on Sword:

> On the second trip, we loaded in Southampton and sailed back to Normandy on our own. Once along the coast we were protected by a destroyer. This time we sailed towards Sword, and we came under heavy fire from the German artillery inland. The Germans tried to sink us before we could get our load of weaponry onto the shore. When a piece of shrapnel pierced the compass house, we got nervous about the big barrage balloon we had up to ward off aircraft attacks, and I let the gas out of it. The German planes only came at night, when they dropped mines all over the waters.[67]

65 Jakob Sørensen, *D-Dag – Operation Overlord 6. Juni 1944* (Copenhagen: People's Press, 2014), pp.248–251.

66 Jakob Sørensen, *D-Dag – Operation Overlord 6. Juni 1944* (Copenhagen: People's Press, 2014), pp.251–252.

67 This and the following are quoted come from an interview journalist, author and editor Jakob Andersen conducted with Hans Juelsdorf in Normandy in 1994.

Evald Brinck, Petty Officer on Board *Empire MT 123*
'I remember it was hit aft and I was told that many were killed.'

When Denmark was occupied, Evald Brinck was on board the Danish ship *Boringia*, and he decided to join The Buffs. The regiment quickly became known as a Danish regiment, where Danes who wanted to fight in Allied service would enlist. Brinck was trained as an infantryman and then reported for duty on board the passenger ship *Highland Princess*, which was in Scotland. Brinck would serve as part of the military crew aboard the ship, which had already been converted into an auxiliary cruiser with guns, depth charges and a rocket battery, but also to transport troops. Brinck sailed countless convoy trips before being transferred to the equivalent ship, *Como*. He was then ordered back to England to prepare an Empire boat at Sunderland, which Brinck did not realise at the time would be part of the Normandy invasion fleet. He arrived at Sword early on the morning of 7 June, and clearly remembers events in the Sword sector:

> We were a convoy of eight Empire boats, carrying troops, tanks and equipment, and we landed off the coast at Sword early in the morning of 7 June. The British had to consolidate the beach area before we could get permission to sail in with the troops. When we reached the beach for the first time, there was still shooting, and I could see a cliff further ahead where the British were firing inland. Here we were also authorised to fire at Caen with our four-inch gun if we thought we could hit something. I wasn't scared, but excited about it all. I think we were used to it from our time on board *Boringia*, where we always wore life jackets and were prepared for the possibility of being torpedoed. The little boats went back and forth all the time to pick up troops and take them to the beach. When we arrived in Normandy in the morning, we were told that in the American Omaha sector, the German soldiers were lying on the beach by the hundreds. I remember that we were close to the beach and the Germans shelled the area and hit a Danish boat that was near us, which was in the process of unloading. I remember it was hit at the stern and I was told that many people were killed. We were told to set up barrage balloons and we were also told not to fire on any German aircraft flying overhead, because the Royal Air Force was flying around up there.[68]

The Empire ships travelled continuously back and forth between England and Normandy to supply the front with soldiers, vehicles and other necessities. Tilbury in England became the fixed base harbour for the Empire boats, and the ships were given a fixed route, sailing 20 ships at a time at convoy speed, which meant they could be at the Normandy coast every three days. However, Brinck experienced delays during the convoy trips – one of which was when a boiler pipe burst on the ship – during bad weather with high seas and German prisoners on board the ship to be guarded. The delays also created greater dangers, as Brinck recalls:

68 Interview with Evald Brinck in March 2017.

> The accident with the steam pipe meant that we couldn't be off Dover until noon the next day. We had to sail as close to the coast as possible, yet the Germans on the French coast saw us and fired two shots at us. One shell hit the sea 50 metres from our starboard side and our gunwale was pierced. Then a corvette came out from Dover and accompanied us the last stretch to the mouth of the Thames.[69]

During the invasion, Brinck made 25 trips to Normandy.

A Precious Cargo

On board the Danish ship S/S *Alf* was perhaps the most unusual cargo compared to the other Danish ships involved in Operation Overlord. The ship carried 450 million invasion dollars to Normandy in the days after D-Day. The specially produced banknotes were to serve as payment to the Allied troops and the citizens of France, as the French franc was, unsurprisingly, at an extremely low rate during the war. 19 lorries aboard various cargo ships, including the S/S *Alf*, transported three billion US-printed invasion francs to the front on D-Day. The currency on board *Alf* was protected by 11 soldiers and 9 officers. The Allied troops taking part in the Normandy invasion were also handed invasion dollars when they boarded the freighters on their way to D-Day. This was noticed by Danish sailor Thorald Nielsen, who sailed for Utah aboard the *Tomsk*:

> Shortly after arrival, the Americans were each given a sum of money, the so-called invasion money, which was decorated with the Tricolour. Then everyone on board knew where the destination was. It wasn't long before the soldiers were in full swing playing poker, and some managed to get cleaned out before the ship had left the harbour.[70]

One of the Danish sailors who transported the invasion currency to the front line aboard S/S *Alf* was Karl Adolph Goth. As part of the upcoming invasion, Goth signed the V Articles and thus underwent training to enter a war situation.

The invasion currency was supposed to bring more balance to the country's economy in cooperation with the country's authorities, but it was not without problems in the countries the Allies reached. *Général* De Gaulle, for example, had to reluctantly accept the new invasion francs despite having proclaimed that it was counterfeit currency. The invasion currency was also introduced in other countries the Allies arrived in during the war such as Germany, Austria, Italy, and Japan.

The Danes who participated in the invasion in the armies of the various Allied countries also received invasion dollars to be spent in the occupied countries. John Andreasen, a gunner in the Canadian Army, describes the special currency that was handed out up to D-Day:

69 Evald Brinck, ... *de vil aldrig blive husket – beretning om danske søfolk 1940 – 1945* (Tåsinge: Evald Springeren Brinck, 2007), p.57.

70 Claus Arboe-Rasmussen & Bent Sørensen, *De befriede os* (Copenhagen: Folk & Sikkerhed, 2005), p.80.

> The location of the invasion was supposed to be a secret, but the next day we were given French invasion money, which consisted of 5-franc notes. The drivers, who were also given French money, gave it to the English girls as souvenirs, so I was quite sure that Hitler knew he was about to have a visitor.[71]

The Danish War Correspondent

Emil Blytgen-Petersen quickly became known as a spokesman for the Free Danish Forces. As editor of the London-based magazine *Frit Danmark*, he was asked by the BBC in early 1944 if he would be willing to act as a war correspondent on the front lines in Europe. After quick consideration and consultation with Christmas Møller, they decided that Blytgen-Petersen should cover the then still top secret invasion of Western Europe. However, he soon realised that he would not be able to participate on D-Day as the BBC's quota for correspondents was full. Good advice was expensive when the news came from the BBC, but shortly after D-Day, he found out that a large group of Danish ships had participated in the invasion, and to cover this participation, he was authorised to go to Normandy on behalf of *Frit Danmark* in London. He was to depart for the invasion area on a Maersk ship from Swansea, and on this occasion, Blytgen-Petersen discovered that the trip was far from harmless, as he had to sign a declaration that any descendants could not claim compensation from the British government if he was killed in Normandy. Worst of all, he was forbidden to leave the ship. However, the eager correspondent was not going to comply, and as he had a letter stating that as a war correspondent he could use the radio stations in Normandy to broadcast his stories, he was of course forced to go ashore.[72]

Blytgen-Petersen's arrival in Normandy was a chaotic affair as he had to find the BBC transmitter, as he recalls:

> At nightfall I was told that the BBC transmitter was in the neighbourhood of Bayeux, and I had driven in the opposite direction – towards Cherbourg… At the press headquarters in Bayeux I was then told that I was to be 'arrested and sent home in chains.' Not only was I a civilian, but I had gone from the American to the British front section. It was also a mortal sin for a war correspondent.[73]

He escaped further prosecution and continued his journey towards Caen, where he reached the Canadian front section after a few close-range German shells. He then made more reports from the front line and returned to London, where there was an entire dossier of reports on 'the mad Dane' who had followed the Allied front-line forces. The reports from Normandy clearly showed a very impressed war correspondent who had never before seen an operation of this calibre with his own eyes:

71 John Andreasen, unpublished war diary, p.32.

72 Emil Blytgen-Petersen, *Dansk Krigskorrespondent* (Copenhagen: Nyt Nordisk Forlag Arnold Busck, 1945), pp.1–13.

73 Emil Blytgen-Petersen, *Dansk Krigskorrespondent* (Copenhagen: Nyt Nordisk Forlag Arnold Busck, 1945), pp.2–3.

> At the very top of the cliff I see one of the greatest panoramas in the history of warfare. As far as the eye can see, I can see ships. Ships are anchored side by side, so that it becomes a forest of masts, and above them hover the silvery balloons that have accompanied the entire convoy journey as companions. Ships come and go, and on the horizon to the right and left I see a row of ship silhouettes with the chimney smoke behind them…. Everywhere, the traffic is directed by military police, and most often the driver drives by code names. Long convoys of lorries roll past, tanks rattling off towards the front. "We don't usually shoot at church towers," says my companion, pointing to a church lying in rubble. "But German snipers had gone up there and set themselves up with a machine gun." We pass camp after camp, lorry park after lorry park, in fields or in the large apple orchards, of which there are so many in this part of France.[74]

Blytgen-Petersen made two trips to Normandy as a war correspondent and was at the front line of the battles. After the Normandy campaign, he continued to report on the war from the front during the Battle of the Bulge in late 1944, after which he returned to London. He finally returned to Denmark on 7 May 1945, two days after the liberation of the country.

Status After D-Day

After D-Day, 6 June 1944, both the Allies and their German opponents could see that the Allied forces had succeeded in gaining a foothold on the Normandy beaches, although the final Allied victory was far from certain. One of the most high-stakes landings in history had begun with brutal and bloody fighting, and around 10,000 Allied soldiers had been killed, wounded or captured on the first day. German statistics estimate anywhere between 4,000–9,000 killed, wounded or missing German soldiers. The German propaganda of an impenetrable Atlantic Wall had suffered a serious blow after 6 June. In the western sector near Utah, the American paratroopers had generally achieved their objectives, despite the fact that the majority had landed outside their drop zones. Likewise, the American landing troops in the sector had penetrated 10 kilometres inland. Despite almost extreme resistance at Omaha, the American troops had also managed to break through the Atlantic Wall here. Likewise, the Canadians and British had broken through at Gold, Juno and Sword and fought their way inland towards the strategically important city of Caen. However, the Allies' plan to take Caen on D-Day had proved far more problematic than expected.

By midnight on 6 June, the 860 transport ships, 31 of which were Danish, had brought around 156,000 soldiers and 20,000 vehicles directly onto the invasion beaches. Despite the nearly 10,000 Allied dead, wounded or missing, the decisive foothold in Normandy had been secured, and the Allies had gained a foothold on an almost 100 kilometre stretch of coastline. The battles that followed during the night of 6/7 June would prove to be just as brutal and bloody as on D-Day itself. The transport ships brought thousands of replacement

74 Emil Blytgen-Petersen, *Dansk Krigskorrespondent* (Copenhagen: Nyt Nordisk Forlag Arnold Busck, 1945), pp.14–18.

troops to relieve the regiments that had been hit the hardest during the last 24 hours of D-Day.

From the landing beaches, the Allied troops worked hard to penetrate further into the areas behind the beaches and fought brutal battles to maintain their foothold on the newly opened front. Some 156,000 Allied soldiers were landed from the ships on D-Day, and five days later, 360,000 soldiers, 54,000 vehicles and over 100,000 tons of equipment and supplies were landed. In comparison, the population of Aarhus was 336,000 as of 1 January 2017. The delivery of troops and supplies continued in the weeks after D-Day, and the Danish warships were an important part of the continued progress of Operation Overlord.[75]

After D-Day, Operation Overlord entered the second phase of the plan. The continued flow of transport supplies was paramount now, but it was equally important to establish airfields in Normandy so that Allied airmen could extend the offensive further into mainland Europe than was possible from bases in England. The beachhead had to be expanded, the Allied bombers had to pave the way for the tanks, which in turn could pave the way for the infantry – the great war machine had to be kept going. Both the harbour city of Cherbourg and the areas south of Caen were of the utmost importance, as Caen in particular provided access to the Seine River for a further offensive against Paris and for the establishment of a number of airfields for fighter aircraft.

Spitfire pilot Kjeld Rønhof was woken before dawn on 7 June to make another morning patrol over the invasion coast. Rønhof's commander, Major Dycker, had reported a successful D-Day from an Allied perspective, with both St Mére Église and Bayeux liberated, but the invasion was highly dependent on continuous supplies to the Norman coast and it was now up to Rønhof and his colleagues to provide air support for the offensive. Despite the Allies dominating the airspace over the coastal area, danger was still present, as Rønhof recalls:

> The sun had not yet risen when we set out on our first morning patrol. When we got to our assigned patrol area, we saw an amazing sight. Everywhere there were tracers, exploding shells and burning buildings. There were several artillery duels below us. We were watching it all as if we were watching a show from the gallery when suddenly we were fired upon. One of our brand new pilots, Sergeant Olufsen, was hit by a shell and we saw him crash in the hills near Creseuilles. It was not a pleasant sight, as the crash ended with a huge explosion that he could not possibly have survived. A little shocked, we flew on with our patrol and came across one of the centre bridgeheads. Surprisingly, an ammunition store exploded, sending flames and smoke masses all the way up to 6,000 feet. It must have made quite a bang. Unfortunately, I think it was one of our own depots that blew up. It was a horrible sight, and yet somehow incredibly impressive.[76]

Although the initial D-Day landings were successful, the war was far from won and more battles were inevitable, as the Allies, including many of the Danish invasion participants, would come to realise.

75 John Keegan, *Six Armies in Normandy*, (London: Penguin Books, 1982), pp.283–292.
76 Kjeld Rønhof, *Vi fløj for Friheden* (Copenhagen: Four Stripes,1991), pp.107–108.

Floating Harbours: Mulberry A and Mulberry B

As Operation Overlord progressed and the Allies pushed deeper into Normandy, there was an increasing need for additional supplies for the fighting troops on the front line. That is why sailors were busy shipping supplies back and forth from England to Normandy. The lack of harbour facilities was also a significant problem for the logistics of shipping. However, this was a perspective the Allies had already considered when they chose Normandy as an invasion area. Winston Churchill was keenly aware of the logistical problems that could arise in the wake of the invasion. Huge floating pontoons were built that could be assembled into one large floating harbour. The individual pontoons would be towed by tugs from England across the Channel to Normandy, where they would then be assembled into a harbour. Danish engineer Oscar Faber was the leading expert on the project, and Danish contractor Peter Lind was also involved in the creation of these huge floating harbours, which consisted of hundreds of floating concrete and steel caissons to be transported to the invasion coast. Two floating harbours were assembled and established in Normandy, one off Saint-Laurent-sur-Mer (Omaha) and one at Arromanches (Gold). These were named Mulberry A and Mulberry B. The floating harbour at Arromanches was commonly called Port Winston, much to Winston Churchill's satisfaction.[77]

Mulberry A would only operate for 10 days. A violent storm ravaged Normandy in the weeks following D-Day, and this proved to be the end of Mulberry A. On 19 June, the floating harbour was destroyed and had to be abandoned as a port facility. After this, the American Omaha sector and the Danish warships that sailed here were once again forced to bring their cargo directly onto the beach using flat-bottomed ships and the DUKW amphibious vehicles. Henrik Bødker Knudsen from Frederikshavn remembers the effect the storm had on the harbour facilities:

> While we were riding out the storm, a lot of debris came drifting past us, including several dead American soldiers sitting in their life jackets as if they were armchairs floating around. When we asked if we should pick them up, we were told that there were other ships whose job it was to do so. When the wind had died down again, we went in to continue unloading. Everything was total chaos where the harbour had been, so we anchored just outside and unloaded the rest of the petrol.[78]

Also on board *Gudrun Mærsk* was J. P. Sørensen, who by now had become a very experienced wartime sailor. Like his shipmate, Bødker Knudsen, Sørensen clearly remembers the artificial harbours and the violent storm:

> Within a couple of days, some huge tugs arrived with concrete boxes. They were to be used for a harbour. They made a big mistake though – outside this harbour a breakwater was made out of some steel boxes. After a few weeks, we had a hurricane and these steel boxes broke loose and smashed the cement boxes. We sailed into all

77 Guy Hartcup, *Code Name Mulberry* (Barnsley: Pen and Sword Books, 1977), pp.15–23.
78 Henrik Bødker Knudsen, *Krigssejler* (Copenhagen: Frihedsmuseets Venners Forlag, 1992), p.100.

> this mess with *Gudrun Maersk*, and the next day we spotted two Danish steamers lying on the beach.[79]

Henrik Bødker Knudsen and J. P. Sørensen on *Gudrun Mærsk* transported petrol to the countless vehicles in Normandy and docked at Mulberry A, which only operated for 10 days. As Operation Overlord progressed, two months into the invasion, a giant pipeline was installed from England to Normandy. This could carry fuel directly from England to the coast of Normandy, making the transport ships that carried fuel to Normandy redundant. The pipeline, codenamed PLUTO (Pipe-Line Under The Ocean*)*, could pump 4,000 tons of fuel from England to Normandy every day. Despite the near total destruction of the Mulberry A, Allied engineers had already made provisions for how exposed the two floating harbours would be in a given storm. Hundreds of old and discarded ships were transported to Normandy. Here they were sunk in a circle around the floating harbours to shield them from wind and weather.*80*

Floating harbours became a central part of the Danish war sailors' work. Jørgen Linnet from Klitmøller arrived off the coast of Omaha on 10 June aboard the *Alan A. Dale*. The ship was loaded with lorries and ammunition, and by this time Omaha had been cleared of bodies and destroyed equipment from D-Day. Linnet clearly remembers the challenges of the Danish sailors when it came to loading, but also the important role he and the other Danish sailors played in general:

> Loading on the open sea was always more challenging than at a harbour. The sea had a lot to say about how the unloading would take place. When the weather is fine, it's no problem, but when it's windy, you have to be careful not to unload anything into an amphibious boat and tip it over. It was very small boats that picked up the equipment. There were no harbour areas. It was all loaded into amphibious boats that constantly travelled back and forth to the shore. They worked around the clock to get as much military materiel as possible to the troops inland. It was also important to get some airfields built over there as soon as possible, as they probably didn't want to go back with their Spitfires et cetera so they could save on fuel and utilise their air force better.[81]

As a naval inspector during Operation Overlord, Holger Jensen was heavily involved in the logistics process that included the floating harbours. He arrived at the normally idyllic Vierville-sur-Mer in Normandy, which by this time was heavily fortified with German gun emplacements painted as bathhouses to fool the Allied airmen. These gun positions had already been neutralised by D-Day, so Jensen was able to focus on his logistics role as a naval inspector. To the west, he could spot the first concrete pontoons that had been shipped in from England. The Phoenix breakwaters were 60 metres long, 18 metres high and 15 metres wide. After arriving on the Normandy coast, the pontoons were lowered and moored to form an entire pier, and anti-aircraft guns were placed on them against possible German

79 J. P. Sørensen interviewed by Ulrik Brandt at Bombebøssen in Christianshavn on 9 August 2005.
80 Guy Hartcup, *Code Name Mulberry* (Barnsley: Pen and Sword Books, 1977), pp.73–93.
81 Quoted from interview with Jørgen Linnet in February 2016.

attacks. Jensen could see how this pier formed an arm on the western side of Omaha, and on the eastern side about 60 ships were moored like a breakwater, codenamed Gooseberry.[82] Establishing the artificial floating harbours was crucial for logistics, Jensen recalls:

> Landing ships with 20 to 30 tanks and as many fully loaded lorries could roll out in 15 minutes, like driving off a ferry. The large number of landed vehicles and soldiers and equipment was becoming a space problem on the beach. It was impossible to get ashore. The Germans had destroyed the existing roads from the beach to the shore and they were simply rendered useless. At the same time, the Germans had concentrated their defences very much around the roads. However, the US Army had the foresight to bring bulldozers to dig a new road up through the dunes and inland. This work lasted 3 days.[83]

Erik Egebak was on board the American Liberty ship, *Joseph Pulitzer*, which made several stops at Mulberry A near Omaha before going down in the storm on 19 June:

> Meanwhile, some large vessels had come up alongside us with some very large pontoons. 2 or 3 or 4 pieces connected together to form a mighty raft with one large regular deck. There were some very large outboard motors on the back. We followed that pattern all summer. We did several trips between Southampton and Omaha Beach.[84]

When establishing the Mulberry harbours, the Allies were well aware that facilities of this size would attract attention, which is why it was necessary to defend against German attacks. For this reason, anti-aircraft gun positions were mounted on top of parts of the harbours. Captain Folmer Clausen on board the Danish ship *Lillian* also noticed this:

> What impressed me most, however, was the sight of the huge artificial harbour that the Americans established on the coast. It has been a demanding job to drag the many storey high caissons across the canal. On top of the caissons, entire gun emplacements were built – the so-called 'storks' nests' – and a large number of ships were lowered to serve as breakwaters, with vessels weighing 20,000 tons between them. It was a huge undertaking.[85]

Another Danish sailor who served aboard the ships of other Allied nations was Chief Engineer Knud Jensen. He was on board an old American steamer that had Omaha as its destination. He arrived at Omaha on D-Day and witnessed the destruction and chaos in the sector. He watched as the American soldiers on board crawled down the side of the ship and

82 Guy Hartcup, *Code Name Mulberry* (Barnsley: Pen and Sword Books, 1977), 77–97.
83 The following quotes come from Holger Jensen's account for the DR radio programme 'Den Store Landgang' by Poul S. Poulsen, 6 June 1969.
84 Quote from Cicerone ApS and Nexus Communication's interview with Erik Egebak and archive material in connection with the production of the documentary 'The War Sailors'.
85 Report from the Mitfanoe.dk archives.

continued in the landing craft towards the shore, where he could only watch as they became fewer and fewer. He later described the sight: 'You can't explain it – it is something not worth looking at. It's horrible.'[86] He also witnessed the sinking of older ships to be used as breakwaters at Mulberry A near Omaha. The older steamer he was on board was to be used as a breakwater. However, the breakwater was not much use, as the Mulberry A was heavily damaged during the storm on 19 June as previously mentioned.

The logistical dilemmas that arose in the aftermath of D-Day were in many ways solved by the Mulberry harbours. Over 2½ million soldiers, ½ million vehicles and 4 million tons of cargo came ashore through these artificial ports during the 77 days of Operation Overlord.[87]

The Allied Advance

However, the overall success on D-Day and the equally successful advance shortly afterwards ran into major problems for the Allies. One of the biggest obstacles, unforeseen by Allied intelligence, was something as simple as the landscape of the Normandy hinterland behind the beaches. *Bocage* is a Norman word meaning, among other things, a small stone wall or small wooded area, and it was precisely this that made the Allied advance so difficult. Everywhere the roads were surrounded by metre-high banks topped by thick hedges, which the Germans could use to great advantage in strategic defence positions. If the Allied infantry tried to leave the narrow roads, the open and wide fields would often be tactically defended by their German opponents. Many times, the German defenders would let the Allied soldiers wander into the open fields and then catch them in a deadly crossfire via machine gun positions placed in the corners of the fields. In addition, German mortars were also often set up in these fields. Similarly, Allied tanks had great difficulty manoeuvring in the Normandy landscape, which was quickly dubbed 'Hedgerow hell'.

The Normandy landings were a success for the Allies, but despite the successful initial phase of the invasion and the fact that the Allies now had a foothold in France, the ultimate success of the invasion was still far from certain. The importance of maintaining a foothold on French soil and the continued advance inland was indisputable, but the focus on supplies was almost more important. Maintaining the constant flow of convoy ships back and forth in the English Channel was paramount. The invasion would simply grind to a halt if supplies did not arrive. Allied dominance in the air was also important in defeating the German defenders and continuing the strategic bombing of the railway network to prevent German supplies from reaching the front. The French Resistance also played a crucial role in intelligence gathering and the destruction of the railway. It is estimated that the French Resistance carried out almost 1,000 acts of sabotage against the railway network on D-Day alone.[88] The Allied air force had its work cut out for it in the attacks after D-Day, which Danish Spitfire pilot Kjeld Rønhof participated in. When the Americans launched a major attack against the German armoured forces on the road to Cherbourg on 17 June, Rønhof's squadron was repeatedly ordered to stand by while a large force of Allied fighters was already in the

86 Christian Tortzen, *Kampen på Havet* (Copenhagen: Information, 2011), p.200.
87 Guy Hartcup, *Code Name Mulberry* (Barnsley: Pen and Sword Books, 1977), pp.138–142.
88 Jakob Sørensen, *D-Dag – Operation Overlord 6. Juni 1944* (Copenhagen: People's Press, 2014), p.262.

vicinity. Only when the army had identified specific targets was Rønhof sent out. However, it was not only the German resistance that posed a danger to the Allied airmen. Allied pilots also had to prepare for and be ready to deal with technical problems on the aircraft, as Kjeld Rønhof himself experienced when he was on patrol on 17 June and the Spitfire's engine suddenly stopped abruptly and he only narrowly manoeuvred between barrage balloons:

> When I couldn't get the engine started again, I had to either find a suitable emergency landing place at breakneck speed or parachute out. Luckily, I spotted an American landing strip carved out of a forest, and I was lucky enough that the strip was directly below me… The strip was very poorly maintained, as several steel mats had come loose after countless take-offs and landings. A Thunderbolt that had landed just before me had loosened the mats even more. Due to my high speed, I was also about to end up outside the square. The Spitfire swayed violently from side to side as the steel mats lifted, and of course a huge cloud of dust rose up. With the rest of my speed, I managed to get close to an air traffic control tent, which I could just make out through the dust cloud.[89]

Rønhof's dramatic landing was known as a 'dead stick landing'. After the emergency landing, he was able to jump out of the plane unharmed, and for the first time since 5 February 1939, when he was a sailor aboard the M/S *Kina* loading at Dunkirk, he was again able to set foot on French soil. Rønhof and the Norwegian squadrons were also involved in an air battle on 15 June, when the German Luftwaffe counter-attacked north of Paris at Evreux Airfield. The 15–20 German Focke-Wulf 190 fighters were promptly attacked and the German and Allied aircraft engaged in prolonged combat from 0 to 15,000 feet. The Allied fighters shot down eight German aircraft and damaged nine.[90] It was crucial for the Allied air force to damage the *Luftwaffe* as much as possible. The Allies did not want to take any chances with the already dangerous *Luftwaffe*, as any German fighters could still be a threat.

On D-Day itself, the Germans had 891 aircraft at their disposal, of which only 497 were combat-ready. The Allied fighters and anti-aircraft units provided a significant counter to the *Luftwaffe* as the Germans lost 208 aircraft over D-Day and the following four days, while another 108 were damaged. The resistance from the *Luftwaffe* was no longer a crucial part of the German defence. The Danish anti-aircraft gunner in Canadian service, John Andreasen, also noted the massive effort to reduce the German threat from above. The Canadian anti-aircraft gunners often acted as support against incoming German aircraft, and three days after D-Day, Andreasen's gun position was close to an Allied airstrip typically used by Spitfire and Typhoon fighters. It was here that Andreasen's platoon shot down their first German fighter:

> Two German fighters came in at a height of 1,000 metres, and when the anti-aircraft guns started firing at them, one of them was hit and crashed to the ground in flames. The other nosed down to get away from the rain of anti-aircraft shells

89 Kjeld Rønhof, *Vi fløj for Friheden* (Copenhagen: Four Stripes,1991), pp.111–112.
90 Susanne Zima Feierskov, *Med vinger og våben* (Copenhagen: Gyldendal, 2011), p.229.

> sent after it, firing almost continuously with its machine guns. At the same time, it was being fired at by the other guns in our platoon. We couldn't fire because there were some trees in the way, but as it was about 20 metres in front of our gun and we could see the pilot in his seat, he probably thought he had made it. When he was right in front of our gun we opened fire. By then he was no more than about 10 metres above the ground and crossed right in front of us. I was in the right seat and had to watch the height, the other seat had to watch the speed. When I got the fighter in my sights, I shouted, "On" and at the same time the other man shouted, "On", and when the machine was right in front of the gun the corporal shouted, "Fire" and everything happened at once, we sent 4 shells at the plane, it was only a matter of a few seconds and then it was over. The first shell hit right in the cabin and when it exploded, the pressurised machine tipped over on its side, one wing hit a roadside tree and the machine crashed to the ground and exploded with a deafening bang about 10 metres from one of our guns.[91]

Andreasen and the Canadian anti-aircraft gunners were frequently in action during the remainder of Operation Overlord and were part of the air defence of the front line, which continued to be pushed further and further into France.

The continuing flow of supplies to the front line was still paramount, which meant that Danish sailors still had a significant role to play in the remaining period of Operation Overlord. The Mulberry harbours were important in the days after D-Day, but it was crucial for the Allies to take larger, regular harbour areas in order to be able to continue the constant delivery of supplies. The capture of the large harbour town of Cherbourg northwest of Utah was thus a priority. The American 4th Infantry Division, of which Henning Møller from Fredericia was a part, was tasked with taking the city, but due to the massive challenges of the *bocage*, with its many high and thick hedges in the area, the advance did not happen as quickly as expected. In the American sector, the continued supplies from the freighters arrived primarily at Omaha. This was also where the majority of the 31 Danish freighters docked, but the disadvantage of the supplies arriving at Omaha instead of Utah was that the vital supplies thus took longer to reach the 4th Infantry Division, which was fighting to take Cherbourg.

The Allied advance towards the strategically important major cities was, in addition to the challenges of the Normandy landscape, also resisted by the *panzerdivisionen* that could do great damage to the Allied troops in the dense landscape. The Allies' overwhelming superiority in the number of tanks deployed in the invasion area was central to the advance. Despite the fact that the Germans had already deployed 600 tanks to the area six days after D-Day, including six of the dreaded Tiger tanks, the Allies had managed to land 2,700 tanks.[92]

Although the German fleet was also severely depleted after D-Day, it still posed a great danger to Allied ships transporting vital supplies across the English Channel. In addition to the threat of mines, a number of German E-Boats and U-Boats still posed an additional threat. On D-Day itself, 35 German E-Boats managed to stay at sea, 16 of which were sent to

91 John Andreasen, unpublished war diary, p.39.

92 Jakob Sørensen, *D-Dag – Operation Overlord 6. Juni 1944* (Copenhagen: People's Press, 2014), p.264.

the area between the Bay of the Seine and the Isle of Wight, while the rest were sent to the Bay of Biscay. Despite the German E-Boats' presence in the waters off Normandy, they only managed to sink one Allied ship – the Allied warship presence and resistance was simply too much for them to handle. The importance of destroying the fast and aggressive smaller German E-Boats was paramount, as they could quickly cause heavy damage to the vulnerable cargo ships.

Danish radio telegrapher Hans Mathiasen, on board *Empire Beatrice*, experienced this first-hand when the ship was on its way to England from Normandy on 27 July:

> An E-Boat, which in itself is a very small target and which, moreover, moves at a speed of about 50 miles, is very difficult to hit. Two E-Boats, however, were hit and blew up with their petrol and torpedoes, but a third came at full speed towards the convoy, fired its two torpedoes, after which it turned off and quickly disappeared in the darkness of the night. On one of the torpedoes was our name.[93]

Danish sailor Evald Brinck, now a British soldier aboard an Empire boat, also witnessed the whole terrifying scenario on board a nearby ship:

> When we came to the mouth of the Thames with the rest of the ships, we came to lie alongside Captain Nielsen's new ship *Empire Beatrice*. As we crossed the English Channel at night, his ship was hit by a German torpedo. It was fired by a German E-Boat, which had managed to sneak in between the ships of the convoy so that we could not fire at it. In the darkness I could see the entire stern of *Empire Beatrice* hung down into the water. Many soldiers died, as well as a number of Danish sailors.[94]

The German E-Boats managed to do extensive damage to the convoy of transport ships, especially SS *Empire Beatrice*. Six Danish sailors, two Danish lighthouse keepers, a gunner and 12 soldiers on board were killed. However, *Empire Beatrice* stayed afloat and the survivors were rescued.

The focus of the Allied air force was also to damage the German fleet as much as possible. On 14 June, a bombing raid was launched against the port of Le Havre, involving 346 Allied bombers. Fortunately for the Allied planes, strict orders had been issued by the Germans not to fire on aircraft near the harbour. This order was presumably issued because the German planes were expected to give cover to a large number of E-Boats that were about to enter the harbour. The Allied bombers thus had more or less free rein and managed to sink 19 tugboats, three torpedo boats, 11 E-Boats, 20 minesweepers as well as damaging 11 other vessels. The following day, another bombing raid was conducted near Boulogne, where another 37 German ships were sunk. These raids were crucial in minimising the threat to Allied transport ships during the remainder of Operation Overlord.[95] The Danish Lancaster

93 Christian Tortzen, *Kampen på Havet* (Copenhagen: Information, 2011), p.201.

94 Evald Brinck, *... de vil aldrig blive husket – beretning om danske søfolk 1940 – 1945* (Tåsinge: Evald Springeren Brinck, 2007), p.58.

95 Jakob Sørensen, *D-Dag – Operation Overlord 6. Juni 1944* (Copenhagen: People's Press, 2014), pp.263–264.

rear gunner, Andreas Moldt, also took part in the continued air offensive after D-Day and participated in the bombing raid on the German ships at Le Havre:

> When we started, there wasn't a cloud in the sky; they only came near Le Havre. As we were approaching the target, I looked up and saw our own fighters, whose presence we had already been informed of. They were to form a protective 'umbrella' over us. Everyone could see that they were in place because they were so high up that they were making contrails. After passing us, one-half of the 'umbrella' turned left, the other half turned right and then came over us again from behind. We saw no German fighters that night. But if there were no fighters, there was flak, and it was so close that we saw several machines being hit and crashing, and felt the smell of burning gunpowder, while small, grey-black clouds flew past to the right and left. There was nothing wrong with their rangefinders, but there was something wrong with their new fuse, which was supposed to make the shells explode when it was near a target or when timed. We bombed and Jack reported, "Bombs gone!" There were 300 aircraft in the attack, and I heard the skipper say that now we had to find a way out of all the confusion that resembled Piccadilly Circus at rush hour.[96]

ITEM turned south and then west, after which Moldt reported that the bombs had hit their target. A German flak battery at Honfleur fired at the aircraft on the return journey, but it was out of range, allowing Moldt and the rest of the crew to return to the safety of England for a while.

The Allied air forces' effective campaign against the *Luftwaffe* in the period after D-Day was a key element in maintaining the constant flow of supplies from the transport ships into Normandy. The Danish ships and sailors aboard other Allied ships also noticed how the pressure and fear of the *Luftwaffe* was removed from the transport convoys after the Allied air force became completely dominant in the air. The combined joint effort to prevent German supplies from reaching the railways and the focus on degrading the German *Kriegsmarine* and *Luftwaffe* helped take the pressure off the merchant ships and transport convoys, ensuring that vital supplies continued to reach the fighting forces in Operation Overlord's offensive.

But there was still no guarantee that Operation Overlord and the Allied invasion of France would end in success. There was still fierce German resistance, as was the case at Caen.

Battle of Caen

Despite the overall Allied success on D-Day and the rapid advance from all five beach sectors, in the days that followed, the German defenders could still find positive trends. After the Allies had gained a foothold in Normandy and the British and Canadian forces had reached the outskirts of Caen relatively quickly, the plan to take this important city in a matter of

96 Andreas P. Moldt, *Natbomber: Slaget om Europa som en Dansker Oplevede det i Invasionssommeren 1944* (Copenhagen: Gyldendal, 1985), p.73.

days would prove far more difficult to realise than expected. Units from *SS Panzerdivision 12* had no intention of letting Caen fall into Allied hands and they waited patiently for the British troops to begin entering the city. Caen and the surrounding area was important to both sides, firstly because of its location along the Caen Canal and the River Orne, which could be used as a natural defence position. Secondly, the terrain around the city itself was relatively flat and open compared to the rest of the *bocage* landscape of Normandy, making the area around Caen ideal for the use of airfields, such as at Carpiquet, where fierce fighting over the airfield would ensue. General Montgomery's troops made three major assaults on the strategically important town before finally managing to drive the Germans out of it. The generally difficult progress of the Allies in the dense and hilly terrain of Normandy also contributed to the fact that Caen was not fully secured until almost two months after D-Day, when the Allies were finally able to break through and hold the medieval city.[97]

Niels Wiesneck was in Canadian service. He had been separated from his regiment before D-Day and was subsequently allowed to transfer back to his old regiment, the Essex Scottish, which also took part in the bitter fighting for Caen. The regiment had helped to put pressure on the Germans, and once the city was taken, they would then attack the area to the south. The Battle of Caen would prove to be one of the most brutal of the battles that Wiesneck participated in:

> Our task was to take Caen. We were sent in from the south side, but we realised it was going to be a difficult task as the Germans had mined the whole area. Roads, doors and rubble, everything was set up with what we called booby traps. Even their fallen soldiers were tied to mines. Thus we were very apprehensive about penetrating further into Caen. So the air forces were sent for, and they did so emphatically that they had almost bombed us along with the Germans. The forces on our flanks suffered heavy losses from the Allied bombers.[98]

The Essex Scottish were later positioned alongside a Polish regiment south of Caen. Before they could advance towards the German positions on the south of the city, the area initially had to be bombed by American bombers to degrade the German defences as much as possible. About 25 large bombers began the bombardment in the regiment's sector, but the planes began the bombardment too short, which resulted in the bombs landing around Wiesneck's regiment and the Polish regiment. This was to have disastrous consequences for the Poles. Wiesneck recalls:

> They were simply wiped off the map. It was a big accident, and there was a big fuss afterwards with fatalities and destroyed equipment… We went around these big bomb holes that had been made… and then there were another 40–50 big Flying Fortresses. We were looking up at these machines, and we could see those bomb doors opening up, and down came these rows of bombs around us. We had a piece of yellow silk and yellow smoke with us, which was just to indicate that we were

97 Antony Beevor, *D-Dag: Kampen om Normandiet* (Copenhagen: Lindhardt & Ringhof, 2009), pp.194–210.

98 Quoted from Kystmuseet Bangsbo Arkiv's material about Niels Wiesneck, where a taped interview is available.

> friendly, and it was shot up so that the American airmen wouldn't bomb us. We were really afraid that they would hit us too. Everyone threw themselves into these bomb craters to seek cover, but it probably wouldn't have made any difference if they had been hit anyway.
>
> But then the Germans were pushed further and further back into Normandy, all the way to Falaise.[99]

Wiesneck and the Canadian Essex Scottish Regiment were part of the 2nd Canadian Infantry Division when, as part of Operation Goodwood, they took part in the attack on Caen on 18 July. The Canadian part of Operation Goodwood was given its very own code name: Operation Atlantic. One of the major battles they fought was at Verrières Ridge outside Caen, a ridge that was fiercely defended by German troops from the *SS Panzerkorps 1*, who had deployed guns, tanks, mortars and infantry from three divisions. On 20 July, the South Saskatchewan Regiment, the Queen's Own Cameron Highlanders and the Sherbrooke Hussars attacked with air support, but they were quickly repulsed by the German defenders on the ridge. The South Saskatchewan lost 282 men during the attack. Two *SS Panzerdivisionen* quickly launched a counter-attack against the Canadian troops, with Wiesneck and the Essex Scottish standing in the way. The regiment held the line of defence, but the Essex Scottish lost close to 300 men during the day. The Canadian defence was then reinforced by troops from the Calgary Highlanders and The Black Watch, and support was provided by the Canadian 3rd Division, after which they did succeed in completely stopping the German counter-attack – but not without heavy losses.

Svend Moustgaard Jensen: Into Battle with The Black Watch

Svend Moustgaard Jensen was born on 22 January 1901 in Filskov near Billund. He travelled to Canada in 1927 to work and to try his luck in a foreign country. When war broke out, he joined the Canadian Army and subsequently became part of the Royal Highland Regiment of Canada, better known as The Black Watch. He joined the army as a private and by the time the Normandy invasion took place, he was 43 years old. The Black Watch landed in Normandy on 6 July as part of the 2nd Canadian Infantry Division. Like Niels Wiesneck, Svend Moustgaard Jensen also participated in the Battle of Caen and the Battle of Verrières Ridge.

The Black Watch functioned as a subdivision of Operation Atlantic called Operation Spring, which aimed to break out of the area near Caen. By taking the Verrières Ridge, the Allies would have a clear advantage because they could then deploy artillery on it and shell the southern parts of Caen, pushing the Germans further back. This would also open the Caen-Falaise Road, allowing two British armoured divisions to advance towards Falaise. On 25 July, The Black Watch attacked the ridge with support from the British 7th Armoured Division and the Canadian 4th Armoured Division. In the target area, *SS Panzerkorps 1*

99 Quoted from Kystmuseet Bangsbo Arkiv's material about Niels Wiesneck, where a taped interview is available.

had already been significantly reinforced with four additional battalions, additional tanks and 500 guns. The Black Watch was due to attack at 05:30, but was delayed until 08:00 due to fierce German resistance at St Martin, which was on the road to the ridge. During the attack, the regiment lost two commanding officers killed, but it was decided nonetheless to continue the advance. When the Canadians began their assault on the ridge at 09:30, they fell easy prey to German artillery, mortars and especially the infamous 88mm guns. The Canadians had to retreat with heavy losses.

During Operation Atlantic, in which Niels Wiesneck and the Essex Scottish took part, the Allies lost 1,349 men, the majority of whom were from the 4th and 6th Canadian Infantry Brigades. After initially failing to capture the strategically important Verrières Ridge, General Montgomery ordered a new offensive codenamed Operation Cobra to break out of Normandy. During the same period, after several attempts the ridge was finally captured. After its capture, the Germans made repeated attempts to recapture it but were repulsed. Operation Cobra and the final offensive to definitively break out of Caen and Normandy could then begin in earnest. When the battle for the ridge was over for The Black Watch, only 15 of the 325 soldiers who began the offensive returned. Svend Moustgaard Jensen was among those who fell during the attack on the German fortified ridge – on 25 July 1944. He was buried in a temporary cemetery before being finally laid to rest in the Canadian cemetery at Bretteville-sur-Laize. The Black Watch's fatal attack on the ridge was statistically the costliest for a Canadian battalion since the raid at Dieppe in 1942.

The casualty statistics for Operation Spring were nearly 500 soldiers killed and nearly 1,000 wounded or captured. It is estimated that the German defenders lost almost 1,300 men, all of whom are buried in the German cemetery La Cambe in Normandy.[100]

The Danish anti-aircraft artilleryman in Canadian service, John Andreasen, also took part in the Battle of Caen. Not far from Niels Wiesneck's regiment, Andreasen was located with other artillery and anti-aircraft positions near Grentheville. After D-Day, Andreasen had been involved in the constant offensive to push the Germans further inland, and during this period, he had experienced several close bombardments from German artillery and bombers. On the evening of 24 July, his platoon had set up their gun, but as they were preparing dinner, a German shell suddenly came hurtling into their position. No one was hurt, but the shell hit directly on the platoon's cooking equipment, and dinner was ruined – much to Andreasen's frustration. At night, German airmen dropped flares in small parachutes to light up the area, and Andreasen describes the terrifying feeling of being completely exposed and visible, so that the German airmen could now see the Canadian positions from a distance. The anti-aircraft defence positions tried to shoot down the small parachutes flares, but without success. Shortly afterwards, Andreasen could hear the German aeroplanes buzzing in front of their position in the darkness, and knew that they would be bombarded shortly:

> …we couldn't do anything, we could hear the machines, but we couldn't see them. It was a nerve-wracking hour. The bombs howled on the way down. I had a feeling that every bomb was going to hit me personally, but again we were lucky, there was

100 David J. Bercuson, *Maple Leaf Against The Axis* (Ontario, Stoddart Publishing, 1998), pp.120–166.

> a lot of shrapnel that hit the gun and the vehicle, and a couple of field guns blew up, but the ammunition was the worst hit.
>
> The grain was burning almost everywhere, we had to go out with our extinguishers and put out the fire, but it didn't look good, many soldiers had been hit and almost all the telephone lines that were on the ground were disconnected, so the guns had no connection with their command post... How close the Germans came that night, I don't know, but when the field guns fired, their shells exploded about half a kilometre before our position. When morning came, everything was quiet again, so we could see how much damage we had taken.[101]

At the end of the morning, the battery reported that 23 gun carriages had been damaged, but that they could be repaired within a short time. On 25 July, the artillery positions around Andreasen's gun position fired continuously at the German lines. They provided support for the infantry who were now on the breakout from Normandy during Operation Cobra. The Canadian anti-aircraft positions followed and provided support against German fighters.

Lancaster gunner Andreas Moldt also took part in the Battle of Caen, as the Allied air force aimed to bomb the German positions in Caen itself in order to force the German defenders to surrender. As we know, this was an almost impossible task, as the Germans had dug into the extremely favourable strategic positions in and around the city. Moldt took part in a bombing raid on the city on 7 July. Lancaster *ITEM* was loaded with 13 x 500kg bombs. Several of them were set on timers so they did not go off at the same time when they hit the ground. The general problem for the Allied air force during these bombing raids was that their own troops were often just a few hundred metres from the German lines. As a result, it was crucial to hit precisely so that the bombs did not land among their own troops, as Niels Wiesneck and others had experienced.

At 19:20, *ITEM* was airborne along with around 550 bombers and fighters. The flight from the coast, which was about 17 kilometres into Caen itself, went smoothly and according to plan until they reached the western part of the City, as Moldt recalls:

> About a kilometre before all hell broke loose; the air was full of tracer bullets of all calibres, 40mm and 20mm, in a veritable fireworks display. They passed all around us and between the small clouds of slightly heavier calibres. Everything the Germans could shoot with was apparently in use. Our own troops had started firing on the German positions before we reached the target, so the enemy was actually under double fire. Several shells exploded close to us, and we didn't get away without holes.[102]

After the bombing, *ITEM* turned right and flew towards the coast again and back to its own lines. For a while, Moldt had a full view of Caen from the rear gunner's seat and told the rest of the crew that Caen was enveloped in dust and smoke.

---

101 John Andreasen, unpublished war diary, pp.45–46.

102 Andreas P. Moldt, *Natbomber: Slaget om Europa som en Dansker Oplevede det i Invasionssommeren 1944* (Copenhagen: Gyldendal, 1985), p.98.

Danish war correspondent Emil Blytgen-Petersen visited war-torn Caen after his arrival in Normandy on 13 July 1944, after the city had been liberated. He arrived after a long jeep ride from the coast, during which several shells had hit close to the car, and he described the extensive destruction the city had been subjected to very aptly:

> At the entrance to Caen there are fires from the German artillery fire, and we drive into the city, liberated a few days ago, which is the worst damaged of the French cities I have seen.
>
> The ruins of shattered houses scrape out towards the street, where there is just enough room for carts to make their way through the rubble. The shops are closed. Unlike Bayeux, which has escaped unscathed from the battle, and where there are stacks of Camembert cheeses in the windows and large butter blocks on the counter, this is almost a dead city, and the few people you see seem unreal.[103]

The Battle of Caen and the surrounding areas was long, bloody and brutal. The Caen area became the last German bastion in north-eastern Normandy. It is estimated that more than 50,000 Allies, Germans and civilians were killed, wounded or missing during the battle for Caen. Before D-Day, the civilian population of Caen was close to 60,000. After the Battle of Caen, the population was 17,000.[104]

The Falaise Pocket

After the breakout from the Caen area, the Allies pushed the Germans even further inland. General Patton and the US Third Army pushed through the German lines and on 1 August, he managed to break through at Avranches. With German forces no longer immediately in front of the armoured column, Patton ordered more forces towards the Brittany peninsula and simultaneously ordered armoured columns to the east and north in an attempt to encircle the Germans. In a desperate attempt to halt the Allied advance, Hitler himself ordered a counter-attack at Mortain, west of Caen, and Falaise on 7 August. It was a desperate plan to try to prevent Patton's supplies from reaching their destination. However, the German counter-attack stalled relatively quickly. There were no longer enough troops or equipment to resist the Allied forces.

At the same time, Canadian and British troops had advanced to Falaise from the north and American forces had reached the area from the south. The German troops were now surrounded and fierce fighting broke out to resist the Allied advance on all sides.

Niels Wiesneck of the Canadian Essex Scottish Regiment took part in the fierce fighting at Falaise and the attacks north of the town. After the war, he reflected on what it was like to be part of the war as a private soldier, where you can do nothing but follow the action:

103 Emil Blytgen-Petersen, *Dansk Krigskorrespondent* (Copenhagen: Nyt Nordisk Forlag Arnold Busck, 1945), p.22.

104 Antony Beevor, *D-Dag: Kampen om Normandiet* (Copenhagen: Lindhardt & Ringhof, 2009), pp.211–233.

> At some point I found a map of Normandy, and of course it helped to clarify approximately where we were in the country. I tried to mark the places we had been on the map. I could see that we had been through Bayeux, Caen and all the way down to Falaise. As we got further down, the Germans' grip on us got looser and looser because the front was getting wider and wider… But we came through this wonderful, beautiful old medieval town called Falaise, and it was in flames. It was all wooden houses from the Middle Ages, so it was all in flames and smoke. We walked down a street where the houses were burning on both sides of us. We rested on the other side of Falaise for 24 hours, where they took stock of how many people had fallen and been wounded… And that was no small thing.[105]

Canadian anti-aircraft gunner John Andreasen also took part in the offensive at Falaise. After taking up a position at Hautmesnil, Andreasen moved on towards Falaise. A daytime bombardment from Allied bombers landed close to the Canadian lines, and as the first bombers naturally hit the target zone first, the other bombers followed suit and dropped their bombs on the same target. This had fatal consequences for many of the Canadian troops, with countless casualties and fatalities. Bombardments from friendly aircraft were not unusual during the invasion, and the consequences were often disastrous. Andreasen experienced being attacked several times by his own air force: 'We now called ourselves "Soldiers of 3 Colours" because we had been bombed by the German, British and American airmen.'[106] Andreasen's sergeant was removed from the front after the bombardment due to a nervous breakdown, and Andreasen also reports that neither he nor his comrades were the same again afterwards.

Despite the fatal bombardment, it was still necessary to press on to surround the Germans at Falaise. On 20 August, Andreasen reached the fleeing German troops and the Canadian anti-aircraft guns were set up on a ridge. Here they had a complete overview of the situation and the artillery was merciless, as Andreasen recalls:

> First we attacked the leading cars in the convoy, and when they were stopped, we targeted the last ones, and when that was done, we destroyed the entire convoy. We went on like this for 3 or 4 days and nights, we didn't get any sleep. At night our airmen dropped large illumination bombs that exploded in the air and sent light into the sky and lit up the whole district for about 10–15 minutes, and when they had fallen to the ground, new ones were dropped, and so they continued all night. Oh, how tired and sleepy we were, because there was a lot of pressure on all of the Canadian troops at the moment.[107]

The Canadian troops were under constant pressure during the invasion and never knew when to be ready for battle:

---

105 Quoted from Kystmuseet Bangsbo Arkiv's material about Niels Wiesneck, where a taped interview is available.

106 John Andreasen, unpublished war diary, p.54.

107 John Andreasen, unpublished war diary, p.58.

> …we never knew when a German tank or armoured car was coming. It was just after dark one evening, as we sat with our binoculars to see if we could find new targets for our shells, when suddenly we heard a machine gun cough out its stream of bullets. We swivelled our 40mm gun so that it pointed in the direction where the noise was coming from. Suddenly we saw a large SS armoured car, which had caterpillar tracks instead of rear wheels, coming out of the woods with the accelerator down. We opened fire on it, got a hit on the engine and stopped it. It contained only four SS soldiers and an American pilot who had been their prisoner, but before our soldiers got to them, the American held them at bay with one of their own machine guns and the Germans were quite happy to be captured.[108]

The German troops' escape from Falaise made them easy targets for Allied artillery and especially fighter planes. The Danish Spitfire pilots in the Norwegian squadrons also took part in overflights near the fleeing German units. One of these was Kjeld Rønhof:

> There was plenty to shoot at. The whole German army, or rather the remnants of the German army in France, was on the run and we did not allow them a moment's peace. On 26 August, I destroyed with my flight 2 lorries that were set on fire and 3 others were totally destroyed. The prize was a Spitfire, slightly damaged near Neufchâtel. All in all, the squadron destroyed 10 lorries that day.[109]

Little John

John Christmas Møller (Little John) was born on 7 October 1924. He was the son of the conservative politician and former foreign minister John Christmas Møller (1894–1948), who during the war was a major political opponent of the Danish Government's cooperation with the German occupying forces. This led Christmas Møller to London, where he made great efforts to promote the Allied cause and to incorporate Danes into the Allied forces. Christmas Møller's son, commonly referred to as Little John, shared his father's mind-set, which led to him entering active service in the British Army. He enlisted in the Grenadier Guards, where he was commissioned as a cadet on 27 November 1942 at the age of 18. During the summer of 1943, he was promoted to second lieutenant just two months before his nineteenth birthday, and in February 1944 he was promoted to first lieutenant. Here he was attached to the 2nd Company of the 1st Motor Battalion, 5th Guards Armoured Brigade of the Guards Armoured Division. He was given command of a reconnaissance platoon, which meant he would be part of the forward units. He had 30 men under him in four half-track vehicles. Given his young age, this was an important role for young Christmas Møller, and the majority of the soldiers he commanded were already battle-experienced, including from the evacuation at Dunkirk. Throughout his active war career, Christmas Møller's platoon operated alongside another platoon consisting of four M4 Sherman tanks.

---

108 John Andreasen, unpublished war diary, p.59.

109 Kjeld Rønhof, *Vi fløj for Friheden* (Copenhagen: Four Stripes,1991), p.136.

After several months of intensive training leading up to the Normandy invasion, the division was ordered to move to Southern England in the spring of 1944, and by this time it was clear to Christmas Møller that something big was in store. When they were ordered to stand shortly before D-Day, it soon became clear to the young officer that the division was to be considered as support after the invasion itself had been launched. Days passed after D-Day and the Allies fought their way forward in Normandy. The men of the Grenadier Guards became more and more eager to get into battle as time passed, and on 15 June they were finally ordered to move to Tilbury to board two Liberty ships that would take them to Normandy. However, as a heavy storm was raging during this period, their departure was delayed, and they only reached Normandy on 24 June where they landed at Arromanches in the Gold sector.

Christmas Møller saw combat for the first time during the fighting at Caen. As part of three armoured divisions, of which the Guards Armoured Division was one, the 1st and 2nd Battalions entered combat near the Orne River northeast of Caen. They managed without major losses and helped push the Germans out of Caen. They then encountered greater resistance near Cagny, including German tanks from *SS Panzerkorps 1*, but the division with 2nd Battalion in the lead eventually cleared the town of German resistance. In the following days, the 1st Battalion dug in near the town, where they were repeatedly subjected to German artillery bombardment. After three hard days, they were ordered away from the front line for a while and replaced by other troops. After the heavy fighting, 1st Battalion reported 15 soldiers killed and 6 officers wounded. 2nd Battalion had 10 soldiers killed, 3 officers killed and 22 tanks destroyed. The two battalions spent the next eight days on the outskirts of the almost completely destroyed city of Caen, where they reported the constant stench of corpses hanging in the air.

On 2 August, Christmas Møller and the rest of the Grenadier group received orders to head south from Caumont to the St Martin Des Besaces area, where they were met almost immediately upon arrival by significant German resistance in the form of buried tanks and anti-tank guns. With support from tanks from the 2nd Battalion, the 1st Battalion was ordered to take the strategically crucial Hill 309, which was ideal for covering an important road junction and where the Germans were located. They succeeded in capturing the hill, but over the next 36 hours the Germans fought hard to retake the ridge. Only when units from the 15th Scottish Division arrived was the ridge finally secured.

During 3 August, the Grenadier group was sent further south to take the high ground near the town of Arclais. The two battalions encountered only scattered resistance along the way, although including German Panther tanks, but they suffered no casualties. However, when they arrived just outside the town, Christmas Møller's 2nd Company came under heavy fire. A platoon leader was killed, there were several wounded and the company's second in command was also badly wounded. The half-tracks and tanks from 3rd Squadron were ordered back to take up a defensive line. At dawn, the Germans attacked, but were repulsed and the fighting continued throughout the day until the Germans finally gave up their counter-attack in the evening. Then the two British companies continued towards the Vire-Falaise main road to push the Germans even further into what would become known as 'the Falaise Pocket'. The fighting on 2 and 3 August had been extremely hard for Møller's company – 50 were dead and wounded. After a few days of rest, the Grenadier Guards arrived at the town of Viessoix, which was on the road to Falaise. Here the Germans had entrenched themselves, mined the roads and set up roadblocks. However, the Germans withdrew when the Grenadier Guards approached the town and instead fired their artillery at the British troops. At the same time, the Americans and Canadians stormed forward from the other sides of Falaise, and the Germans were increasingly squeezed into the pocket. On 13 August, the fighting in Normandy was over for Møller and the Grenadier Guards when they were assembled near the town of Fleur.[110]

The Allied attack on the German Army at Falaise had disastrous consequences for Hitler's forces, and the battle was the Germans' final defeat in Normandy. Although 50,000 German soldiers managed to escape from Falaise, more than 40,000 were taken prisoner and around 100,000 were killed, 10,000 German soldiers fell until 21 August 1944 alone.[111]

Christmas Møller, with the rest of the Grenadier Guards, continued with the Allied advance, which led them to Belgium, where they fought and later took part in the overambitious Operation Market Garden in The Netherlands in September 1944. An operation that was an Allied attempt to end the war before Christmas, 1944. Christmas Møller was part of the forces that were to reach Nijmegen and capture one of the strategically important bridges. Among other things, he made a name for himself by rescuing a wounded American soldier; a soldier who was caught in the crossfire and unable to get to safety on his own. Operation Market Garden was a major disaster and the Allies had to withdraw and regroup. By 24 March 1945, however, the tide of the war had turned in the Allies' favour. The Germans were in retreat and a large-scale crossing of the Rhine was imminent. Møller took part in this crossing, which targeted the city of Wesel. The fierce fighting continued, and in the coming weeks the Allies advanced slowly but steadily. However, 9 April 1945 proved fatal for John Christmas Møller:

> 2nd Coy/3rd Sqn had been warned that it might meet resistance in Dalum. So when they were met by machinegun fire on the outskirts of the village, the leader of the attack, Platoon Commander Lt Møller, jumped onto the front Troop Commander's Sherman tank to coordinate the effort. This was normal procedure on such occasions and usually posed no risk, but just then a hidden body of men fired on Lt Møller and mortally wounded him, and shortly afterwards Lt A. R. Ryan met the same fate. After this, Major A. M. H. Gregory-Hood decided to counter the resistance with a full scale attack.[112]

The city was then taken. John Christmas Møller was killed on the same day as Victoria Cross recipient, Major Anders Lassen.

---

110 Aksel Willumsen, *Lille John – I Britisk Tjeneste* (Copenhagen: Frihedsmuseets Venners Forlag, 2017), pp.13–19.

111 Antony Beevor, *D-Dag: Kampen om Normandiet* (Copenhagen: Lindhardt & Ringhof, 2009), pp.496–505.

112 Aksel Willumsen, *Lille John – I Britisk Tjeneste* (Copenhagen: Frihedsmuseets Venners Forlag, 2017), pp.79–88.

Disembarkation in the South of France

On 15 August a less extensive landing than the Normandy operation took place in the South of France between Toulon and Cannes under the code name of Operation Dragoon. The plan was originally intended to be part of the overall Overlord operations, but due to lack of resources, Dragoon became a standalone operation.

The purpose of the landing was to secure important harbours on the French Mediterranean coast, putting additional pressure on the remaining German forces in the area and opening another front. Dragoon was dependent on several factors: firstly, Rome had to be secured in June, and secondly, Operation Cobra in Normandy had to be completed. As both operations went according to plan, the landing in Southern France could also proceed as planned. The Free French and American Forces were initially selected to take Toulon and then Marseille. However, this plan was changed to include a landing at Saint-Tropez.

The Dane Verner Jensen took part in the landing at St Tropez. He was a sailor when war broke out in Denmark and experienced being torpedoed. He later enlisted in the American Army. He took part in the landing at Anzio in Italy and fought in Italy before taking part in the landing in Southern France:

> We landed on 'Red Beach' just off St Tropez. Here we took 500 prisoners. Most of the bodies on the coast were Poles, the Germans had fled north and left the Poles to defend the coast. The company commander ordered 12 infantrymen to sit on each tank, and then the three tanks drove along the road until someone started shooting at us. We were driving through a small forest when all hell broke loose around us. We jumped down from the tanks and started shooting again when we heard someone shouting in French and the shooting stopped. They were civilians from the Free French. They came running and embraced us. They thought we were Germans.[113]

Several Danish ships also took part in the invasion of Southern France, transporting supplies and troops to the area. One of the sailors who took part was Captain Martin Bantz, who had sailed out from Frederikshavn in March 1940 and only returned to Denmark 5 years, 8 months and 6 days later in December 1945. During the landing in Southern France, he transported troops to the coast and vividly recalls what it was like to participate in an operation of this scale:

> The troops we had on board were Americans, and they were some of the finest people I have ever met. We shipped up to the South of France, where the invasion took place. Our place was a little west of Nice around St Raphael. It was very exciting to be there and it was the first time I really saw the DUKWs at work. The invasion was led by the Americans and I have to say that it was American all the way through. It was fast-paced and everything was done in a jiffy.[114]

113 Claus Arboe-Rasmussen & Bent Sørensen, *De Befriede os* (Copenhagen: Folk & Sikkerhed, 2005), p.37.

114 Kåre Lauring, *Mellem Bomber og Torpedoer* (Copenhagen: Gyldendal, 2004), pp.140–165.

Over 94,000 soldiers and 11,000 vehicles were landed during the first day of 15 August. Due to the progress of the battle during and after Operation Overlord in Normandy, a majority of the Germans in Southern France had been transferred to fight the Allies in the north. This made the landing in Southern France less difficult than in Normandy. The Allied forces met relatively little resistance from the German defenders and within 24 hours they had already penetrated 30 kilometres inland.[115]

Elsie Margaret Hansen, Nurse, 36th General Hospital 'It was only in France that I got access to penicillin for the wounded'

Elsie Margaret Hansen was a surgical nurse aboard the hospital ship *Arcadia* during the landings in the South of France. She was born in Stubbekøbing, Denmark in 1918 and emigrated to the US with her family in 1929 when her father wanted to find work. She spoke a little English when she arrived in the US, so she had a relatively easy time mastering the language. Leading up to World War II, Elsie enlisted in the army as a surgical nurse, serving mainly aboard the hospital ship *Arcadia*. During the war, the ship was present during the campaigns in Italy, Africa, Germany and, not least, in France. Elsie Hansen achieved the rank of first lieutenant during the war in 36th General Hospital. In connection with the landing in Southern France, she tended wounded soldiers from the fighting and assisted in operations on the wounded around the clock for three days. When the ship was full, it sailed to Italy, where the wounded were treated in a hospital. There were several advantages to embarking on *Arcadia* – advantages that may seem trivial today:

> We were stationed at Naples when I was ordered to embark on the hospital ship, *Arcadia*. It was wonderful at first as we had clean sheets and milk. It was something I hadn't seen in a very long time. Our unit manned three hospital ships. The soldiers would be shipped out to us on barges and then I would receive them in the operating theatre. We never left the ship as we were always needed.[116]

After *Arcadia* had delivered the wounded to the hospital in Italy, the ship returned to the South of France to repeat the procedure. Here, a field hospital was set up in a large villa near St Tropez that had been abandoned. Elsie and the other nurses were stationed there for a period of time with strict orders not to approach the beaches as there were still mines in place. Later they also received German prisoners. The German doctors assisted and cared for them in their operating theatres. 'It was only in France that I had access to penicillin for the wounded – in fact, it was the first time I saw penicillin in the war.'

After two months in the villa, on 5 October 1944, when the roads were passable again, Elsie's unit moved on to Dijon. Here they stayed for 6 months, treating the wounded. In October 1945, they were sent to Le Havre, from where they sailed home to the USA.

115 William B. Breuer, *Operation Dragoon: The Allied Invasion of the South of France*, (New York: Presidio Press, 1996), pp.83–90.

116 This, with the following quotes, are from a Veterans History Project interview with Elsie Margaret Hansen <http://memory.loc.gov/diglib/vhp/bib/loc.natlib.afc2001001.33436>.

The Aftermath of Operation Overlord

The Normandy invasion was one of the major turning points of the Second World War and marked the beginning of the end for the Nazi regime after the Allies gained a firm foothold on French soil. The invasion operation, which began with Operation Overlord, lasted 77 days and was highly costly for both sides. The statistics speak for themselves: around 225,000 Allied casualties and close to 500,000 German casualties. In addition to large numbers of civilians who perished.[117] The Battle of Normandy also had a huge materiel cost, but it was necessary to open the second front. The retreat of Hitler's troops was the result of a combined Allied effort on the Western and Eastern Fronts. The retreat in the West, which started on D-Day on 6 June 1944, ended in 1945 with the surrender of Germany on 8 May 1945 – VE Day (Victory in Europe Day). The opening of a Western Front would be decisive for the outcome of the war, as both the Allies and the German troops knew.

The invasion itself became an important focal point leading up to D-Day itself – either the Germans would succeed in defending the Normandy coastline, knocking the Allies back into the sea and winning a battle that – if large enough – could decimate the Allied forces; or the Allies would manage to break through the defences and gain the foothold in Europe that was so extremely important to shorten the war. If the Allies were thrown back into the sea by the German defences, it would have prolonged the war considerably, and it is not possible to say anything for certain about when the Allies could gain a foothold in the West. At this point in the war, the Germans were already under tremendous pressure, but a possible victory over the Allies in Normandy did not mean that they could win. One of the most important factors was that the US had become part of the war after the Japanese attack on Pearl Harbor on 7 December 1941, thus increasing the Allies' chances significantly.

One of the reasons why D-Day and the preliminary exercises for Operation Overlord succeeded was the intense confusion the Allies managed to create around the invasion. The German General Staff in Normandy considered the invasion on 6 June to be a feint, and they understood the actual gravity of the situation far too late. Despite the German Atlantic defences, the Allies' numerical superiority on land, sea and air was crucial to the outcome of D-Day and the subsequent offensive. In several landing sectors, the Atlantic Wall was far from complete, and the German troops on the beaches were of mixed quality. Despite all this, the Germans still managed to put up strong resistance. This was definitely the case in the defence of Caen, and it characterises the effectiveness of German troops during the Second World War. The German Waffen-SS divisions fought with a manic belief in the defence of Nazi ideology, and this had an impact on the effectiveness of the troops. Despite the superior Allied presence, the outcome of the invasion was not a foregone conclusion and the military strategy of both sides was crucial. The scenario might have been different if the German panzer divisions had been positioned at the landing beaches and not at Calais and inland on that fateful 6 June 1944.

For those involved in the invasion, the foothold in Normandy and the massive subsequent pressure against the Germans inland was a sign of hope ahead – a hope that the tide of

117 Antony Beevor, *D-Dag: Kampen om Normandiet* (Copenhagen: Lindhardt & Ringhof, 2009), pp.557–563.

war was turning. This was of utmost importance to the Allied war participants, as Henrik Bødker Knudsen, who arrived in Omaha aboard *Gudrun Maersk*, recalls:

> Once the Allied armies broke out of the bridgeheads and seized the major harbours along the French Channel coast, you had the feeling that the tide of war had turned. You could once again go to bed and go to sleep with your eyes closed.[118]

The invasion of Normandy was a step towards breaking the Nazi regime. For the Allies, after Operation Overlord, almost another year of constant fighting awaited before the final victory was secured – it was still a long and bloody road to Berlin. The German troops in the West were defeated in Normandy, but not yet defeated in Europe. The Allied victory over the Nazi occupiers would not have been possible without the sacrifices made by every single combatant to liberate a Europe on its knees.

Without each individual's effort, will to win and sacrifice for the good and the free, our world could have been very different today.

The Danish Losses

The Battle of Normandy was of great importance to the more than 800 Danish sailors aboard the 31 Danish ships and the dozens of Danes in other Allied forces. Although the statistics are not complete, it is estimated that approximately 20 Danish sailors died during Operation Overlord.[119] Four of the Danish ships that took part in the attack were lost during and after the Battle of Normandy. *Aarø* was the first Danish ship to arrive on the Normandy coast on 6 June and continued to carry supplies to the ports there even after Operation Overlord had ended. On 6 October, the ship arrived in Omaha during a heavy storm. The crew was unable to manoeuvre the vessel, which resulted in it colliding with a coaster and sinking. Another Danish ship, *Empire Beatrice*, was hit by a torpedo from a German E-Boat on 27 July while in England to pick up more supplies. 21 men died on board the ship, including six Danish sailors and two Danish stokers. Additionally, the Danish ship *Outlook* (formerly *Anna Mærsk*) was sunk near Antwerp on 12 December 1944 when it struck an underwater wreck.

Jørgen Linnet's ship, *Alan A. Dale*, which also came to Omaha, was torpedoed off Antwerp on Christmas Eve 1944. The ship was lost, although everyone on board was rescued. The dramatic event is still vivid in Jørgen Linnet's memory:

> On Christmas Eve we were torpedoed near Antwerp. It was probably one of the small two-man submarines that had fired a torpedo at our ship. On our way towards Antwerp at half past two or three in the afternoon, there was a huge bang. I was sitting with the second mate down in the saloon, and we could feel how the ship gave a big jump. He shouted for us to hurry out, and we got out and headed for

118 Henrik Bødker Knudsen, *Krigssejler* (Copenhagen: Frihedsmuseets Venners Forlag, 1992), p.101.

119 The following is based on the research of Erik Kragelund, former chairman of the Danish War Sailors' Association. The number of Danes killed in Operation Overlord was previously estimated to be 10–15, but current statistics point to around 20 casualties.

> the deck. Everything went completely dark, because the light went out all over the ship. When I got out on deck, the ship started to heel over to port, and I thought we were going to tip over. But luckily we didn't. The ship stabilised itself in a 45-degree list. The lifeboats were hanging outside the ship, so I headed towards one of them. However, the crash had caused the lifeboat I was near to land in the centre of the deck, so I had to rush to the other side to jump into the lifeboat that was there, but there were already 12 people in it. The anchor was lowered to anchor the ship so it wouldn't drift further away. A fire had started on board, which we then tried to extinguish. We had a cargo full of mail for the soldiers, which burnt up.[120]

The outcome of Operation Overlord was clear when the 77 days of the operation were over. The Allies had pushed the Germans all the way back to Falaise, and an Allied landing was also carried out in Southern France. The goal of opening the second front was officially a reality. The efforts of the Allied sailors were an essential part of Operation Overlord's success – the tons of supplies were key to keeping the Allied machine running.[121] Participation in the invasion was not only of great personal importance to the Danes involved, but the overall effort also had a huge impact on Denmark's reputation after the invasion was over. This was a fact that the King George VI of Great Britain also wanted to emphasise when he gave a speech in the House of Commons in November 1944, after the success of Operation Overlord was a reality. He wanted to thank all the countries that took part in Operation Overlord and fought for the united Allied cause. However, he had a problem with how to refer to the Danish sailors, as they were not officially allies:

> My fleets secured the passage of the great invasion convoys to attack the coasts of Western Europe; they still maintain the flow of supplies to my armies and ensure that the food and materials on which the life and labour of the nation depend arrive safely and on time. All this could not have been accomplished without the splendid valour displayed by our sailors and by those of the United Nations and Denmark.[122]

Of the more than 800 Danish sailors who took part in the invasion, around 20 perished. One of those who became part of the Danish casualty statistics was Svend Aage Christensen (b. 1917) from Skagen. Before the Danish occupation, he was a fisherman in the North Sea, but later enlisted under the Allied flag as a wartime sailor. In connection with the invasion, he boarded a Norwegian steamer. After the bow of the ship was damaged during an attack during the Normandy landings, he jumped into the sea and was never seen again. It is believed that he was killed by the ship's propeller. He was decorated with both a Danish and a Norwegian medal.

The approximately 20 Danish sailors who died in Operation Overlord may seem like a drop in the ocean compared to the overall statistics for the invasion. However, the more than 800 Danish sailors were an essential part of the Danish merchant fleet and its overall contribution to the Allies' transport supplies. Of the 245 Danish ships that sailed for the

120 Quoted from an interview with Jørgen Linnet in February 2016.
121 Christian Tortzen, *Kampen på Havet* (Copenhagen: Information, 2011), pp.195–203.
122 Christian Tortzen, *Søfolk og Skibe 1939–1945, bind 4* (Copenhagen: Lindhardt & Ringhof, 1985), p.440.

Allies during the war, 128 never returned to Denmark, and 83 of them were torpedoed during the war. Furthermore, close to 1,100 of the 6,300 Danish wartime sailors in Allied service died during the war. Based on these statistics, these sailors were the group in the Danish population with the most fatalities. Overall, around 2,300 of the approximately 13,000 Danish sailors who were part of both the home and foreign navies perished.[123]

Some of the Danes mentioned in this book who fought for the Allies in other armies and those who emigrated to other Allied countries also became part of the casualty statistics. This book includes the fates of those who belonged to Denmark and made the ultimate sacrifice for freedom in the world. These were primarily represented in the armies from England, Canada and the USA. What these individuals had in common was that they all had a connection to Denmark and all wanted to fight for the Allies. These casualty figures may seem minimal compared to how many people participated and died in the invasion, but their efforts were an important part of the overall Normandy landings.

Even more important was their contribution to the image of the overall Danish effort for and to the Allies.

Around 1,000 Danes served in the Allied forces during the Second World War, including dozens who participated in the Normandy invasion in addition to the more than 800 Danish sailors. Despite this number of Danes in Allied service, there was no actual Danish unit where they were all officially gathered. However, several Danes were part of smaller groups: Seven Danish-manned minesweepers in 137 Minesweeping Flotilla went into action in early 1945, a significant number of Danes served in the British regiment of *The Buffs*, and there were a number of Danish pilots in the Norwegian Air Force Squadrons, but specific Danish units did not exist as they did for their Norwegian colleagues. Danish involvement in Allied service during the Normandy invasion was therefore generally characterised by sporadic participation, which means that the overall picture of Danish participation in Operation Overlord has never been comprehensively collated.[124]

Invasion Beachhead in Denmark

In the period after Operation Overlord, when the war had shifted to the countries north of France, it was still uncertain when Germany and eventually Berlin could be taken. With Denmark and Norway still occupied by German combat-ready divisions, Allied commanders assessed that there was a risk that the Germans would retreat to Denmark and Norway to make a stand there.

This also led to wild rumours that there might be a need for some kind of Allied invasion in Jutland, albeit on a smaller scale than the one that had taken place in Operation Overlord. However, these rumours of an invasion into Denmark took on a more concrete character than just wild rumours. Erik Schmidt-Hansen, a Dane who had been in Allied

123 The following is based on the research of Erik Kragelund, former chairman of the Danish War Sailors' Association. As more archives and databases have become available in recent times, casualty statistics have become more accurate and especially for the statistics of Danish wartime sailors killed in Allied service, which have increased in number compared with Tortzen's research.

124 Jakob Sørensen, *For Danmarks Ære* (Copenhagen: People's Press, 2011), pp.277–284.

service during the war had subsequently returned to Denmark, where he was tasked with translating American invasion books in the event of a landing in there.

> We were to make an invasion manual in Danish for the American Army when it entered Danish soil. Was an invasion of Denmark being prepared? You will naturally ask, and the answer is: Exactly the same invasion manuals were made in this building in 22 different languages.[125]

Invasion manuals were typically prepared in countries where Allied troops were to operate. However, rumours of a potential landing in Denmark became even more tangible when specific plans were drawn up in North Jutland for a possible landing, and the North Jutland resistance movement was to play a significant role in such an invasion. In January 1945, the Resistance in Vendsyssel drew up a specific operation plan for the active military groups in the area. The overall plan was to capture and secure a bridgehead in Vendsyssel in connection with an Allied invasion of Denmark. The establishment of this bridgehead was to be done in collaboration with Allied airborne troops and other Allied forces, but the main part of the plan, in relation to securing access for the Allies, was largely up to the resistance. In other words, the resistance would be part of an actual military operation, similar to the way the French Resistance had acted in cooperation with the Allies when a large part of the Normandy railway network was sabotaged before D-Day.

The German Support Point Group Hirtshals was carefully selected by the resistance to act as the invasion bridgehead. Several factors suggested that the area around Hirtshals was optimal for an Allied landing, and the harbour area in particular was an important part of the plan. Support Point Group Hirtshals consisted of two coastal batteries located east and west of the town with various concrete positions with anti-aircraft guns, anti-tank positions and powerful 10.5cm guns. In addition, infantry support points and more concentrated fortifications were placed around the harbour itself. Despite this, the harbour at Hirtshals was the most realistic to possibly take, as both Skagen and Frederikshavn were significantly more fortified. Danish military intelligence estimated that during the summer of 1944, between 1,200 and 2,000 troops had been placed in the harbour.

But because of the progress of the war, more troops had moved south, reducing the German fortification's garrison at Hirtshals to just 685 men in January 1945. The majority of these 685 soldiers were Czechs and Poles in German service, and only 21 of them were actually German! This was also a crucial fact for establishing an invasion bridgehead in Denmark, as morale would be lower than with a dedicated German unit. Crucial to the Danish Resistance was also the fact that during the summer of 1944, significantly more arms deliveries arrived from England to them, increasing the chances of success in attacking and defeating German battle groups.

In addition, the Resistance in Vendsyssel had been successful in recruiting one of the Czechs in German service to carry out espionage missions for them. Ludvig Batka had been forced into German service; he had been captured by the Germans in 1941 and deported to the Dachau concentration camp near Munich, where he was then allegedly forced to

125 Erik Schmidt-Hansen, *5 Aar i Allieret Tjeneste* (Copenhagen: Branner, 1946), p.119.

enter German service. He arrived in Hirtshals in 1943, was entrusted with the function of telephone operator and was able to listen in on telephone conversations. It was partly on the basis of Batka's intelligence to the resistance that the final decision to attack Support Centre Group Hirtshals in connection with an Allied invasion was made. He submitted documents, maps of gun positions, machine gun nests, trenches and the number of soldiers in the area. Central to Batka's intelligence was also his assessment that the conscripted troops in German service would not resist an Allied invasion.

If the Allied invasion took place at Hirtshals, the resistance movement was prepared with 400 combat-ready men, which was roughly the total strength of the resistance movement in Vendsyssel in January 1945. Before the operation, the resistance fighters were to meet and conduct specific training and exercises with weapons and maps to simulate the capture of Support Point Group Hirtshals. At the same time, in cooperation with England, it was planned that two groups of Allied paratroopers would be dropped in Vendsyssel in parallel with the resistance's attack on the German strongpoint to confuse and disperse the approximately 20,000 German soldiers who were located throughout Vendsyssel. One group of paratroopers was to attack a hill near Sindal to distract the Germans from the real primary action. At the same time, the other group of paratroopers would attack south of Hirtshals, where heavy artillery was positioned and keep the access roads to Hirtshals under fire so that German reinforcements could not reach the town. While the resistance and paratroopers attacked the German defenders, an Allied naval squadron with landing forces was to begin the approach to Hirtshals.

Additionally, the North Jutland branch of the Civil Beskyttelses Udrykningskorpset (the CBU, the Civil Defence Emergency Corps), which was established in 1941, was to act as support for the paratroopers. Despite their civilian purpose, the CBU column had already undergone training in partisan warfare in connection with the plans.

The attack was to take place while the German main company was lined up in the barracks camp in Hirtshals town, leaving only a few sentries in the large fortress. At the same time, Czech Ludvig Batka had to disconnect the position's telephone connections.

The idea of taking the German position was that the Germans would then have to attack their own defence positions, which would undeniably be a difficult task due to the strong armament, especially as the Germans also had little field artillery and only a handful of tanks in Vendsyssel in January 1945. After the capture of Support Point Group Hirtshals, the aim was to secure a naval base for the Allies. In addition to securing a harbour, the Allies needed an air base. Due to its isolated location and the fact that the Germans had effectively abandoned the facility, Knivholt's flat area west of Frederikshavn was chosen. The Germans had already established an airfield here in 1940. As part of the grand invasion plan by the resistance and intelligence services, additionally discreet reconnaissance was also carried out at the airfield to assess the defences.

The invasion of Hirtshals, and Denmark for that matter, never materialised, but the plans existed in case the Allies had chosen this solution. The plans were largely inspired by the Normandy landings, where all the elements of the Normandy landings were transferred in a scaled-down format to the invasion plans for Denmark. Navy, airborne forces, landing troops and cooperation with the resistance were all key elements of the Danish invasion plans. The plan was large scale and daring, and whether the outcome would have been favourable to the resistance and the Allies is anyone's guess. The resistance movement was not a battle-hardened military unit, and it was significantly inferior to the German troops in Vendsyssel in both numbers and armament. In addition to the German troops' willingness to fight, they were also still better trained and armed than the Danish freedom fighters. However, the plan for the Danish invasion is concrete and visible proof that the war in January 1945 was by no means considered as won by the Allies. If the German leadership had decided to retreat to Denmark and fight to the last man in one last great battle, it was not inconceivable that an invasion along the west coast of Jutland would have been considered, but the reality was that it never happened and instead Berlin was taken in April-May 1945, with Hitler committing suicide on 30 April as a result of the series of defeats leading to the inevitable conclusion.[126]

126 Henrik Gjøde Nielsen, *Storm Fæstning Hirtshals – Den nordjyske modstandsbevægelses planer om et invasionsbrohoved i Vendsyssel* (Copenhagen: Vendsyssel årbog, 2008), pp.21–31.

Engineer Oscar Faber, one of the driving forces behind the Mulberry Harbours. (Faber & Partners)

Modern photo of the remains of Mulberry B at Arromanches. (Private collection)

Mulberry A off Omaha was destroyed in one of the worst June storms in 80 years. (US National Archives)

Vehicles arrive on Gold via Mulberry B on 16 June 1944. (Library of Congress)

American troops entering open fields surrounded by the thick hedges. (US Army)

Contemporary view of the area near Sainte Marie du Mont behind Utah beach, showing the high and dense hedges that caused the Allied advance so much trouble. (Private collection)

Aerial view of the Normandy landscape. The hedged fields are clearly visible. (US National Archives)

Allied reinforcements poured into Normandy in the period after D-Day. In this photograph replacement troops from the 4th Infantry Division arrive in the Utah sector. (US National Archives)

The French railway network at Tourcoing is bombed by Allied bombers from the 2nd Tactical Air Force in the weeks after D-Day. (Imperial War Museum)

American soldiers pass the church at Colleville-sur-Mer in the Omaha sector in the days after D-Day. (US National Archives)

The church at Colleville-sur-Mer today in what was, in 1944, the Omaha sector. (Private collection)

German E-boats (speedboats) posed a significant danger to the slow transport ships. The image shows E-boat *S204*, with white flag, surrendering at Felixstowe in England on 13 May 1945. (Imperial War Museum)

The Danish ship *Avance* unloading pipelines in St Vaast harbour in the months after D-Day. Note the Dannebrog. (M/S Museet For Søfart)

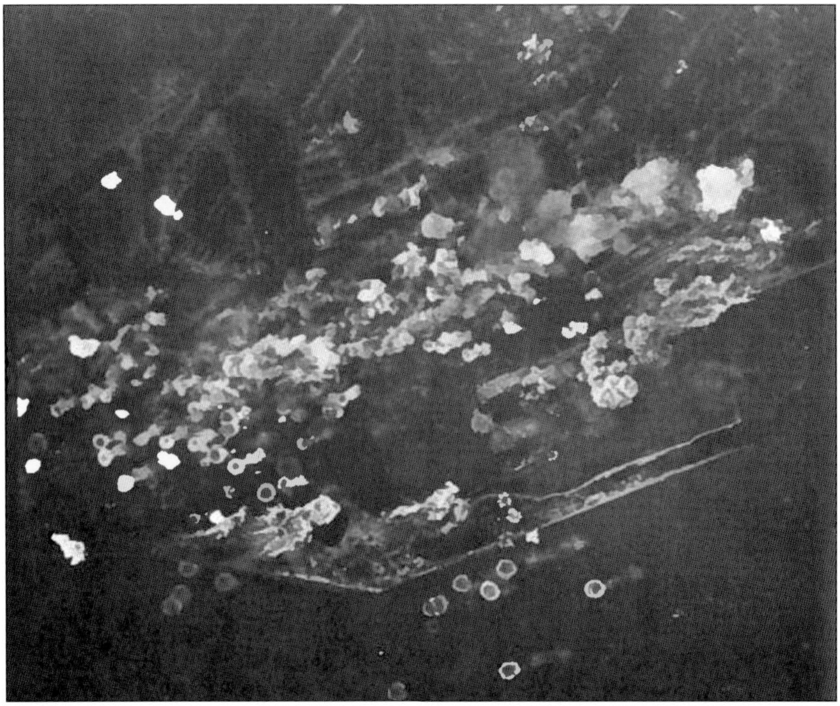

Target photo taken from Moldt's *ITEM* Lancaster bomber. The photo is from the attack on Le Havre on 14 June 1944, when the aircraft targeted the city's harbour area. The aircraft's bombs hit the dry dock, which can be seen to the right of centre. At the top are the docks in the inner harbour. (Moldt)

Canadian soldiers patrolling along the destroyed street Rue Saint-Pierre in Caen, July 1944. (Library and Archives Canada)

Top: Wiesneck brought several items home after the war, including this German belt buckle with eagle and swastika. (Finn Wiesneck) Left: Niels Wiesneck gets a cup of water while the regiment is in a withdrawn position from the front in Normandy. He would later take part in brutal fighting at Caen. (Finn Wiesneck)

Niels Wiesneck also brought these three pieces of silk back to Denmark after the war. When the troops were at the front line, they often relied on supplies from the air, so containers of supplies were parachuted down to the troops. The colour indicated what kind of supply was in the container: Green was food, red was ammunition and yellow was explosives. (Finn Wiesneck)

Svend Moustgaard Jensen in Canada in the pre-war period. (Ole Moustgaard)

Svend Moustgaard Jensen's temporary burial place in Normandy before he was permanently laid to rest at the Canadian cemetery at Brettevillesur-Laize between Caen and Falaise. (Ole Moustgaard)

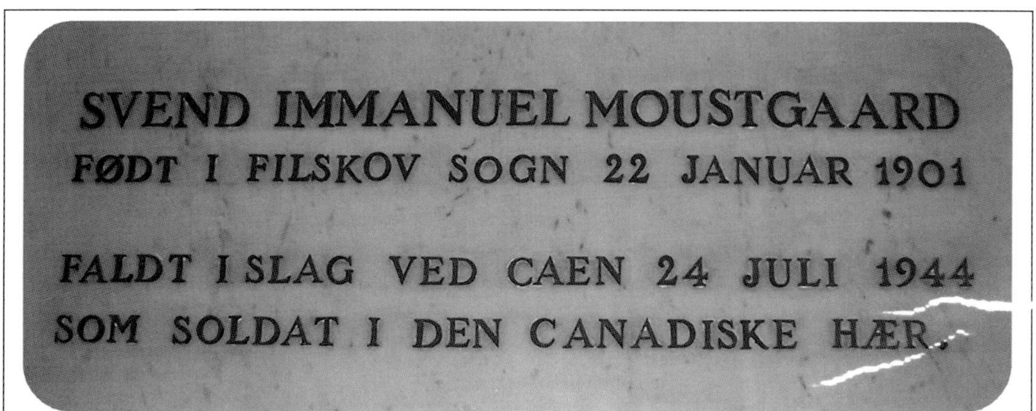

Memorial plaque for Svend Moustgaard in Filskov Church. (Ole Moustgaard)

Target photo from the attack on Caen on 7 July 1944, as seen from *ITEM* Lancaster bomber. The square to the right of the centre was a landmark. Under the smoke to the left, a large number German tanks were positioned. (Moldt)

The devastation after the Battle of Caen. The bombardment of the city has left its mark. (US National Archives)

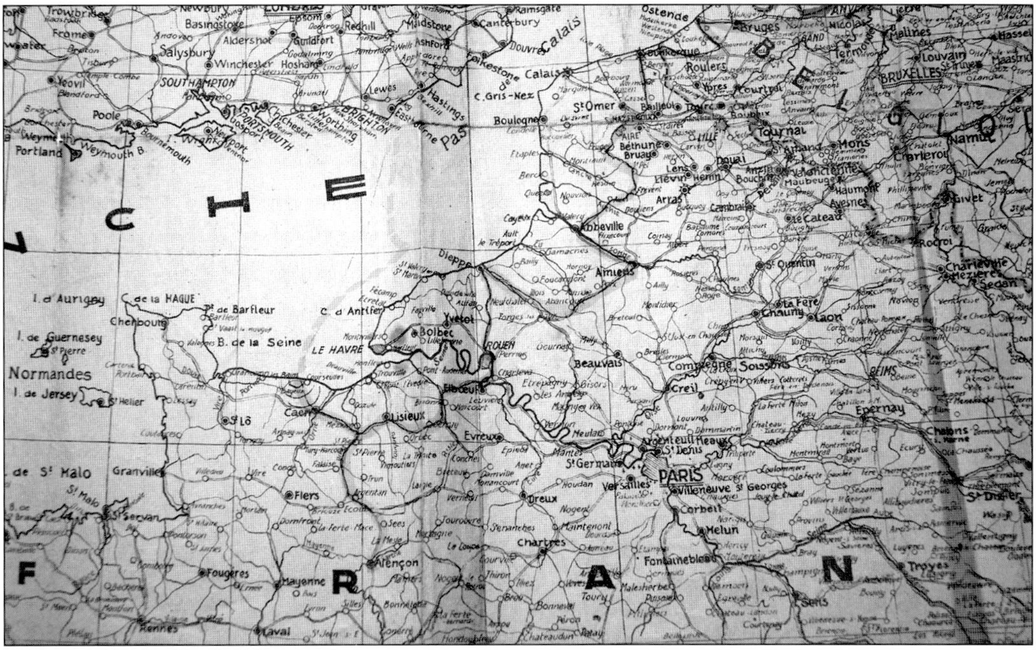

Niels Wiesneck's personal landing map of the invasion of Normandy, where he also recorded the Essex Scottish Regiment's progress after the fighting in France. Note the route from Eastbourne in England to the Gold sector, Bayeux, Caen, Falaise and down to Alencon. Wiesneck brought the map home to Denmark after the war. (Finn Wiesneck)

A dramatic photo from the Battle of Falaise. Allied bombers have just bombed a German transport convoy on 8 August, destroying several vehicles on the Caen-Falaise Road. Canadian troops have taken cover in the ditch. (Library and Archives Canada)

John Christmas Møller in British uniform.
(The Royal Library)

Verner T. Jensen in American uniform.
(Claus Arboe-Rasmussen)

Elsie Margaret Hansen, third from left, served as a nurse aboard the hospital ship *Arcadia* in France.
(Veterans History Project)

The Allied landings in southern France on 15 August 1944. (US National Archives)

The hospital ship *Arcadia*. (Veterans History Project)

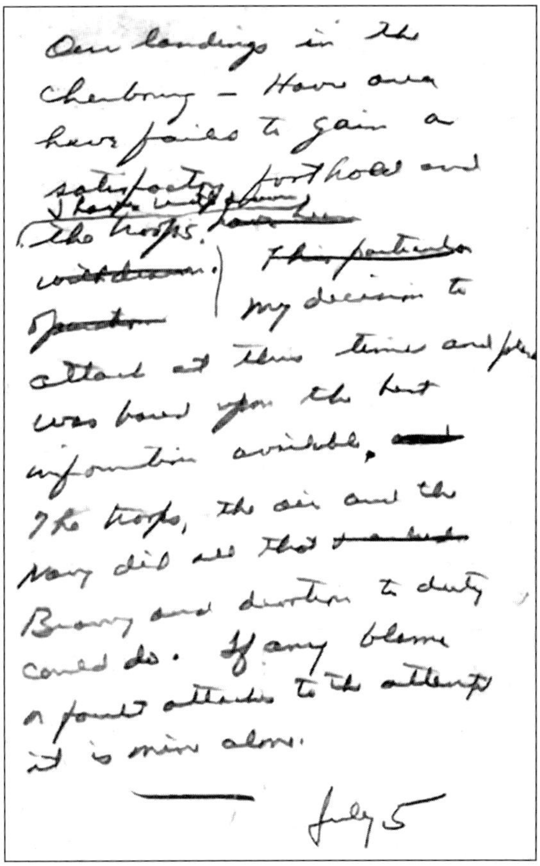

Our landings in the Cherbourg – Havre area have failed to gain a satisfactory foothold and the troops have been withdrawn. My decision to attack at this time and place was based upon the best information available. The troops, the air and the Navy did all that Bravery and devotion to duty could do. If any blame or fault attaches to the attempt it is mine alone.

July 5

There was no guarantee that D-Day and the invasion would be a success. The Commander-in-Chief, General Dwight D. Eisenhower, knew this, and although the famous D-Day leaflet had already been delivered to the troops before the day, Eisenhower was not sure of the outcome of the battle. On 5 June, he wrote a draft message in case the Allied landing failed, he mistakenly dated the letter 5 July. The letter reads: 'Our landing in the Cherbourg-Havre area has failed establish a satisfactory foothold and I have withdrawn the troops. My decision to attack at this time and place was based the best possible information available. The troops, air force and navy displayed all forms of courage and determination in the line of duty. If any blame is attempted to be attached, I alone bear the responsibility.' (US National Archives)

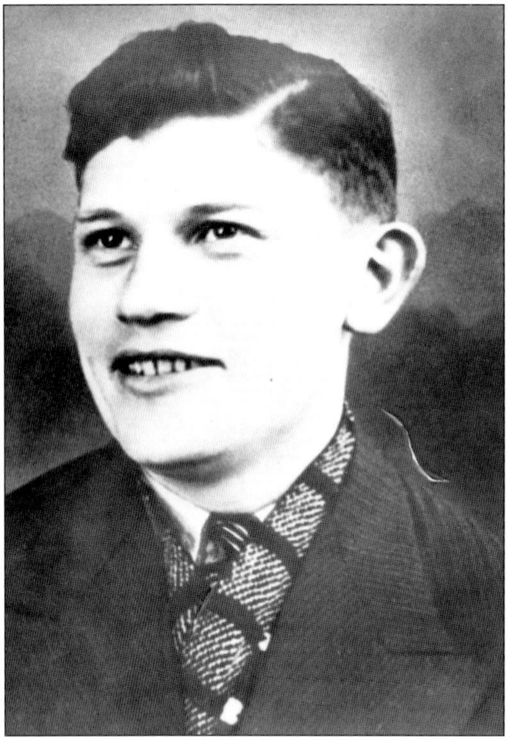

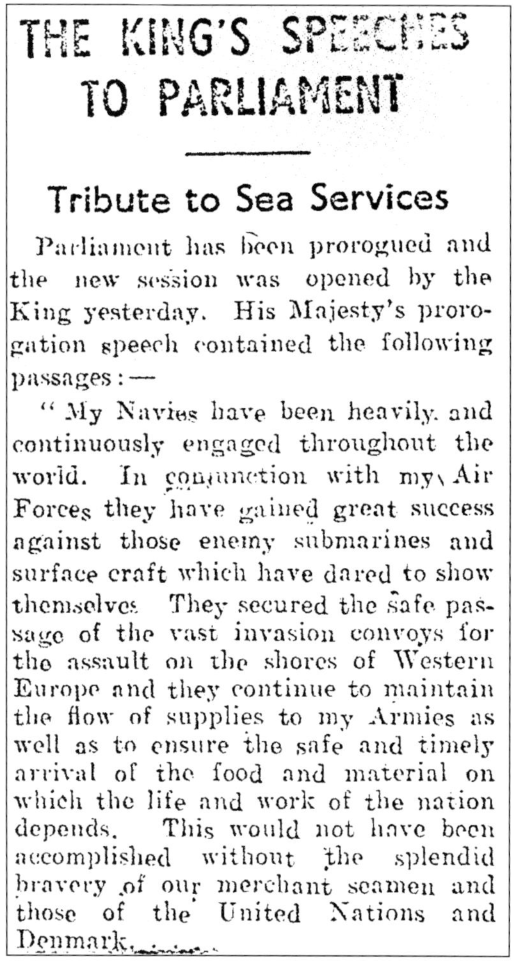

THE KING'S SPEECHES TO PARLIAMENT

Tribute to Sea Services

Parliament has been prorogued and the new session was opened by the King yesterday. His Majesty's prorogation speech contained the following passages:—

"My Navies have been heavily and continuously engaged throughout the world. In conjunction with my Air Forces they have gained great success against those enemy submarines and surface craft which have dared to show themselves. They secured the safe passage of the vast invasion convoys for the assault on the shores of Western Europe and they continue to maintain the flow of supplies to my Armies as well as to ensure the safe and timely arrival of the food and material on which the life and work of the nation depends. This would not have been accomplished without the splendid bravery of our merchant seamen and those of the United Nations and Denmark.

Above: Svend Aage Christensen from Skagen died during the Normandy invasion. (Local History Archive Skagen)
Right: King George VI's speech in the House of Commons after Operation Overlord where Denmark is mentioned. (Imperial War Museum)

US cemetery at Colleville-sur-Mer.

Svend A. Holmstrup's grave at the American cemetery above Omaha at Colleville-sur-Mer in Normandy. Holmstrup was one of the many Americans with Danish ancestry. He was killed on D-Day at Omaha. 9,387 American soldiers are buried in the cemetery, including several Danish-Americans. (Private collection)

The fire control bunker in the 10th battery at Hirtshals before its dismantling, *c* 1945. (Museum Centre Hanstholm, Photographer: Orla Jensen)

The fire control bunker in the 10th battery at Hirtshals today. (Vendsyssel Historical Museum, Photographer: Chrestina Dahl)

Tage Pedersen in uniform. (Torben Vildner Pedersen)

TAGE PEDERSEN

To you who answered the call of your country and served in its Armed Forces to bring about the total defeat of the enemy, I extend the heartfelt thanks of a grateful Nation. As one of the Nation's finest, you undertook the most severe task one can be called upon to perform. Because you demonstrated the fortitude, resourcefulness and calm judgment necessary to carry out that task, we now look to you for leadership and example in further exalting our country in peace.

Harry Truman

THE WHITE HOUSE

President Truman's letter of thanks to Tage Pedersen for his service in the US Army. (Torben Vildner Pedersen)

Part 4

Liberation of Denmark, VE Day and VJ Day

Allied forces began the final push into war-torn Germany in April 1945 with Russian forces leading the race to take Berlin. The outcome was a foregone conclusion – the Nazi regime was defeated. For Denmark, this meant that the euphoria of liberation broke out on 4 and 5 May 1945. On 8 May, VE Day – Victory in Europe was declared, and for the European Continent, the Second World War was officially over. The rush of joy in Denmark and the other liberated countries characterised the post-liberation period. The news of Europe's liberation and peace in Europe was also extremely uplifting for Danish sailors and other Danes in Allied service. Danish war correspondent Emil Blytgen-Pedersen returned to Denmark during Liberation Week in May 1945 and experienced the Danish people's great joy at being free:

> We know that liberation has come from within as it has come from without. The sabotage, the resistance in all its variations, the developments that led to a 29 August, and the organisation of the freedom fighters are liberation from within, just as the Allies' victorious advances after D-Day are liberation from without.... The free Denmark we have dreamed of for over five long years is today an almost unbelievable reality. Danes from abroad thank the Home Front for its perseverance and efforts and is pleased to feel that the work of free Danes abroad is appreciated, and that we are welcome at home. To earn the right to come home to a free Denmark has animated the Danes abroad. First and foremost, this applies to our free Danish seafarers. I have sailed with them to the invasion coast of Normandy. They were proud to be there, and I was proud to be with them and their ships, which since 9 April have represented the largest Danish contribution to the fight on the Allied side.[1]

For the Danes in Allied service and the sailors aboard the ships, the news of Denmark's liberation was joyous news, but despite peace having officially arrived in the homeland, sporadic fighting was still taking place across Europe. John Andreasen, a Danish anti-aircraft gunner in Canadian service, was five kilometres outside the north-western German

1 Emil Blytgen-Petersen, *Dansk Krigskorrespondent* (Copenhagen: Nyt Nordisk Forlag Arnold Busck, 1945), pp.157–158.

town of Emden. On 4 May, despite the news of the German surrender on 5 May at 8 a.m., there was still sporadic fighting in the area. John Andreasen's regiment came under heavy artillery fire near Emden when German troops were still in the town. During the bombardment of the town and the subsequent tank attacks, the German soldiers in the town were beaten. In the evening, John Andreasen's platoon received word that the Germans would surrender the next morning at 8 a.m. and that the Canadian troops should remain passive at all costs to avoid further casualties. Despite this, a small group of German soldiers attacked the Canadians during the night of 5 May, but were resolutely beaten. Throughout the night, the Canadians continued to be subjected to sporadic artillery attacks, and the Canadian artillery positions responded with everything they had. Needless to say, there was no sleep for Andreasen that night because of the German artillery strikes. In the morning, the Canadian troops were greeted by an eerie silence, and no one could quite understand if the war was over. No one cheered or looked happy, as the focus was still on whether there would be more sporadic German attacks. However, Andreasen could see with his own eyes that the Germans had effectively surrendered on the morning of 5 May:

> At eight o'clock on the 5th of May, 1945, the Germans laid down their arms and surrendered to our armies of good fortune and piety, and by morning all the roads were blocked by German soldiers, one battery and regiment after another with their officers at the head. As their administration had completely broken down, there was a great confusion in the soldiers on the roads, but as they had received their orders to proceed to certain camps which were established, and that they were not to proceed to these camps without being under the command of their own officers, the business was quickly sorted.[2]

After the German surrender in Europe, however, the need for supplies around the world was still huge. In addition, the war against Japan in the Pacific was not over, and a large number of Danish warships contributed to supplying the American forces. The Danish sailors in the British merchant fleet could not be discharged without further discussions, as there had been negotiations in London in early 1945 between the British authorities and the Danish Council. It was decided that it was also important to ensure the presence of Danish seamen on board the ships after Germany was defeated, and it was also important to retain Danish seamen for a period of up to six months after Japan was defeated to continue the flow of supplies.

The majority of these sailors had been away from Denmark and their families for more than five years at this point. They had experienced war and destruction first-hand, and they had lived with the constant danger of German E-Boats and mines throughout this period. They had become accustomed to 12-hour shifts on board ship. Lifejackets were always worn and were used as a pillow so they were always at hand. The little red light attached to the lifejacket gave the sailors hope that they would be picked up if the ship was torpedoed – despite the fact that the men knew full well that there were strict orders not to pick up men in the water while part of a convoy. Life as a wartime sailor was stressful and harsh, and when the

2 John Andreasen, unpublished war diary, p.99.

Danish sailors finally reached safe harbour, they did what they could to forget the dangers of the sea, as Erik Egebak recalls:

> When we got back to Southampton, we let our hair down. Because now it wasn't our business for a while. The dockers and soldiers took over loading and we went from one pub to another.[3]

Even though the war in Europe was officially over and the Danes in Allied service who had participated in the Normandy invasion rightfully felt part of the victorious party, being a Dane was still not smooth sailing. Danish paratrooper Niels Christensen, who was dropped during the night on D-Day, also realised this. Christensen had experienced the D-Day inferno and seen his friends killed, and he had himself subsequently been captured by the Germans. Despite having fought with the 101st Airborne Division, the fact that he was Danish still caused him problems when he had to return to the US. After Christensen and the other prisoners were liberated in the Limburg prison camp, they were transported to Paris to catch a plane to England. As Christensen was about to board the plane, he was stopped and denied permission to board because of his Danish accent. Panicked about not being able to return home, Christensen recounted growing up in Denmark and travelling to the US, where he enlisted in the US Army. He mentioned that an officer told him the day before D-Day that he did not really need to participate in the invasion as he was not an American citizen, to which Christensen replied that he was determined to fight the Germans. He also started mentioning which bases he had been stationed at, and when he said that he had been recommended by an officer to go to a soldiers' ball when he was on leave, it paid off. Incredibly, it was the same officer who stood guard at the aircraft in Paris, and Christensen was subsequently allowed to board to begin his return journey to the USA.

Niels Wiesneck from Copenhagen, who had been a sailor in the first year of the war but had later joined the Canadian Army, continued the advance across Europe with his regiment after Operation Overlord. He was involved in bitter and intense battles at Antwerp in Belgium and Arnhem in The Netherlands before finally helping to occupy Oldenburg in Germany in 1945. Wiesneck served as an interpreter in the Essex Scottish Regiment at the end of the war, as he had studied German at school. After VE Day, the regiment served in the occupying army in Germany before Wiesneck eventually returned home to Denmark in December 1945. It was very characteristic that the troops in the regiment knew nothing about what was going to happen. They became a kind of 'now' people who lived from day to day, as Wiesneck recalls:

> I was just a soldier with a rifle. Where we were and what we were to do, that was always the big question. We were given an order and then we did what we were told. There wasn't much else to do.[4]

---

3 Quote is taken from Cicerone ApS and Nexus Communication's interview with Erik Egebak and archive material in connection with the production of the documentary 'The War Sailors'.

4 The quotes come from the Bangsbo Archive's material on Niels Wiesneck, where a taped interview is available.

In July, Wiesneck received permission to drive a supply lorry up through Germany to visit his family in Copenhagen:

> We had to avoid the big cities as they were heavily bombed and riddled with holes. After a while we came up to the German border. There was a lot of control with British, Canadian and American customs officers at the border. When I crossed the German border, heaven just opened up. Big Danish flags and farms everywhere. Green fields and straw on the roofs. On top of all this, it was pure idyll – I could hardly believe my eyes.[5]

Wiesneck then travelled across Denmark and sailed on the Great Belt ferry, and after 5½ years away from his homeland, he was reunited with his family. However, 14 days later he had to report back to the Essex Scottish Regiment in Germany, which now acted as a part of the occupying army and had to take care of the refugees in the area. The regiment would then drive all equipment, such as ammunition and daily supplies, to the coast, after which they would sail across the Channel to some large camps in England. After a week or so, Wiesneck was discharged in London and signed out of the Canadian Army. He was then paid a salary, given civilian clothes and a one-way ticket to Denmark, where he arrived at Copenhagen Central Station on 19 December 1945.

For many Danish sailors, the war was not over when Denmark was officially liberated on 5 May 1945. Joy and celebration erupted as the message of freedom poured out of the radios and the Danish people could finally enjoy freedom after five years of occupation. But, as mentioned, there was still a huge need to transport supplies to rebuild the war-torn countries. Furthermore, the war was still continuing in the Pacific, as Japan had no intention of surrendering to the Allies. Many Danish sailors volunteered for this task. One of the last to return home was Erik Egebak from Vrå in Vendsyssel, who volunteered to continue sailing supplies in the Pacific. He even experienced the end of the war in the Pacific first-hand when Japan unofficially surrendered on 15 August – VJ Day (Victory in Japan) and later formally signed the surrender on 2 September after the atomic bombs destroyed Hiroshima and Nagasaki on 6 and 9 August respectively. In August 1945, Egebak's ship was docked in Guam when he saw two American planes carrying huge bombs take off from the airfield:

> At the time, of course, we didn't know that the planes were carrying these things, but we were able to follow them when they started their bombing runs. They also took off from Saipan. So we were right in the middle of it. When we heard about what had happened, I remember three or four of us sat in the officers' mess with a couple of British officers and played a game of hearts. Then we heard on the radio that there had been this bombing of Japan, and I remember everyone turned round and one of the officers said that it was just propaganda, so we played on until another message came through, and then we believed it was true.... And then all hell broke loose. There were shouts of joy and aeroplanes were flying all over the

5 The quotes come from Kystmuseet Bangsbo Arkiv's material about Niels Wiesneck, where a taped interview is available.

> place. It's hard to describe how much happiness there was all of a sudden that the war was over.[6]

The Second World War was officially over, and for the Danish sailors and other Danes in service, depending on the length of the contract, it was now possible to return to Denmark after more than 5 years in allied service.

Homecoming and the Aftermath of War 'Get those rags down so we can get unloading'

The first Danish sailors began returning home after the liberation of Denmark in 1945, but the majority did not return until the end of 1945 and up until the end of 1946. At this point, Denmark and the Danish population were already going about their daily lives as they had before the war broke out. The wartime sailors came home in small groups or individually.

Life continued for them after the war ended and they returned home to Denmark, but slowly the experiences of war began to intrude. They had been active during the war for more than five years and now had to get used to living a life in peaceful conditions. There was great joy when the individual sailors set sail for their homeland, and expectations of a warm welcome in Denmark after more than five years of war in Allied service were equally high. Erik Egebak, who had sailed aboard an American Liberty ship during the Normandy invasion, arrived in Aarhus on 23 December 1945. The ship's crew had decided that when they arrived in Aarhus, they would present themselves at their best, as they were representatives of Denmark and had been away from home for more than five years. The ship was cleaned, they put on their best clothes and the signal flags were hoisted. However, the crew had to look far and wide for a warm welcome:

> We docked at the coal harbour, where a group of dockers arrived. All they said was 'get the bloody rags down (signalling flags) so we can unload.'[7]

Egebak's sister and father had travelled from Vrå to Aarhus to welcome him, as he had telegraphed in advance that he was on his way home to Denmark. After an overnight stay in Aarhus, he travelled home to North Jutland. He was delighted when he arrived home in Vrå:

> The next morning, we started the journey back to Vrå by train and arrived around noon. Of course, I got a big welcome from the family, and my mum was especially affected. During the war, I had sent many letters through the Red Cross, but I don't think any of them ever really got through. So it was obviously a great day.[8]

6 Quote is taken from Cicerone ApS and Nexus Communication's interview with Erik Egebak and archive material in connection with the production of the documentary 'The War Sailors'.

7 Quote is taken from Cicerone ApS and Nexus Communication's interview with Erik Egebak and archive material in connection with the production of the documentary 'The War Sailors'.

8 Quote is taken from Cicerone ApS and Nexus Communication's interview with Erik Egebak and archive material in connection with the production of the documentary 'The War Sailors'.

However, life in Denmark after the war for these Danish sailors would prove to be extremely problematic, not only in terms of living with the trauma of war, but also in terms of the state's help for them. A large number of the sailors who had been at sea for more than five years were among the first to receive a letter from the tax authorities stating that they had not paid taxes during the war and that they would be claimed back. The sailors saw this as an insult to all those who had sailed in Allied service. In addition, the sailors were also upset that there was no official thanks or recognition for their efforts from the Danish state.

Viggo Hans Nielsen was in the same situation as many of his colleagues. He returned to Denmark on 29 August 1945. He had been away from Denmark for seven years:

> I had barely set foot on land before the tax authorities were there. They demanded tax for three years back. I asked what for? He said it was the law. I thought that was mean – I had paid tax through my work in England, but now I was told I had to pay again.[9]

Furthermore, the majority were called into conscription as, according to the Danish state, they had never officially been part of Denmark's forces. This was also the case for Erik Egebak:

> The next message I got from the authorities was that I had to turn up for conscription service. 'You cheated to get out of the conscription, and where have you really been?' So I had to be conscripted, and they quickly announced that I was suitable for the field artillery. So I told them that firstly, I'm a skilled seaman, and as such I'm entitled to do my military service in the navy. They could see that from my papers. Secondly, I said, I've heard that those of us who have served in allied service are exempt from military service. Well, they said. They didn't know anything about that.[10]

In many ways, Denmark was still on its knees, just like the other countries in Europe after the war. The economy was on the up, but still not optimal. This also had an effect on the Danish merchant fleet, so work (and pay) for Danish sailors was extremely scarce. All of these factors did not make it any easier for the sailors who had participated in the war and contributed to the majority being affected by what is now commonly known as 'the war sailor syndrome'. After the liberation of Denmark, the then government introduced Act on the Victims of the Occupation, which would benefit Danes who had fought and assisted the Allies against the German regime.[11] The Act meant financial compensation and war pension and was in many ways a great gesture by the Danish Government. Participants in the resistance movement could naturally receive these forms of compensation, but it was different for

9 The quotes are from an interview with Viggo Hans Nielsen conducted by Kjeld Sasbye on 16 February 1984.

10 Quote is taken from Cicerone ApS and Nexus Communication's interview with Erik Egebak and archive material in connection with the production of the documentary 'The War Sailors'.

11 Act on Compensation for Victims of the Occupation. <https://www.retsinformation.dk/Forms/r0710.aspx?id=145690>.

the sailors. When the first sailors came home in 1945 and early 1946, they naturally applied for this type of compensation for the typically up to 5–7 years at sea, far away from their families and homeland. But they received rejection after rejection. At the time, Denmark had no overall picture of the efforts of the Danish Merchant Navy and sailors in Operation Overlord and during the war in general. The Danish Government hardly realised at the time the importance of the sailors' efforts during the Normandy invasion. The first war pension for sailors was not introduced until 1969, by which time many of the traumatised sailors had already succumbed to the pressure of the lack of help and the memories of war.

Alcoholism and suicide became more and more common among the group of sailors who were active in the Royal Danish Navy. Erik Egebak recalls the impact of the Victims of Occupation Act – a law that until 1969 did not include Danish war sailors:

> I didn't even know anything about it – no one had ever told me that such a law had been made. At the same time, more and more sailors were dying like human wrecks. Alcoholics and maybe even drug addicts. Without knowing why, they were feeling bad. But they suffered from bad nerves to such an extent that they were complete strangers to the family they came home to. So there was an equally great need for the same law for Danish seafarers.[12]

The description of the late effects as post-traumatic stress disorder was not widely known in the period just after the Second World War. Back then it was known as shell shock or war fatigue. For many seafarers, these injuries did not manifest themselves until years later.

Around 1944–1945, H. H. Koch, head of the Ministry of Social Affairs, had the idea that an independent body should be established after the war that was not strictly bound by legal provisions, but could make decisions based on purely subjective judgement, and thus the Freedom Fund was established. 24 years after the resistance fighters had received their compensation, the war sailors were given the same opportunity.

Furthermore, there were approximately 100 Danish sailors in Japanese captivity during the war, but the Occupation Victims Act stipulated that they had to have been in German captivity. Therefore, this group received no compensation until 1984, when the law was changed. The Freedom Fund initiated the procedures to have the war sailors incorporated into the law, but the fund was closed in 1995 and the tasks were transferred to the National Board of Industrial Injuries. The state took over the majority of the many millions collected for the Freedom Fund. The tax authorities also demanded tax on the money collected. When the money was paid out to the veterans, the tax authorities demanded that approximately 50 percent of the veterans' pensions be deducted in taxes.[13] Many of the Danish veteran sailors who took part in the Normandy invasion also suffered from 'war sailor syndrome'. Holger Jensen from Hou remembers the effect of the war on his own life:

> In terms of nerves after the war, it's hard to get over it. Obviously, it's inevitable that it sometimes comes up when you go back five years to when you first sailed and

12 Quote taken from Cicerone ApS and Nexus Communication's interview with Erik Egebak and archive material in connection with the production of the documentary 'The War Sailors'.

13 Christian Tortzen, *Kampen på Havet* (Copenhagen: Information, 2011), pp.299–334.

> didn't know when a torpedo was coming or if there was a mine in front of the ship. It took 21–23 days to get from the US to an English harbour. All that time you wore clothes and life jackets, and when you had to go to the toilet you sat with one leg out in front to get out as quickly as possible in case of an attack. You never knew when it was going to happen. When you do that for several years in a row, day in and day out, it leaves its mark in one way or another. It can't be avoided. There are many things I think are too drastic to mention, it's too brutal.[14]

The harsh experiences during the war had left their mark on the Danish war sailors. Sven Arvid Birkeland, Chief Physician at the Rehabilitation and Research Centre for Torture Victims, has previously worked with the Danish Freedom Foundation's pilot studies, which were based on interviews with 578 sailors. 75 percent of these had significant problems as a result of the war. The interviewees were divided into two groups: those who had experienced physical problems, such as reduced mobility, and those who suffered from mental health problems: anxiety, obsessive thoughts, depression and suicidal thoughts.[15] Henrik Bødker Knudsen describes the aftermath of the war in his memoirs:

> It is probably not the physical wounds inflicted by war that are the hardest to bear, the psychological ones are far worse. Many have probably had to realise that.[16]

42 percent of the 578 sailors surveyed in the Freedom Foundation pilot study had experienced being attacked more than 30 times, while 35 percent had experienced being attacked regularly (5–30 times). Only 11 percent of respondents had been attacked less than five times.[17] Jørgen Linnet from Klitmøller, who experienced being torpedoed, did not feel the same kind of psychological aftereffects as many of his friends and colleagues. But even though Jørgen Linnet avoided the psychological scars, he was naturally affected by the war:

> Losing mates has made a big impression, but I also think that because I was as young as I was, you get a little less damage from such experiences. Lying in your bunk with your clothes on and not knowing when [you may have] to storm out of it and get to a lifeboat is a big burden, but as a very young person, I think you can sleep a little from it anyway.... But I think the slightly older people who have experienced the horrors of war have been more damaged by it. But it makes a big impression to lose your mates, but I never suffered psychologically like many others did.[18]

---

14 Quoted from Holger Jensen's account come from the DR radio programme 'Den Store Landgang' by Poul S. Poulsen, 6 June 1969.

15 Sven Arvid Birkeland, *Sænket af tyskerne – Danske krigssejlere i 2. Verdenskrig* (Copenhagen: Gyldendal, 2012), pp.442–455.

16 Henrik Bødker Knudsen, *Krigssejler* (Copenhagen: Frihedsmuseets Venners Forlag, 1992), p.106.

17 Sven Arvid Birkeland, *Sænket af tyskerne – Danske krigssejlere i 2. Verdenskrig* (Copenhagen: Gyldendal, 2012), pp.450–455.

18 Quoted from an interview with Jørgen Linnet in February 2016.

The war sailors and other Danes in Allied service who were involved in the war had constantly been under massive mental and physical pressure. Many did not experience the aftereffects until several years later and in many ways found it difficult to come to terms with the psychological consequences. Professional psychological counselling was also lacking, as these men were not offered the same kind of help that, for example, soldiers who participated in the Allied forces received. Niels Wiesneck, who was a sailor in the early years of the war but later joined the Canadian Army, also felt the trauma of war when he returned to Denmark. As he had been in Canadian service, he was offered psychological counselling, unlike those who had only been sailors during the war. Wiesneck became a teacher at the Maritime School in Frederikshavn after the war, but after 15 years of service, he had to stop because of the war trauma:

> My heart started beating wrong, and then my nerves started to snap, and I had flashbacks from the war. So I had to stop at the maritime school. After a while, I recovered so much that I became a teacher at Fladstrand School. I had some great years there.[19]

Many wartime sailors felt the aftermath of the horrific events of the war. Another blow to Danes who had sailed for the Allies came on 3 May 1946, when King Christian X's commemorative medal for participation in the 1940–1945 war was awarded to Danes who participated in the Allied forces in the fight against the German occupying forces. The medal was given to the Danish resistance fighters who worked in cooperation with the British intelligence service SOE, as well as other Danes in Allied service. It was decided that the sailors were civilians and thus could not be considered. Stauning's New Year's speech in 1940, which also addressed the wartime sailors, still symbolises their perception of the government's treatment of them after the war. 'You shall not be forgotten,' Stauning said, but the Danish sailors felt to a great extent that their efforts were forgotten[20].

J. P. Sørensen, who was served on board *Gudrun Mærsk* during the Normandy invasion, also found his return to Denmark a sad affair:

> Fortunately, I had family in Gentofte who could help me, but many of my friends had no money when they came home and no place to live, so many of them had to beg for money on the various benches at Kongens Nytorv. The Danish state could not help. Personally, I clearly remember that I had to renew my passport – I didn't have a real passport, just a consular passport on a piece of paper. So I went to the police station to get a new passport, but when I showed the sergeant my English passport and registration book, I was practically thrown out with the comment: "You could be a Nazi for all I know." Then I had to find three witnesses who could sign that I was actually Danish. It was as if every public place you went, you got the feeling that it was bad that you had sailed over in England – it was bad that you had only sailed during the war.[21]

19 The following quotes come from Kystmuseet Bangsbo Arkiv's material about Niels Wiesneck, where a taped interview is available.

20 Christian Tortzen, *Kampen på Havet* (Copenhagen: Information, 2011), page 56.

21 J. P. Sørensen interview by Ulrik Brandt. Recorded at Bombebøssen in Christianshavn on 9 August 2005.

However, it was not just the Danish Government's neglect of the wartime sailors. Initiatives such as the Home Leave and Holidays Act and the Honours Act were all rewritten in 1945 to include war sailors, regardless of whether they had served on board a foreign or Danish ship. However, the most important law in the eyes of the sailors regarding compensation claims for participation in the war was far from optimal from their perspective.

Danish fighter pilot Kjeld Rønhof, who was a sailor at the start of the war, specifically mentions the feelings of being at war, engaging in bitter fighting and watching his friends die. When the Germans surrendered in May 1945, Rønhof was given the opportunity to fly to Norway in a Stirling bomber.

He landed at Gardermoen Airport north-east of Oslo, which was packed with German prisoners of war. A German major came up to Rønhof and saluted, and for the first time, Rønhof came face to face with the enemy he had been fighting for more than five years:

> How strange it was to be face to face with the enemy. I had to make an effort to speak in a civilised manner – not to lose my temper and smash a fist right into this major's face. It wasn't easy when you think of Belsen, Buchenwalde, Neuengamme, Dachau and the other horror camps. It wasn't easy when you thought of comrades at sea who had been mowed down defenceless in lifeboats, as I had seen when S/S *Enid* of Tronhjem had been sunk in 1940. It wasn't easy when you thought of the ruins in Coventry, Hull, Rotterdam, London, Warsaw and countless other places. It wasn't easy when you thought of the Gestapo's underground execution rooms, torture chambers, violent crimes against young girls from occupied countries. It wasn't easy thinking about human guinea pigs, lampshades made of tattooed human skin. It wasn't easy when I thought about the execution of my comrades Halvor Espelid and Niels Jørgen Fuglsang. It wasn't easy when I thought about the murder of my brother on 12 April 1945, just a few days before the war ended.[22]

The bitterness, feelings of powerlessness, anger and grief and the deep scars that the Danes who took part in the Second World War and the Normandy invasion all possessed stayed with them for the rest of their lives, but the Danes who assisted the Allies during the war and who were not recognised for their efforts until decades later were more deeply scarred.

22 Kjeld Rønhof, *Vi fløj for Friheden* (Copenhagen: Four Stripes,1991), pp.184–185.

The liberation of Denmark is celebrated on 5 May 1945 at Strøget in Copenhagen. (Freedom Museum)

Niels Christensen visiting Yosemite National Park on leave in July 1945. (Mary Christensen)

KAPUT. Troops of the Canadian Royal Artillery Regiment read the 8 May issue of the Canadian magazine, *The Maple Leaf*, near Aurich, Germany. (Library and Archives Canada)

Niels Wiesneck's medals. From left to right: King Christian X's medal for participation in Allied service 1940-1945, The 1939-1945 Star, The France and Germany Star, The Defence Medal 1939-1945, George IV 1939-1945 medal, Canadian volunteer medal 1939-1945. (Finn Wiesneck)

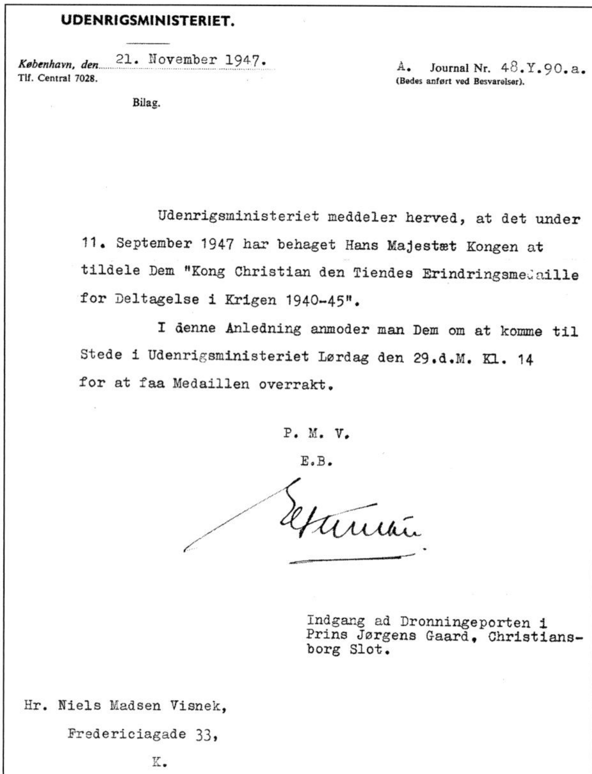

UDENRIGSMINISTERIET.

København, den 21. November 1947.
Tlf. Central 7028.

A. Journal Nr. 48.Y.90.a.
(Bedes anført ved Besvarelser).

Bilag.

Udenrigsministeriet meddeler herved, at det under 11. September 1947 har behaget Hans Majestæt Kongen at tildele Dem "Kong Christian den Tiendes Erindringsmedaille for Deltagelse i Krigen 1940-45".

I denne Anledning anmoder man Dem om at komme til Stede i Udenrigsministeriet Lørdag den 29.d.M. Kl. 14 for at faa Medaillen overrakt.

P. M. V.
E.B.

Indgang ad Dronningeporten i Prins Jørgens Gaard, Christiansborg Slot.

Hr. Niels Madsen Visnek,
Fredericiagade 33,
K.

Niels Wiesneck received the King's Commemorative Medal for his services with the Allies in the war. He was a sailor to the bone, but made a decision to become a Canadian soldier. For his service, he was awarded the King's Commemorative Medal. Many of the 6,300 sailors who 'simply' chose to sail for the Allies did not receive the Commemorative Medal as the authorities did not believe there was concrete and visible proof of their efforts during the war. (Finn Wiesneck)

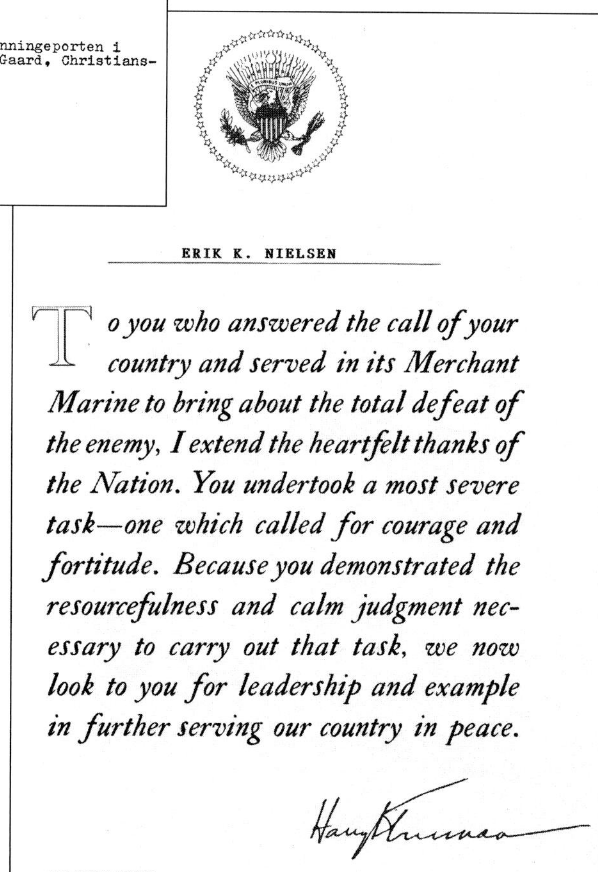

ERIK K. NIELSEN

To you who answered the call of your country and served in its Merchant Marine to bring about the total defeat of the enemy, I extend the heartfelt thanks of the Nation. You undertook a most severe task—one which called for courage and fortitude. Because you demonstrated the resourcefulness and calm judgment necessary to carry out that task, we now look to you for leadership and example in further serving our country in peace.

THE WHITE HOUSE

Danish sailors in Allied service received honours from the nations they had assisted during the war, but it would be many years before they received official recognition from the Danish Government. This is President Truman's letter of thanks to Erik Kragelund Nielsen for his service in the US Merchant Marine. (Private collection)

S/S *Thyra* and S/S *Frigga* on their return to Copenhagen after being in Allied service. Both sailed for DFDS. (M/S Museet for Søfart)

The stamp with the motif of the Danish war sailor was sold around Denmark to support the financing of the statue in Normandy. (Private collection)

The inscription on the Danish war sailors' monument in Normandy: 'In memory of 800 Danish sailors' participation in the invasion of June 1944'. (Private collection)

The Queen of Denmark, HM Queen Margrethe II, inaugurates the Danish exhibition at the Utah Beach Museum in connection with the 70th anniversary of D-Day in 2014. From left to right is the Deputy Mayor of Sainte Marie du Mont Charles De Vallavieille, whose father was shot on D-Day, founded the museum in 1962, the author, HM The Queen. (Private collection)

Danish war sailor Viggo Hans Nielsen at the inauguration of the Danish War Sailors Monument in 1984. Nielsen arrived on Juno Beach on D-Day with *Thyra III*. The monument is located behind Utah in Normandy. (Fyens Stiftstidende)

John Andreasen, who was an anti-aircraft gunner in Canadian service, visits the American cemetery at Colleville-sur-Mer in connection with the 40th anniversary of D-Day in 1984. (Familie Journalen/ Karl Ravn)

In connection with the 80th anniversary of D-Day in 2024, a new Danish memorial wall at Utah Beach was inaugurated by HM King Frederik X. Danish Prime Minister Mette Frederiksen also participated in a ceremony at the Danish memorial. The wall bears the names of Danes and those with Danish ancestry who participated in the invasion of Normandy in 1944 in Allied service. That is, all those besides the 800 who participated in the merchant navy, including those who were part of the American, British and Canadian armies, were in the Royal Air Force and in the Canadian and US Air Force. The wall is continuous, so more memorial stones with names can be added over time. In the background is the memorial to the Danish sailors. (Photo Stine Tisvilde / Private collection)

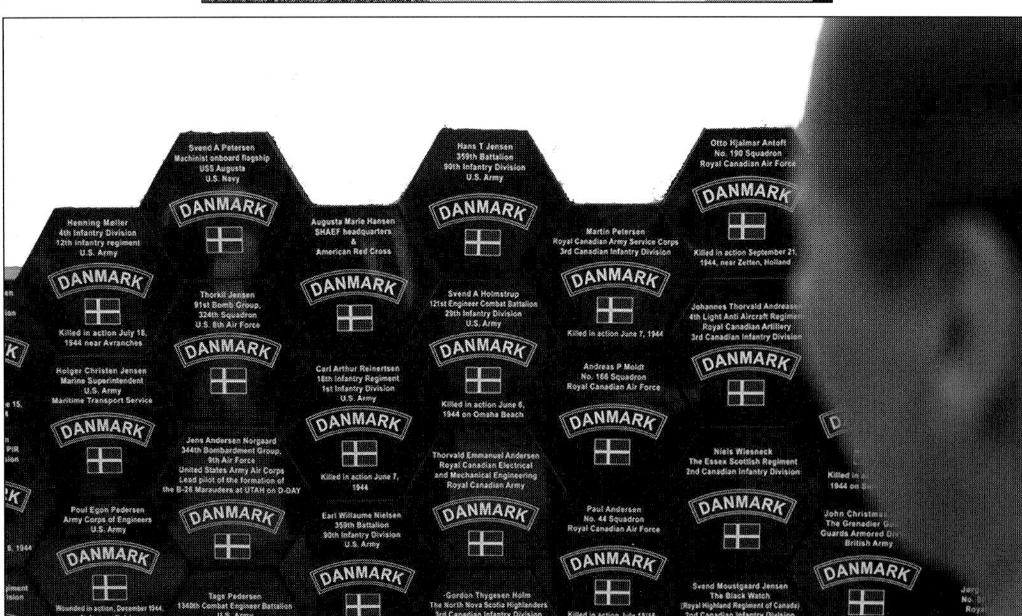
Svend A Petersen
Machinist onboard flagship
USS Augusta
U.S. Navy
DANMARK
Henning Møller
4th Infantry Division
12th infantry regiment
U.S. Army
DANMARK
Killed in action July 18,
1944 near Avranches
Augusta Marie Hansen
SHAEF headquarters
&
American Red Cross
DANMARK
Thorkil Jensen
91st Bomb Group,
324th Squadron
U.S. 8th Air Force
DANMARK
Holger Christen Jensen
Marine Superintendent
U.S. Army
Maritime Transport Service
DANMARK
Carl Arthur Reinertsen
18th Infantry Regiment
1st Infantry Division
U.S. Army
DANMARK
Killed in action June 7,
1944
Jens Andersen Norgaard
344th Bombardment Group,
9th Air Force
United States Army Air Corps
Lead pilot of the formation of
the B-26 Marauders at UTAH on D-DAY
DANMARK
Poul Egon Pedersen
Army Corps of Engineers
U.S. Army
DANMARK
Wounded in action, December 1944,
Ardennes, Belgium
Earl Willaume Nielsen
359th Battalion
90th Infantry Division
U.S. Army
DANMARK
Tage Pedersen
1340th Combat Engineer Battalion
U.S. Army
Hans T Jensen
359th Battalion
90th Infantry Division
U.S. Army
DANMARK
Svend A Holmstrup
121st Engineer Combat Battalion
29th Infantry Division
U.S. Army
DANMARK
Killed in action June 6,
1944 on Omaha Beach
Thorvald Emmanuel Andersen
Royal Canadian Electrical
and Mechanical Engineering
Royal Canadian Army
DANMARK
Gordon Thygesen Holm
The North Nova Scotia Highlanders
3rd Canadian Infantry Division
Martin Petersen
Royal Canadian Army Service Corps
3rd Canadian Infantry Division
DANMARK
Killed in action June 7, 1944
Andreas P Moldt
No. 166 Squadron
Royal Canadian Air Force
DANMARK
Paul Andersen
No. 44 Squadron
Royal Canadian Air Force
DANMARK
Killed in action July 15/16,
1944, over Danish waters
Otto Hjalmar Antoft
No. 190 Squadron
Royal Canadian Air Force
DANMARK
Killed in action September 21,
1944, near Zetten, Holland
DANMARK
Niels Wiesneck
The Essex Scottish Regiment
2nd Canadian Infantry Division
DANMARK
Svend Moustgaard Jensen
The Black Watch
(Royal Highland Regiment of Canada)
2nd Canadian Infantry Division
DANMARK

Epilogue, A New Focus on The Danish Effort

The Danes who took part in Operation Overlord not only fought a physical enemy during the war, but in many ways they also fought a battle to be recognised as equals in the eyes of the Allies. The Danish sailors who participated in the Normandy invasion helped solve Overlord's major logistical challenges, but they did so in a highly unofficial role. They were all volunteers and civilians, acting out of their own convictions and not at the behest of their home government. Despite this, more than 800 Danish sailors chose to sail supplies directly into one of the bloodiest landing operations in history. They did this despite the fact that their foreign colleagues, especially Norwegians, considered the Danes to be pro-German, and so the Danes in Allied service had to keep fighting to prove their worth. But after Operation Overlord, there was more clarity about Denmark's relationship with the Allies. The participation of Danish sailors in the invasion and the violent August uprising in Denmark of 1943 helped put Denmark as a nation in a better light. This also made living conditions easier for the Danish sailors in the foreign fleets.

Historian Jakob Sørensen has previously covered the story of Danes in Allied service during World War II. Sørensen has estimated that there were around 1,000 Danish citizens who served in the Allied forces, in addition to the Danish sailors who sailed for the Allies. This book has contributed additional stories to the history of Danes in Allied service, and digging deeper into foreign archives will undoubtedly reveal more. Characteristic of Danes in Allied service, and especially those who participated in the Normandy invasion, was that apart from the Danish sailors, Danes were sporadically placed in the various Allied forces. The closest thing to a Danish unit during the was the Danes in The Buffs as well as the Danish-manned minesweepers, which were combined into one unit but primarily only came into service in 1945.[1] In contrast to the history of the sailors, the recognition perspective seemed easier for the Danes who officially served in the Allied forces during the Normandy invasion. By joining the Canadian Army, for example, there were automatically other bodies that viewed the efforts of these Danes in Allied service in an equal perspective. It also meant that their status and living conditions after the war in the form of compensation, war pension and certificates and medals recognising their achievements were secured. For the Danish sailors who participated in the Second World War invasion of Normandy, compensation was generally out of reach.

The Danes who were in Allied service during the Normandy invasion and the sailors who continued to sail supplies for the Allies long after the war ended in May 1945, apart from

1 Jakob Sørensen, *For Danmarks Ære* (Copenhagen: People's Press, 2011), p.281.

a lukewarm welcome at home, never had the same feeling of liberation on 5 May 1945 that the Danish Resistance and population had experienced. The Danes who had been in Allied service had a different attitude to the excitement surrounding the great public celebration that 5 May 1945 was full of. In many ways, they felt alienated from the feeling that the domestic Danish population had in relation to liberation – not because they could not be part of the euphoria and joy of liberation, but because they simply did not perceive liberation in the same way as the Danes who had been only in Denmark during the occupation. They had this perception because they had typically encountered the Germans – the enemy – in open conflict. Another fact that historians Anette Warring and Claus Bryld have previously discussed is that there has been a general perception that the domestic occupation during the war has been one category, whereas the great story of World War II and the Danish volunteers in Allied service who participated in the war has been a completely different category. As a result, the Danish volunteers have never really been part of the Danish story about the Second World War, as has the case with the history of the Danish resistance movement in particular. Roughly speaking, it can be said that the Danes who served in Allied service have taken a back seat when it comes to communicating the history of the Second World War. Typically, the veterans who participated in Operation Overlord preferred the commemorations abroad, such as the anniversary of D-Day in Normandy, rather than the commemorations associated with the liberation of Denmark.[2]

Danish volunteers in Allied service made an important contribution to the Allied fight in World War II and the Normandy invasion – but in comparison to the entire Allied effort, where it is estimated that there were six million British and 16 million American troops mobilised during the war, the Danish statistics were obviously a drop in the ocean.

The importance of the Danes who served in Allied service, and in particular the efforts of the sailors during the Normandy invasion, was to have a central and decisive impact on the way Denmark is viewed today. The dissemination of the history of these sailors, or lack thereof, has had an equally decisive effect on the collective memory and the late recognition of the Danish sailors' efforts. The Danish sailors played a special dual role during the invasion, because Denmark was effectively occupied by and apparently did not oppose the Germans until August 1943 it was therefore, quite rightly, not considered an Allied nation. Despite this, this group of Danes still fought alongside the Allies during the invasion, but these efforts were not officially recognised until 70 years after D-Day. From the very beginning of the war, the sailors thus acted against the will of the Government and were viewed unfavourably by their Allied colleagues – especially the Norwegians.

When the government resigned and broke off cooperation with the German occupying forces in 1943, the sailors continued their efforts, but now in a completely new role where they felt they had the support of their home country. The sailors' dual role began with them being hunted for their support of the Allies when the Danish Government cooperated with the German occupying forces, only to cross over to the other side and be hailed for sailing for the Allies after that cooperation policy ended. This strange role reversal contributed to the sailors' efforts being overlooked in the post-war period, and as there was no overall

2 Claus C. Bryld & Anette Warring, *The Occupation as Collective Memory*, (Copenhagen: Samfundslitteratur, 1998), p.41.

picture of their achievements, their importance remained overlooked for many decades. It should also be taken into account that the war sailors' dual role and changing status actually emphasised and exposed a very unpleasant fact in Danish official policy after the liberation: Before August 1943, the Allies did not know where Denmark actually stood because of the cooperation policy. Was Denmark not really a pro-German nation? Only after the collapse of the cooperation policy in August 1943 did it become clear that Denmark was an occupied country, and had been one before August 1943. Politicians spoke out against the German occupation, parts of the population resisted, and the Allies could now see Denmark as a potential Allied nation. Before August 1943, based on official Danish policy, it is fair to say that the Allies' sceptical view of Danish sailors from the official level down to the individual sailors was appropriate, and it was not until after August 1943 that it became clear where Denmark stood.

The lack of recognition of the efforts of Danish sailors in Normandy has therefore naturally been a controversial topic for many years. Various organisations and veteran sailors have fought long and hard to create more focus on their efforts. In 1984, Danish sailors were honoured for the first time in Normandy when a statue was erected in connection with the 40th anniversary of D-Day. The statue was designed by the artist Svend Lindhardt and inaugurated by Prince Henrik. The project was funded through a national collection, where you could buy a stamp showing the statue to be erected in Normandy. The then Minister of Defence, Hans Engell, also participated in the inauguration of the monument in 1984 and said in connection with the inauguration:

> Danish sailors made a remarkable effort for their country. An effort that is worth remembering. It is my hope that this monument will always stand for the ability to do, the will to want and the courage to act.[3]

The placement of the monument on the road between Utah Beach and the town of Sainte-Marie-du-Mont was largely realised thanks to goodwill and cooperation with the then mayor of Sainte-Marie-du-Mont, Michel De Vallavieille. For many years, the mayor had been aware of the Danish efforts during the invasion and wanted to do everything in his power to help make that effort visible.

De Vallavieille himself was wounded on D-Day in 1944 when an American paratrooper landed near De Vallavieille's farm at Brecourt Manor. The paratrooper dropped into the darkness of the courtyard and instinctively shot him, believing De Vallavieille to be German. De Vallavieille was subsequently hospitalised in England and made a full recovery. In 1962, he founded the current Utah Beach Museum. Today, the Danish war sailor monument is located a few kilometres inland behind the museum and the Utah Beaches.

Despite the Danish participation in the inauguration of the monument in Normandy in 1984, none of the Danish veterans were officially invited. Similarly, there was no official Danish invitation to the veterans in connection with the 50th anniversary of D-Day in 1994. However, this was the year when Germany was officially invited to the ceremonies for the

3 Thomas Oldrup, *Danske Søfolk ved D-Dag – en Vigtig Indsats for Danmark (Helsingør: Museet for Søfarts årbog: Søfolk i Krig – nedslag i den maritime historie, 2014)*, p.191.

first time. The still living sailors tried once again to be officially invited in 2004 in connection with the 60th anniversary ceremonies, but to little avail. It was not until 2014, after a persistent and ongoing project, that the remaining sailors were officially invited to the 70th anniversary of D-Day ceremonies. For the first time, a Danish sailor was represented at the major international ceremonies alongside the veterans of the other Allied countries.

Denmark was officially invited to the ceremonies in Normandy by the then French President, Hollande. As an official representative of Denmark, H.M. Queen Margrethe was officially invited along with heads of state from the other Allied countries that participated in the Normandy invasion. On the same occasion, a large-scale Danish ceremony was held at the Danish memorial and an exhibition about the Danish efforts in Normandy was set up at the Utah Beach Museum. At the inauguration, Her Majesty said in her speech

> However, during and after the war, the efforts of the Danish war sailors were almost forgotten; it was undeserved, and we must learn from it in the future; learn to recognise our heroes before it is too late. So today we can pay tribute to the war sailors and the other Danes who took part in the invasion, who now get the recognition they all deserve. Today's 'Dannebrog to Normandy' day helps to establish that Danish sailors are not forgotten – and will not be forgotten.[4]

Denmark as a nation is very much seen as an equal at these official ceremonies in Normandy today. From a historical perspective, the big question about Denmark's participation has been: How do you assess whether a country is an ally? Is it based on the government's behaviour with the occupying forces, or is it based on the people's defiance, rebellion and willingness to assist the Allies? Shortly after the New Year in 1945, a group from the Danish Freedom Council and leading Danish politicians expressed their wish to the British Foreign Office to change Denmark's status to that of an Ally after the efforts in the war and the break with the German occupying power in 1943. It was believed that the petition was greatly justified. The British Foreign Office was immediately in favour of the proposal, the Americans were also positive, but dragged their feet, while the Russians were decidedly opposed. The efforts of the Danish sailors only weighed heavily in British eyes, as the effort was most visible here.[5] For this reason, the Danish historical perspective in the post-war period has largely been characterised by the fact that Denmark could in no way be considered an ally.

Denmark's participation in connection with the 70th anniversary of D-Day is also seen by some historians as a seance with the character of a contemporary political game, as the Normandy invasion was the common denominator for both the Western and Eastern Allies during the war, and these allies have historically had a strained relationship with each other since the end of World War II. This has created a perception that the D-Day ceremonies were the link between the two warring parties, and the ceremonies could help to galvanise and unite the Allies.

However, the fact is that the Dannebrog is now a permanent part of the international ceremonies in Normandy and has been since the 70th anniversary in 2014, and this is solely

4 <http://kongehuset.dk/menu/nyheder/hm-dronningens-tale-ved-den-danske-markering-af-70-aret-for-de- allied-invasion-of-norway>.

5 Christian Tortzen, *Kampen på Havet* (Copenhagen: Information, 2011), pp.344–345.

due to the fact that the history of the Danish efforts in Normandy, and especially the history of the Danish sailors, has been brought to public attention.

Regardless of the political motives involved, the story is that a group of Danes selflessly chose to assist the Allies during the invasion to help liberate the European population from the Nazi dictatorship, and therefore their story alone must be told. The final symbol of the French recognition of the Danes' efforts can be seen in the form of the last living Danish veteran of the invasion, Evald Brinck, who sailed to Sword in 1944. In 2018, he received the highest French order for his efforts, the *Legion d'Honneur.* So far, only veterans from Allied countries have received this honour.

This book is therefore the history of these Danes and them alone. They made a great sacrifice for the free world, and it is our foremost task as occupation historians to pass on their stories. However, the Danish stories and the history of the Danish contribution to the invasion of Normandy in 1944 are still not fully explored. This book contributes with an extract from some Danish accounts that are representative of the Danish effort in Normandy, but there are still accounts, mainly in relation to the Danish emigrants, that need to be researched and disseminated. The Danish efforts in Normandy were of fundamental importance, not only for Denmark's participation in the war, but also for Denmark's reputation after the war. Through this book project, more and more stories with a Danish connection have emerged that, for various reasons, it has not been possible to include. What they all have in common, however, is that many with a Danish background chose to fight for the Allies in the Normandy invasion. These accounts provide fertile ground for more research on the subject. It is the author's hope that with this study we have come some way and have increased interest in further research into a subject that has both historical and current significance.

Bibliography

Archives

The list below provides further references for the images contained within the book.

Frihedsmuseet/Nationalmuseet (Copenhagen, Denmark)
Tyske bombemaskiner over København d. 9. April 1940. På gaden ligger nedkastede flyveblade 'OPROP'. I baggrunden ses Palads Biografen. Fotograf/skaber: Krause og Johansen. (Fil-ID: 295153. Filnavn: 02A6001001.tif)
Kjeld Rønhof (15B-15)
Tilfangetagne englændere og franskmænd ved Dunkirk. Fotografskaber Presse-Bild-Zentrale Berlin. (Fil-Id-285726. Filnavn 01B0112002.tif)
Dieppe og tyske soldater (FHM-285950 + FHM-285874)
Flådens sænkning (Fil id 14361)
Kaj Birksted (15B-26)
Jørgen Kjeldbæk (Fil-ID 204727)
S/S *Aarø* (FHM-237687)
Kikkert og kniv som Holger Jensen bragte med hjem til Danmark
Frit Danmark forside (Fil-ID 237599)
Fejring af 5. maj (Fil-ID 250577)

Imperial War Museum (London, England)
Dunkirk (Catalogue number HU 93157)
Dunkirk (Catalogue number HU 41240)
Den falske flåde (Catalogue number H 42527)
DD-kampvogn (Catalogue number MH 3660)
Landgang på Gold (Catalogue number B 5245)
Kampvogne på vej ind fra Gold (Catalogue number B 5251)
Landgang på Sword-stranden (Catalogue number B 5114)
Lovats tropper (Catalogue number B 5103)
Soldater under angreb på Sword-stranden (Catalogue number B 5091)
D-dagsfrancs (Catalogue number B 5149)
Bombefly over Tourcoing (Catalogue number C 4399)
Tysk E-båd (Catalogue number A 28559)
Kongens tale (Catalogue number 1628)

Bundesarchiv (Koblenz, Germany)
V-1 bombe (Bundesarchiv, Bild 146-1975-117-26 / Lysiak / CC-BY-SA 3.0)

Commonwealth War Graves Commission (Maidenhead, Berkshire, United Kingdom)
Otto Hjalmar Antofts grav

Fyens Stiftstidende (Odense, Fyn, Denmark)
Foto af Viggo Hans Nielsen i Normandiet, 6. juni 1984

Library and Archives Canada (Ottawa, Ontario, Canada)
Photo: Scout car abandoned during the raid on Dieppe, Dieppe, France., 19 Aug. 1942 Source: Library and Archives Canada/Department of National Defence fonds/c029861
Photo: Unidentified Canadian soldiers landing on Juno Beach, Courseulles-sur-Mer, France, 6 June 1944 Source: Library and Archives Canada/Department of National Defence fonds/a132655
Photo: Troops of the 9th Canadian Infantry Brigade (Stormont, Dundas, and Glengarry Highlanders) going ashore from LCI (L) 299 [Landing Craft Infantry], Bernières-sur-mer, Normandy, France, 6 June 1944. Source: Library and Archives Canada/ Department of National Defence fonds/a122765
Photo: Wounded Canadian soldiers awaitingtransfer to a Casualty Clearing Station of the Royal Canadian Army Medical Corps (R.C.A.M.C.) on D-Day, Courseulles-sur-Mer, France, 6 June 1944. Source: Library and Archives Canada/Department of National Defence fonds/a132384
Photo: German personnel captured on D-Day embarking for England, Bernières-sur-Mer, France, ca. 6 June 1944. Source: Library and Archives Canada/Department of National Defence fonds/a132474
Bofors AA (MIKAN 3229979)
Rue Saint-Pierre, Caen (MIKAN 3465533)
Photo: A dramatic war picture showing fires caused by bombing with transports and men taking cover on the Caen-Falaise Road, 8 August 1944. Source: Library and Archives Canada/Department of National Defence fonds/e010858649
Photo: Gunners of the 12th Field Regiment, Royal Canadian Artillery (R.C.A.), with the Victory issue of the Maple Leaf newspaper, Aurich, Germany, 20 May 1945. Source: Library and ArchivesCanada/Department of National Defence fonds/a150931

M/S Museet for Søfart (Helsingør, Denmark)
Dansk propaganda plakat (Filnummer 000005296)
S/S *Dagmar* (Filnummer 000008677)
S/S *Avance* (Filnummer 000005276)
S/S *Avance* (Filnummer 000005278)
M/S *Gudrun Mærsk* (Filnummer 000002034)
Danske skibe i konvoj (Filnummer 000004666)
'DUCKS' amfibiekøretøjer (Filnummer 000013955)
S/S *Avance* (Filnummer 000005294)
S/S *Tomsk* (Filnummer 000014425)
S/S *Alf* (Filnummer 0000053762)

Emil Blytgen-Petersen (Filnummer 000033581)
S/S *Avance* (Filnummer 000009075)
S/S *Thyra* og S/S *Friggas* hjemkomst til København (Filnummer 000008675) *308 309*

US National Archives / NARA (Maryland, USA)
Evening Standard avisforside
Skitsering af strandforhindringer
Amerikanske tropper før D-dag
Eisenhower
Turqueville
Oberstløjtnant Robert Wolverton
Bombning af Pointe du Hoc
2. Rangerbataljon ved Pointe du Hoc + Len Goodgal
Pointe du Hoc luftfoto
Pointe du Hoc kanonstilling
Niels Christensen dokument
Sainte-Marie-du-Mont
Utah landgangskort
AM-125 synker ved Utah
Det røde hus på Utah-stranden
Kampvognsmuren på Utah-stranden
Samaritter på Utah-stranden
Soldater søger dækning på vej mod Omaha
Omaha landgangskort
Amerikanske soldater på vej mod Omaha i Higginsbåde
USS *Augusta* + Svend A. Petersen
Soldater og køretøjer på vej mod Omaha
Amerikanske tropper går i land på Omaha
Sårede soldater fra 1. Infanteridivision på Omaha
St. Laurent-sur-Mer
Vierville-sur-Mer
Omaha efter D-dag
Mulberry A ud for Omaha
Amerikanske tropper på vej ind I åbent markområde
Bocage fra luften
Erstatningssoldater på vej til Utah-sektoren
Kirken ved Colleville-sur-mer
Ødelæggelserne efter slaget om Caen
Operation Dragoon
Eisenhower note

US Library of Congress (Washington DC, USA)
Teheran konference (U.S. Signal Corps photo – Library of Congress Reproduction Number: LC-USZ62-32833)
Exercise Tiger (digital ID cph.3c32795)
Køretøjer ankommer til Gold via Mulberry B

The Pima Air and Space Museum (Tuscon, Arizona, USA)
B-26 Marauder

Kystmuseet Bangsbo Arkiv & Bangsbo Fort (Frederikshavn, Denmark)
Rommel på Pikkerbakken + bunker med kanon
Henning Møller

Lokalhistorisk Arkiv Skagen (Skagen, Denmark)
Svend Aage Christensen

Cicerone ApS og Nexus Kommunikaiton (Hillerød, Denmark)
Diverse råmateriale ifm. interview med Erik Egebak og J.P. Sørensen, samt arkivmateriale i forbindelse
med udarbejdelsen af dokumentaren ›Krigssejlerne‹.

Det Kongelige Biblioteks Billedsamling (Copenhagen, Denmark)
John Christmas Møller (Lille John – ID DH001347)

Danmarks Radio (Copenhagen, Denmark)
Interview med Kjeld Rønhof og Niels Wiesneck i DR-udsendelsen: ›D-Dag Den Længste Dag‹, genudsendt juni 2004.
Interview med »Jens Jensen», Holger Jensen og Arthur Larsen i DR-radioprogrammet: »Den store
landgang« ved Poul S. Poulsen. Sendt første gang d. 6. juni 1969. Følgende citater stammer herfra. Jens Jensen er et opdigtet navn i forbindelse med interviewet.

Nordjyske Historiske Arkiv (Aalborg, Denmark)
D-dags forside

Hadsten Lokalarkiv (Hadsten, Denmark)
Hans Erik Jepsen

Marinemuseet (Lillehammer, Norway)
Svenner (Identifier MMU.945740)

Historisk Arkiv – Vendsyssel Historiske Museum (Hjørring, Denmark)
Erik Egebak (Nummer I901804)
Ildlederbunkeren i 10. batteri ved Hirtshals (Fotograf: Chrestina Dahl)

Museumscenter Hanstholm (Hanstholm, Denmark)
Ildlederbunkeren i 10. batteri ved Hirtshals (Fotograf: Orla Jensen)

Familie Journalen / Karl Ravn (Copenhagen, Denmark)
John Andreasen i uniform
John Andreasens deling

John Andreasen med krigsbytte
John Andreasen ved den amerikanske kirkegård ved Colleville-sur-Mer

Nordby Sognearkiv (Fanø, Denmark)
Avisudskrift om danske skibe

Randbøl Lokalhistoriske Arkiv (Vandel, Denmark))
Information om Kjeld Seyer-Hansen stammer fra diverse avisudklip fra Randbøl Lokalhistoriske Arkiv, 19/8 1979 *310 311*

Private Arkiver
Jørgen Linnet i uniform (Jørgen Linnet)
Niels Wiesneck i uniform og tegning af havn og skib (Finn Wiesneck)
Henrik Bødker Knudsen i uniform (Aksel Bødker Knudsen)
Holger Jensen i uniform (Jørgen Aarlo Jensen)
Evald Brinck i uniform (Evald Brinck)
J.P. Sørensen i 2005 (Ebbe Kyrø)
331. Eskadrille (Jon Tvedte)
Hans Erik Jepsen, mindesmærke (Canadian Virtual Memorial)
Henning Rudolph Calberg gravsten (K. Falconer & J. Stephens)
Viggo Hans Nielsen i 1943 (Lis Nielsen)
Nordvest (Jørgen Linnet)
Niels Wiesnecks røde kors brev (Finn Wiesneck)
Foto af Essex Scottish Regiment (Finn Wiesneck)
Moldt og *ITEMS* besætning (Moldt)
Lancasterflyet, *ITEM* (Moldt)
Erik Christiansens lønopgørelse + V-artikler (Christian Tortzen)
Niels Wiesneck med ven (Finn Wiesneck)
Waco-svævefly (442nd Fighter Wing archives)
Niels Christensen + familie (Mary Christensen)
Besætning fra 3. bataljon, 506. Luftvåben (Michel De Trez via Ian Gardner)
Kort over nedkastningszone (Gardner & Day)
Jens Nørgaard (Karl Leach)
Thorkil Jensen (Veterans History Project)
De norske eskadriller (Jon Tvedte)
Svenners anker (Normandywarguide.com)
Hans Mathiasen (Kromann)
Andreas Moldt i agtertårn (Moldt)
Thorald Nielsen (Claus Arboe-Rasmussen)
Poul Egon Petersen (Carl Steffensen)
Foto af Holger Jensen + dokument (Jørgen Aarlo Jensen)
Einar Sørensen modtager medalje (Krish Harsh)
Carl E. Nielsens grav (Fields of Honor database)
Niels Wiesneck i canadisk uniform (Finn Wiesneck)
Niels Wiesnecks krigsbytte (Finn Wiesneck)

Hans Juelsdorf (foto: Jakob Andersen)
Viggo Hans Nielsen i uniform (Lis Nielsen)
HNoMS *Glaisdale* (Navy Photos Collection)
Eric arnold Aage Kiaer + gravsten (Commandoveterans.org)
Evald Brinck i britisk uniform (Evald Brinck)
Karl Adolph Goths søfartspapirer (Simon Bang)
Niels Wiesnecks invasionsvaluta (Finn Wiesneck)
Oscar Faber (Faber & Partners)
Målfoto, Le Havre (Moldt)
Foto af Niels Wiesneck, bæltespænde
og faldskærmssilke (Finn Wiesneck)
Foto af Svend Moustgaard + grav og mindesten (Ole Moustgaard)
Målfoto, Caen (Moldt)
Niels Wiesnecks personlige landgangskort (Finn Wiesneck)
Verner T. Jensen (Claus Arboe-Rasmussen)
Elsie Margaret Hansen + *Arcadia* (Veterans History Project)
Niels Christensen på orlov (Mary Christensen)
Niels Wiesnecks dokumenter + medaljer (Finn Wiesneck)

Published Works

Arboe-Rasmussen, Claus & Sørensen, Bent, *De befriede os* (Copenhagen: Folk & Sikkerhed, 2005)

Austin, Lambert: *344th Bomb Group m "Silver Streaks": History & Remembrances World War II*, (St Petersburg, Fl: Southern Heritage, 1996)

Balkoski, Joseph: *Omaha Beach: D-Day, June 6, 1944* (Mechanicsburg: Stackpole Books, 2006)

Balkoski, Joseph, *Utah Beach: The Amphibious Landing and Airborne Operations on D-Day, June 6, 1944* (Mechanicsburg: Stackpole Books, 2006)

Bando, Mark, *The 101st at Normandy* (Minneapolis: Zenith, 1994)

Barber, Nigel, *The Day the Devils Dropped In* (Barnsley: Pen & Sword, 2010)

Beevor, Antony, *D-Dag: Kampen om Normandiet* (Copenhagen: Lindhardt & Ringhof, 2009)

Bercuson, David J., *Our Finest Hour: Canada fights the Second World War* (London: Harper Collins, 2015)

Bercuson, David J., *Maple Leaf Against The Axis* (Ontario, Stoddart Publishing, 1998)

Birkeland, Sven Arvid, *Sænket af tyskerne - Danske krigssejlere i 2. Verdenskrig* (Copenhagen: Gyldendal, 2012)

Bjerg, Hans Chr., Kieler, Svend, Laub, Søren: *For Flaget og flåden – om marines personel og dets Virke 1943-45* (Copenhagen: Søværnet, 1995)

Blytgen-Petersen, Emil, *Dansk Krigskorrespondent* (Copenhagen: Nyt Nordisk Forlag Arnold Busck, 1945)

Breuer, William B., *Operation Dragoon: The Allied Invasion of the South of France*, (New York: Presidio Press, 1996)

Brinck, Evald, *... de vil aldrig blive husket – beretning om danske søfolk 1940 – 1945* (Tåsinge: Evald Springeren Brinck, 2007)

Brown, Anthony Cave, *Bodyguard of Lies: The Extraordinary True Story Behind D-Day* (New York: The Lyons Press, 2007)
Bryld, Claus C. & Warring, Anette, *The Occupation as Collective Memory*, (Copenhagen: Samfundslitteratur, 1998)
Churchill, Winston, *Erindringer om Den Anden Verdenskrig, Bind 1, 1939–1942* (Copenhagen: Rosenkilde, 2010)
Christensen, Claus Bundgård, Lund, Joachim, Olsesen, Niels Wium, Sørensen, Jakob: *Danmark besat - krig og hverdag 1940–1945* (Copenhagen: Gyldendals, 2005)
Crookenden, Napier, *Drop Zone Normandy: The Story of The American And British Airborne Assault On D Day 1944* (Abingdon: Purnell Book Services, 1976)
D'Este, Carlo, *Decision in Normandy*, (Old Saybrook: Konecky and Konecky Military Books, 1994)
Edwards, Kenneth, *Operation Neptune: The Normandy Landings, 1944* (Stroud: Fonthill Media, 2013)
Feierskov, Susanne Zima, *Med vinger og våben* (Copenhagen: Gyldendal, 2011)
Flintholm, Jørgen, *Normandiet og D-Dag - Dengang og nu* (Denmark: Flintholm, 2014)
Ford, Ken, *D-Day 1944 (3): Sword Beach & the British Airborne Landings* (Oxford: Osprey, 2002)
Ford, Ken, *D-Day 1944 (4): Gold and Juno Beaches* (Oxford: Osprey, 2002)
Fowler, Will, *The Commandos of Dieppe: Rehearsal for D-Day* (London: Collins, 2002)
Gardner, Ian, *Tonight We Die As Men* (Oxford: Osprey, 2010)
Gjøde Nielsen, Henrik, *Storm Fæstning Hirtshals - Den nordjyske modstandsbevægelses planer om et invasionsbrohoved i Vendsyssel* (Copenhagen: Vendsyssel årbog, 2008)
Granov, Torsten: *D-Dag: Optakten, Dramaet og Efterspillet* (Denmark: Cultours, 2012)
Hansen, Anders Bjørn, *Breve fra Anders* (Copenhagen: Gyldendal, 2012)
Hargreaves, Richard: *The Germans in Normandy* (Barnsley: Pen and Sword Books, 2013)
Hartcup, Guy, *Code Name Mulberry* (Barnsley: Pen and Sword Books, 1977)
Hoyt, Edwin P., *The Invasion Before Normandy* (London: Robert Hale, 1987)
Jensen, Verner, *Frederikshavn under besættelsen* (Frederikshavn: Bangsbomuseet, 1985)
Jeppesen, Torben Grøngaard, *Danske i USA 1850–2000: En demografisk, social og kulturgeografisk undersøgelse af de danske immigranter og deres efterkommere* ((Odense: Museum Odense, 2005)
Keegan, John, *Six Armies in Normandy*, (London: Penguin Books, 1982)
Kjølsen, F. H., *Da Danmarks Flåde Blev Sænket* (Copenhagen: H. Hagerup, 1945)
Knudsen, Henrik Bødker, *Krigssejler* (Copenhagen: Frihedsmuseets Venners Forlag, 1992)
Kragelund, Erik, *Overlord - Den Danske Deltagelse i Invasionen i Normandiet i 1944* (Copenhagen: Radius, 2013)
Kromann, N. M., *Fanø Sømænd i Storm og Stille* (Fanø: Kromann, 1960)
Lauring, Kåre, *Mellem Bomber og Torpedoer* (Copenhagen: Gyldendal, 2004)
Levine, Joshua, *Operation Fortitude: The Greatest Hoax of The Second World War* (London: Collins, 2011)
Lovat, Lord: *March Past: A Memoir* (London: Weidenfeld & Nicholson, 1978)
Meanwell, R. W., *1st Battalion The Essex Scottish Regiment 1939–1945: A Brief Narrative* (Aldershot: Wellington Press, 1946)
Moldt, Andreas P., *Natbomber: Slaget om Europa som en Dansker Oplevede det i Invasionssommeren 1944* (Copenhagen: Gyldendal, 1985)

Mosgaard, Arne, *Monumenter, Mindesmærker og Fredede Grave i Herning Kommune* (Herning: Ubirex, 2012)

Oldrup, Thomas, *Danske Søfolk ved D-Dag – en Vigtig Indsats for Danmark (Helsingør: Museet for Søfarts årbog: Søfolk i Krig – nedslag i den maritime historie, 2014)*

Plannthin, Mikkel, *Britain's Victory, Denmark's Freedom* (Stroud: Fonthill Media, 2017)

Robertson, Stuart C, Booth, Dale, *Following in the Footsteps of Heroes: D-Day June 6th 1944*, (Devizes: Sabrestorm, 2014)

Robinson, Wayne C. & Hamilton, Norman E., *Move Out, Verify: The Combat Story of the 743rd Tank Battalion* (United States Army, 1945)

Røder, H. C., *De Sejlede Bare* (Copenhagen: Høst & Søn,1974)

Rønhof, Kjeld, *Vi fløj for Friheden* (Copenhagen: Four Stripes,1991)

Rønhof, Kjeld, *Vi Startede fra England: En Dansk Jagerflyvers Oplevelser* (Copenhagen: Berlingske, 1945)

Sebag-Montefiore, Hugh: *Dunkirk*: Fight to the Last Man (London: Viking, 2006)

Schmidt-Hansen, Erik, *5 aar i Allieret Tjeneste* (Copenhagen: Branner, 1946)

Sørensen, Erling, *Fanø under Besættelsen* (Copenhagen: Erling Sørensen, 2010)

Sørensen, Jakob, *D-Dag – Operation Overlord 6. Juni 1944* (Copenhagen: People's Press, 2014)

Sørensen, Jakob, *For Danmarks Ære* (Copenhagen: People's Press, 2011)

Tortzen, Christian, *Kampen på Havet* (Copenhagen: Information, 2011)

Tortzen, Christian, *Søfolk og Skibe 1939–1945, bind 1* (Copenhagen: Lindhardt & Ringhof, 1981)

Tortzen, Christian, *Søfolk og Skibe 1939–1945, bind 2* (Copenhagen: Lindhardt & Ringhof, 1982)

Tortzen, Christian, *Søfolk og Skibe 1939–1945, bind 3* (Copenhagen: Lindhardt & Ringhof, 1983)

Tortzen, Christian, *Søfolk og Skibe 1939–1945, bind 4* (Copenhagen: Lindhardt & Ringhof, 1985)

Tout, Ken, *Roads to Falaise* (Cheltenham: The History Press, 2003)

Tvedte, Jon, *Flyvningen – Det Moderne Eventyr* (Fall: Norsk Faglitteratur, 1958)

Tzu, Sun, *Kunsten at Føre Krig* (Copenhagen: Gyldendal Business, 2015)

Willumsen, Aksel, *Lille John – I Britisk Tjeneste* (Copenhagen: Frihedsmuseets Venners Forlag, 2017)

Zaloga, Steven, *D-Day Fortifications in Normandy* (Oxford: Osprey, 2005), Fortress series no.37

Zaloga, Steven: *Rangers Lead the Way, Pointe-du-Hoc, D-Day, 1944* (Oxford: Osprey, 2009), Raid series no.1

Websites

https://www.loc.gov/vets/

https://www.retsinformation.dk/Forms/r0710.aspx?id=145690

http://kongehuset.dk/menu/nyheder/hm-dronningens-tale-ved-den-danske-markering-af-70- aret-for-the-allied-invasion-of-nor

www.mitfanoe.dk www.commandoveterans.org

www.normandywarguide.com

https://www.fieldsofhonor-database.com/index.php/en/ https://www.veterans.gc.ca/eng/remembrance/memorials/canadian-virtual-war-memorial https://www.history.navy.mil/our-collections/photography.html